TRUE NORTH CABIN COOKBOOK

volume two

TRUE NORTH CABIN COOKBOOK

Stephanie Hansen

volume two
SEASONAL RECIPES
FROM A COZY KITCHEN

MINNESOTA HISTORICAL SOCIETY PRESS

To Kurt

*My favorite adventurer,
pizza maker, and grilling champion*

Text and images copyright © 2025 by Stephanie Hansen unless noted below. Other materials copyright © 2025 by the Minnesota Historical Society. All rights reserved. No part of this book may be used or reproduced in any manner whatsoever without written permission except in the case of brief quotations embodied in critical articles and reviews. For information, write to the Minnesota Historical Society Press, 345 Kellogg Blvd. W., St. Paul, MN 55102-1906.

mnhspress.org   @mnhspress

The Minnesota Historical Society Press is a member of the Association of University Presses.

Images on pages 11, 17, and 190 from iStock by Getty Images.

Manufactured in Canada.

10 9 8 7 6 5 4 3 2 1

∞ The paper used in this publication meets the minimum requirements of the American National Standard for Information Sciences — Permanence for Printed Library Materials, ANSI Z39.48-1984.

ISBN: 978-1-68134-322-8 (hardcover)

Library of Congress Control Number: 2025934336

True North Cabin Cookbook: Volume Two was designed and set in type by Susan Everson in St. Paul, Minnesota. The typefaces are Montebello, Rockeby, MultipleSlab, and MultipleSans.

2 *Introduction: My Food Origin Story*

4 *October*

1991 Halloween Blizzard 5

Pumpkin Spice Cream 8 · Pumpkin Spice Espresso Martini 9 · Curried Pumpkin Soup 10 · Herb Drop Biscuits 11 · Weeknight Enchilada Soup 12 · Big Beefy Chili 13 · Autumn Harvest Sheet Pan Roasted Veggies 14 · Baked Brussels Sprouts with Lemon and Goat Cheese 15 · Maple Roasted Butternut Squash with Sage Browned Butter 16 · Braised Red Cabbage with Apples 17 · Double Potato Gratin with Apples and Onions 19 · Skillet Shells with Sausage, Ricotta, and Greens 20 · Sheet Pan Shawarma Two Ways 22 · Roast Chicken with Autumn Vegetables 24 · Short Rib Bolognese 26 · Mom's Meatloaf 27 · Pork Chop and Scalloped Potato Casserole 28 · Pumpkin Dark Chocolate Snack Cake 30 · Pumpkin Muffins 31 · Pumpkin Snickerdoodle Cookies 33 · Salted Caramel Apple Bars 34 · Apple Donut Cake 36 · Tarte Tatin 37

38 *November*

Thanksgiving Memories 39

Cranberry French 75 42 · Pomegranate Old-Fashioned 43 · Thanksgiving Punch 44 · Roasted Carrot Hummus 45 · Butternut Squash Soup with Crispy Prosciutto Croutons 46 · Thanksgiving Leftovers Turkey Wild Rice Soup 47 · Mom's Chili Mac 48 · Asian Pear Spinach Salad with Maple Pecans and Ginger Vinaigrette 49 · Kale, Pomegranate, and Apple Salad with Roasted Pumpkin Seeds 50 · Sesame Almond Chicken Salad 51 · Cranberry Wild Rice Salad with Candied Pecans and Bitter Greens 52 · Roasted Parmesan Delicata Squash 54 · Roasted Brussels Sprouts with Pomegranate Seeds 55 · Wild Rice Stuffing 56 · Pan-Seared Ribeye Steaks with Shallot Cream Sauce 57 · Cranberry Orange Sauce 58 · Pecan Bars 59 · Pumpkin Pudding, aka Crustless Pumpkin Pie 60 · Pumpkin Bars with Cream Cheese Frosting 61 · Pumpkin Cheesecake 62

64 December

The Christmas Eve Party 65

Homemade Irish Cream 68 · Cranberry Old-Fashioned 69 · Eggnog 70 · Spiced Nuts 71 · Baked Party Brie 72 · Gruyère Puff Pastry with Sun-Dried Tomatoes 73 · Beth's Chex Party Mix 74 · Ham Hock and Split Pea Soup 75 · Beef Barley Soup 76 · Christmas Eve Cheesy Artichokes 77 · Scalloped Potatoes with Gruyère Cheese 78 · Creamed Corn 79 · Lila's Swedish Meatballs with Gravy 80 · Reverse-Seared Prime Rib with Horseradish Cream 82 · Popovers with Honey Butter 83 · Aebleskivers 84 · Eggnog Croissant Christmas Casserole 85 · Savory Sausage Breakfast Bread Pudding 86 · Cranberry Orange Bread 87 · Mom's Toffee Bars 88 · Easiest Roll-Out Sugar Cookies 89 · Cherries in the Snow 90 · Ginger Molasses Cookies 91 · Cookie Exchange Salted Caramels 92

94 January

Amateur Night 95

Beth's Spinach Dip 98 · Artichoke Dip 99 · Thai Chicken Rice Soup 100 · Italian Sausage Soup 101 · Arugula Clementine Salad with Dried Cherries 102 · Spinach Salad with Instant Pot Jammy Eggs and Bacon Vinaigrette 103 · Broiled Scallops à la Simpson's with Oven-Baked Lemon Risotto 104 · Cheesy Sausage Lasagna 106 · Heavenly Chicken and Rice 107 · Stuffed Chicken Breasts 108 · Apple Cider–Braised Lamb Shanks with Parmesan Risotto 110 · Lentil and Sausage Stew with Spinach and Lemon 112 · Mom's Oven Barbecue Spare Ribs 113 · Old-School Beef Stroganoff 114 · Thai Pork Noodle Goulash 115 · Pork Shoulder Ragu with Cheesy Polenta 117 · Swedish Meatloaf with Brown Gravy 118 · Cabbage Almond Pasta with Toasted Breadcrumbs 120 · Banana Bread Cookies with Cream Cheese Frosting 121

122 February

Winter on True North Island 123

Hot Pickle Dip 126 · Oven-Baked Chicken Wings 127 · Oven-Baked Jalapeño Poppers 128 · Beer Cheese Wild Rice Soup 129 · Spicy Chicken Sausage and Sweet Potato Soup 130 · Broccoli Cheese Soup 131 · Buffalo Chicken Chili 132 · Easiest From-Scratch Focaccia 133 · Easy Shortcut Focaccia 134 · Roasted Brussels Sprouts Caesar Salad 135 · Brussels Sprouts and Butternut Squash Salad with Tahini Vinaigrette 136 · Arugula and Wild Rice Salad with Pear Vinaigrette 137 · Grandma's Scalloped Cabbage 138 · Miso Mashed Potatoes with Horseradish 139 · Hungarian Goulash with Horseradish 140 · Ground Turkey Red Curry 142 · Gochujang Kimchi Meatloaf Muffins 143 · Juicy Lucy Cheeseburger Tater Tot Hot Dish 145 · Creamy Lemon Pasta with Crispy Breadcrumbs 146 · Marry Me One-Pot Shrimp 148 · Orange Madeleines 149 · Gluten-Free Bourbon Brownies 150

152 March

Breast Vacation Ever 153

Boozy Shamrock Shakes 156 · Tuna Pâté 157 · Thai Winter Squash Soup 158 · Coconut Curry Soup with Salmon 159 · Fish Chowder with Bacon 160 · Dill Pickle and Ham Soup 161 · Irish Soda Bread 162 · Twice-Baked Potato Casserole 163 · Dill Pickle Pot Roast 164 · Oven-Baked Corned Beef Brisket 165 · Chicken and Biscuits 166 · Grilled Jerk Chicken with Coconut Rice and Mango Salsa 168 · Cajun Shrimp Pasta 170 · Linguine and Clam Sauce 171 · One-Pot Turkey Meatballs with Lemon Orzo 172 · Skillet Baked Ziti with Meatballs 174 · Cowboy Bread 175 · Blueberry-Lemon Bread 176 · Salted Peanut Butter Rice Crispy Treats 177

178 April

Easter 179

Mason Jar Basil Lemonade 182 · Cheddar and Chive Shortbreads 183 · Orzo Vegetable Bean Soup 184 · Clam Chowder 185 · Creamy Chicken Broccoli Soup 186 · Roasted Asparagus Quinoa Salad 188 · Arugula, Parmesan, and Pine Nut Salad 189 · Kathy's Cheesy Potatoes 190 · Gluten-Free Ham and Cheese Egg Bake 191 · Asparagus Quiche with Hash Brown Crust 193 · Crispy Skillet Hash Brown Cake with Kale Pesto 194 · Gnocchi with Spring Pesto 197 · Roast Rack of Lamb 198 · Green Sauce 199 · Old Bay Crab Cakes with Mustard Sauce 200 · Baked Haddock with Buttered Breadcrumbs 202 · Roasted Salmon with Lemon 203 · Roasted Salmon Caesar 204 · Pan-Roasted Chicken Thighs with Roasted Grapes 205 · Rhubarb Almond Bread 206 · Gooey Butter Bars 207 · Lemon Bars 208

210 Acknowledgments

211 Index

224 About the Author

TRUE NORTH CABIN COOKBOOK

volume two

MY FOOD ORIGIN STORY

One of my first food memories is standing on a kitchen chair next to the stove as my mother made her chili mac (recipe on page 48). She wore the red-and-green-striped apron my oldest half-sister Laura had given her for Christmas. My mother had me stir the pot of macaroni, reminding me not to let the noodles stick together. Minutes later, she asked if the noodles were done. I don't think she'd ever asked my opinion before, and now I had that responsibility. I lifted out a few pieces with the spoon and blew on the noodles to let them cool. I pinched one and then tasted. It was still tough, and I told my mother just that. She said, "A couple more minutes, then." I let the noodles cook, watching as they tumbled in the boiling water. I waited, and my mother said nothing. The responsibility was all mine. I tested again, and they were done. I offered the cooled spoon to Mom for her opinion. She put a noodle to her teeth and then smiled and said, "Perfect." She strained the macaroni and added the noodles to the pot of chili. *Perfect*, I thought. Maybe that was when it all started — the impulse to create something perfect that I knew my family would consume and enjoy.

Fifteen years later, I moved with my husband, Kurt, to Baltimore. My mother was a great midwestern home cook, and many of her recipes are in my cookbooks. But in Baltimore Kurt and I went to the public market and sat at the oyster bar, where men shucked oysters at blinding speed and served them on a bed of crushed ice with cocktail sauce and Tabasco. We ordered a dozen, along with pints of Bass Ale. I had my first oyster, and then my second. I was hooked. In Baltimore, I worked as a server for the Chart House restaurant in the Inner Harbor and was exposed to seafood I'd rarely encountered at my family's dinner table. Kurt and I had more food experiences: eating steamed crabs thrown out on a butcher paper–covered picnic table, savoring hand-rolled sushi at our local bar, and munching crab cakes with luscious chunks of claw meat. Once, Kurt's mother, Dolores, visited us from Houston, where she managed the Grand Opera. She took us to a French restaurant with more tableware than I'd ever seen. I knew enough from working at the Chart House to start with the outside fork and move in, but there was one bent knife that was a total mystery. I thought maybe it was for butter, but I was too intimidated by Dolores to actually use it for that purpose. To my relief, she held up the knife to the server and asked; she had no idea either. The server replied that it was for removing the fish meat from the bones. Over time I became less intimidated by new foods and kitchen gadgets and, like Dolores, simply asked. Food for me is a lifelong learning experience that I love to share.

After Baltimore, we moved back to Minneapolis, living in a duplex near the Institute of Art with our yellow lab, Sophie, who had a crooked nose. Kurt went to graduate school and bartended while I sold classified ads for the *Twin Cities Reader*. I worked there when the writer Brett Anderson — later a James Beard Award–winning restaurant critic at the New Orleans *Times-Picayune* and the *New York Times* — was our intern and for lunch would eat only pizza from our local pizzeria. I'd learned to love exploring new restaurants and new foods. Back then it was the New French Café, which we could rarely afford, King and I Thai, Cuban food at a funky place called Chez Bananas, artichoke dip at the Loring, and ribs at Market Bar-B-Que. Of course, because we were making little money, we mostly cooked at home. Kurt made, among other things, Caesar salad and fettuccine alfredo, while I perfected roast chicken and pot roast. We gave each other kitchen gadgets for birthdays and Christmas.

Fast-forward ten years. I was selling ads for Hubbard Broadcasting and doing guest appearances on the *Lori & Julia Show* on myTalk 107. When a daytime slot opened up, I jumped at the opportunity. I remember that first day on air with my partner, Meredith Teplitz, scared out of my mind. I hadn't slept the night before, obsessing about each fifteen-minute increment, all laid out on a spreadsheet the previous week. The thought of holding a conversation for three hours was daunting, to say the least. But I got through those three long hours — and through another 750 hours over the next year. Then that show was canceled, but miraculously I picked up a weekend food show, *The Weekly Dish*, with my cohost, Stephanie March, then a freelance writer at *Rake Magazine* and subsequently a food editor at *Mpls.St.Paul Magazine*. That was over fifteen years ago, and we're still going strong.

Who am I now? Stephanie March (or "Smarch," to differentiate between the two Stephanies) always had the restaurant and writer chops. I'm the home cook. While Smarch gives the insider knowledge of the dining experience, I am the eater, experiencing the food, the restaurant ambiance, and the hospitality from the average patron's perspective. I bring that curiosity and love of food to my television series, *Taste Buds with Stephanie* on Fox. I meet people in the industry: chefs, food growers, and product makers. I see how they do their thing and then take a small piece of what I learned from them back into my own kitchen. This sequel to *True North Cabin Cookbook* reflects that impulse to gather and explore and share. It's written for the home cook who needs simple recipes and seasonal ideas to prepare for a family meal or a gathering of friends. Ready to explore with me? Let's go!

1991 HALLOWEEN BLIZZARD

Where were you during the Halloween Blizzard of 1991? Kurt and I weren't yet married, but we had a "fur baby," a yellow lab named Sophie we'd adopted in Baltimore a year earlier. We'd both decided to start fresh in Minnesota. I worked for the *Twin Cities Reader* selling classified ads, probably the lowest sales position you can have (or maybe one up from selling Kirby vacuum cleaners door-to-door, which a few friends were doing then). Kurt worked at a dilapidated conference center in Arden Hills, selling meeting space to corporate planners and cut-rate wedding receptions to strapped couples. We lived in a duplex near the Minneapolis Institute of Art at the base of a twenty-foot sound barrier that barely masked the traffic on Interstate 35W. We were broke and living paycheck to paycheck.

It was a community of sorts, with neighbors in much closer contact with each other than what we have now. We shared the duplex with a gay couple who threw great parties and invited us over for dinner from time to time. Paul was the cook and taught me to make crepes with seafood and beurre blanc sauce — buttery and tangy. (Remember when crepes were all the rage?) In one nearby house lived a multigenerational Hmong family with five kids. They liked playing with Sophie — until she bit one of them when they came into the house without knocking (sorry!). We would buy Creamsicles from an ice cream truck that also sold forty-ouncers of Colt 45 malt liquor. We had a hand-waving relationship with the weed dealer who worked the corner just down the block on Twenty-Sixth Street.

We ate cheap but well. My specialty was pasta with a can of Hunt's basil, garlic, and oregano diced tomatoes: add some grated Parmesan cheese and you're good to go. For a real special treat, add a link of sliced hot Italian sausage, and if you're feeling really fancy, a half cup of heavy cream. On special occasions I made my mother's spaghetti sauce that oddly included black olives. And back then, a whole chicken was inexpensive, and a Sunday supper of roast chicken, buttered spring potatoes, and green beans (frozen, from a silver paper–lined box) could last well into the next week. Then I was not above Hamburger Helper or Rice-A-Roni (the San Francisco treat!), though I would not let Kurt purchase Dinty Moore Beef Stew or canned chicken. I don't think I'm a snob, but there is a line I will not cross, and while tinned fish seems fine, tinned meat does not.

6

The snow started falling on a Thursday evening. We all knew it was coming but not how much. It was Halloween and we passed out some candy, but the neighborhood kids who knew any better were working the affluent homes closer to the lakes.

Over two feet of snow eventually clogged the sidewalks and streets. There was no going to work. All the meetings Kurt had scheduled had been canceled, and we settled in to enjoy the early snow and day off. At noon the sun came out, and many of the neighbors were out shoveling and helping to push cars out of their on-street parking spots and into the ruts of the unplowed streets. The corner drug dealer had a shovel of his own and did his part.

That evening we decided to splurge and walked the few blocks to Nicollet Avenue and a bar called Porter's, where the locals hung out. That Friday it was packed. Our neighborhood was diverse, and so was this place — gay, straight, artsy, working-class, white, Black, Latino, Hmong. Some had nabbed tables and chairs, but most just stood around talking, drinking, and smoking. Yes, back then I smoked too, and the place was filled with a cigarette haze, loud conversations, and laughter. Our duplex neighbors were there, and then I recognized one woman my age, Julie; I'd gone to the Children's Theatre Conservatory School with her seven years earlier. We all talked about the storm. Then Kurt and I talked to a few strangers who we learned were also our neighbors. Interesting people with stories to tell, and we had our own to share.

Then, suddenly, something happened. The place was packed, and all of us had trudged through the partially cleared streets to the bar, most wearing heavy snow boots, tracking snow inside. Since we'd been enjoying ourselves, we hadn't noticed that the snow had melted and left us standing in a slick of mud. The bartender turned the music up, so we danced. The place had a great sound system, and what blasted over the speakers was some solid funk — Prince of course, but also Kool & the Gang; Earth, Wind & Fire; Parliament; James Brown; and Kurt's favorite eighties band, Cameo. He still gets excited when he hears the opening bars of "Word Up." Porter's had no real dance floor, and everyone just started dancing where they stood. We were all shoulder to shoulder, singing to the music and shuffling our feet, dancing in the slippery winter goo. To me it was like swirling on ice, but like on ice, someone went down. All I saw was a wool-capped head that suddenly wasn't there, then a major gap as people moved away from the fallen victim. I was close and moved closer. I didn't recognize the guy, but it was hard to recognize anyone whose face was covered in blood, with a gash like a thick leech stretched over his eye.

Someone yelled, "Call an ambulance!"

Someone else said, "Fat chance." I guess it was obvious to everyone that getting an ambulance through the clogged streets could take hours. And there were probably worse medical emergencies.

October

A woman said, "I got a truck." It was Julie.

I decided to help her. Kurt headed home to let the dog out.

Neighbors picked the man up and helped him outside to Julie's four-wheel-drive pickup. The bartender had given the man a bar towel, and now he sat between us, holding it to his head, careful not to get blood on the seats. We drove to the Abbott Northwestern emergency room and dropped him off.

That's my 1991 Halloween Blizzard story. It was a time in our life when we lived hand to mouth in one of the worst neighborhoods in Minneapolis. Bad things happened in that neighborhood (a twelve-year-old stole my car), but most of my memories are good. What every Minnesotan knows is that a powerful winter blizzard might be deadly, but it might also bring out the best in people. We help each other; we dig each other out. We have shared responsibilities, like working together to get a neighborhood guy with a forehead gash to the emergency room.

Julie! Are you still out there?

Pumpkin Spice Cream

Serves 4

Fall is one of my favorite seasons. The air gets crisp and refreshing, the leaves turn tie-dyed shades of red and orange, and Starbucks announces its recurring pumpkin spice latte. It used to be that we didn't get Pumpkin Spice season until at least September, but like fall on Burntside Lake, it seems to be creeping upon us in late August. My Pumpkin Spice Cream and subsequent cold brew might have been inspired by Starbucks, but it came together when one of the largest cold brew coffee makers in the United States (Bizzy Cold Brew — from Minnesota, of course!) sent me a case of cold brew concentrate. I used it to make my own pumpkin spice cold brew at home.

1 cup half-and-half

⅓ cup pumpkin puree (not pumpkin pie filling)

½ teaspoon pumpkin pie spice

pinch ground cloves

pinch salt

1 teaspoon vanilla extract

¼ cup maple syrup

Blend all ingredients together with an immersion blender or stand blender and store in a jar in your refrigerator. Use the cream to make pumpkin spice–flavored cold brews and lattes.

FOR PUMPKIN SPICE COLD BREW

Fill a glass with ice and pour in 1 cup cold brew. Top with ⅓ cup Pumpkin Spice Cream and stir.

FOR PUMPKIN SPICE LATTE

Froth ⅓ cup Pumpkin Spice Cream and pour over hot espresso. Stir to combine; top with cinnamon.

Pumpkin Spice Espresso Martini

October 9

Serves 1

In the late 1980s when I was a cocktail waitress at the Heartthrob Café in St. Paul, dancing on the tables in a poodle skirt, we served an espresso martini. What I remember is a concoction of vodka, Kahlúa, and freeze-dried coffee crystals all shaken up and served with a hazelnut. This was definitely not the rarified boutique espresso martini served today. I've always loved espresso martinis, and this iteration with pumpkin spice gives me all those warm and fuzzy fall feelings. I never tire of pumpkin spice, though I draw the line at pumpkin spice hummus, pumpkin spice chicken sausage, and Pumpkin Pie Spice Pringles. Aren't we getting just a little carried away?

1½ ounces vodka

1½ ounces Irish cream (Baileys)

2 tablespoons pumpkin puree (not pumpkin pie filling)

2 ounces espresso cold press coffee

½ teaspoon pumpkin pie spice

ground cinnamon, for garnish

Fill a cocktail shaker with ice. Add vodka, Irish cream, pumpkin puree, espresso, and pumpkin pie spice. Shake for 30 seconds to combine. Strain into a martini glass and sprinkle with cinnamon.

Curried Pumpkin Soup

Serves 6

By now you're probably getting the idea: I love most things pumpkin. I've long been a fan of squash soup, and during the pandemic, in lieu of roasted squash, I found myself using the disaster-proof cans of pumpkin puree I'd stocked in my pantry. When I added warm garam masala spice, I loved the texture and taste of this easy-to-make soup.

- ¼ cup plus 2 tablespoons olive oil
- 2 cups chopped onion
- 4 cloves garlic, minced
- 2 teaspoons garam masala
- 1 teaspoon turmeric
- 1 teaspoon chopped fresh thyme
- 3 cups pumpkin puree
- 4 cups chicken broth
- 3 tablespoons maple syrup
- 1 teaspoon kosher salt
- ½ teaspoon freshly grated nutmeg, plus more for garnish
- 12 sage leaves
- 2 tablespoons toasted pumpkin seeds
- ⅓ cup heavy cream

TIP: Be very careful blending hot soup in a stand blender. It's recommended to blend half of the soup at a time and to not fill up the blender more than halfway. Take out the center of the blender lid and cover the hole with a towel, allowing the steam to vent but keeping the hot soup from spraying all over your kitchen. I speak from experience on this one.

Heat 2 tablespoons olive oil in a large pot over medium-high heat. Add onion and cook, stirring occasionally, for about 10 minutes. Add the garlic, garam masala, turmeric, and thyme, and cook for 2 minutes more. Stir in pumpkin puree and cook until it becomes darker and more concentrated, about 5 more minutes. Stir in chicken broth, maple syrup, salt, and nutmeg. Simmer, uncovered, stirring occasionally, until slightly reduced and flavors have melded, about 30 minutes.

Heat remaining ¼ cup olive oil in a small frying pan over medium-high heat. Add sage leaves and cook until dark green, about 2 minutes, using tongs to flip. Remove sage and set aside on paper towel to cool.

Remove soup from heat and blend with an immersion blender to create a smooth texture. Alternatively, use a stand blender (see tip). Finish by stirring in the heavy cream. Taste and adjust seasonings, then serve, garnished with toasted sage leaves, pumpkin seeds, and a bit of fresh nutmeg.

Herb Drop Biscuits

Makes 12 drop biscuits

This biscuit recipe is easy, with no kneading or rolling required. You get a crisp exterior and a soft, pillowy interior full of craggy holes to trap butter. The recipe is super versatile, depending on the types of garden herbs you prefer, like rosemary, sage, or thyme. You can also add shredded cheese like Parmesan, Gruyère, or cheddar. If you aren't a fan of goat cheese, substitute cream cheese. Try chocolate chips if your inner ten-year-old absolutely demands it.

2 cups all-purpose flour

2 teaspoons baking powder

1 teaspoon kosher salt

½ cup (1 stick) unsalted butter, melted

½ cup goat cheese (herbed or plain), crumbled or softened, at room temperature

½ cup milk (try using goat or sheep milk for a tangier biscuit)

2 tablespoons fresh chopped chives (or dill, basil, rosemary, or thyme; or sliced green onions)

Heat oven to 400 degrees.

Mix flour, baking powder, and salt together in a large bowl. Add melted butter and goat cheese crumbles and milk, then add herbs. Stir together until a shaggy dough forms, being careful not to overmix.

Place heaping tablespoonfuls of dough on an ungreased baking sheet about 1½ inches apart. Bake 12–15 minutes, until the bottoms are golden brown.

11 October

Weeknight Enchilada Soup

Serves 6

Every year I make my own salsa verde. Lots of it. The 3b zone of the Ely Hilltop Garden makes growing tomatoes difficult, with the majority maturing in late August and early September, right before the first frost. As a result, I'm stuck with dozens of green tomatoes that make a good substitute for tomatillos in salsa verde. I blend the green tomatoes with jalapeños, onions, cilantro, and lime juice. The pectin in the green tomatoes gives the salsa a rich thickness. Or you can purchase the not-too-bad Herdez salsa verde at your local supermarket.

This soup comes together quickly, making it perfect for a weeknight dinner when the October chill sets in. The tortilla strips and toppings add texture and more flavor to the meal.

2 tablespoons olive oil

1 medium onion, chopped

1 poblano pepper, cut into quarter-inch dice

4 cloves garlic, finely chopped

4 cups vegetable or chicken broth

1 cup salsa verde

3 (15.5-ounce) cans great northern or navy beans, rinsed and drained

1 cup corn (frozen, fresh, or canned)

1 tablespoon paprika

1 tablespoon chili powder

2 teaspoons cumin

2 teaspoons kosher salt

1 teaspoon dried oregano

juice of ½ lime

1 cup sour cream

Tortilla Strips
6 (6-inch) corn tortillas, piled into a stack and cut into quarter-inch strips

1 tablespoon olive oil

1 teaspoon kosher salt

¼ teaspoon chili powder

Optional Toppings
sliced avocado, chopped green onions, lime wedges, shredded pepper jack cheese, sliced jalapeños, queso fresco, cilantro, pulled rotisserie chicken

For the Soup
Heat 2 tablespoons olive oil in a medium pot on medium heat. Add onions and poblano peppers and cook for 5 minutes, until softened. Add the garlic and cook, stirring, for 2 minutes more. Add the broth, salsa verde, beans, corn, and seasonings and mix until well combined. Bring to a boil, reduce heat, and simmer for 15 minutes. Remove from heat and whisk in lime juice and sour cream until well combined.

For the Tortilla Strips
Heat oven to 400 degrees. Toss tortilla strips with 1 tablespoon olive oil. Place the strips on an ungreased sheet pan and spread in an even layer. Bake for 6 minutes, toss lightly to redistribute, and bake for 6 minutes more, until crispy, golden brown, and toasty. Sprinkle kosher salt and chili powder on the strips while warm from the oven.

Garnish soup with tortilla strips and desired toppings.

Big Beefy Chili

Serves 6-8

Chili comes in many varieties. Do you use ground meat or chuck steak? Beans or no beans? I find that a big beefy chili loaded with steak and tons of rich, deeply flavored chili powder is my fall favorite on a Sunday game day, as a pregame for trick or treating, or for a Halloween party potluck. A smidge of pumpkin puree in this recipe adds sweetness and creaminess, but feel free to skip it . . . if you dare.

- 1 tablespoon extra-virgin olive oil
- 2 pounds chuck roast, cut into cubes (or substitute ground beef)
- 1 large onion, diced
- 1 bell pepper (green, red, yellow, or orange), diced
- 1 jalapeño, seeds removed, diced
- 4 cloves garlic, minced
- 3 tablespoons chili powder
- 2 teaspoons kosher salt
- 1 teaspoon black pepper
- 1 teaspoon cumin
- ½ teaspoon cinnamon
- 1 cup beer (light or dark is fine)
- 1 (28-ounce) can crushed tomatoes
- 1 (14.5-ounce) can diced tomatoes
- 2 (15-ounce) cans kidney beans, drained
- ¼ cup pumpkin puree (not pumpkin pie filling)
- juice of 1 lime
- for serving: sour cream, pickled jalapeños, chopped cilantro, tortilla chips

Heat the oil in a large Dutch oven over medium heat and, working in batches, brown the meat to sear well on all sides. Set the seared beef aside.

Add the onions and peppers to the pot and cook for 5 minutes, until soft. Add the jalapeño, garlic, chili powder, salt, pepper, cumin, and cinnamon and cook for 2 minutes more. Add the beef and the juices back into the pot. Add the beer, crushed tomatoes, diced tomatoes, and kidney beans and give everything a good stir. Simmer on low for 2 hours, then stir in the pumpkin puree and lime juice.

Serve with sour cream, pickled jalapeños, chopped cilantro, and tortilla chips.

13

October

Autumn Harvest Sheet Pan Roasted Veggies

Serves 6

Sheet pan veggies have been a game changer for me. It's just so easy. I love how you can mix up the combination of vegetables based on what might be available at a late-season farmers market or CSA and roast them all at once. Roasted vegetables are probably my number-one fall side dish, and I always make extra for lunches or to top with an over-easy egg.

3 cups brussels sprouts, trimmed and halved

3 cups butternut squash, peeled and cut into half-inch cubes

12–15 small red potatoes, halved or quartered if larger

2 medium parsnips, peeled and cut into half-inch chunks

2 medium carrots, peeled and cut into half-inch chunks

1 red onion, cut into half-inch wedges

⅓ cup olive oil

2 tablespoons fresh thyme

2 teaspoons kosher salt

2 teaspoons fresh ground black pepper or 1 teaspoon fine-ground black pepper

3 teaspoons fresh or dried rosemary leaves, divided

¾ cup apple cider vinegar

¼ cup honey

2 tablespoons maple syrup

1 tablespoon Dijon mustard

Heat oven to 400 degrees.

Combine vegetables on a sheet pan and toss with the olive oil, thyme, salt, pepper, and 2 teaspoons rosemary. Distribute the vegetables evenly so they can get nice and roasted. Bake for 30 minutes, until the vegetables are caramelized.

Meanwhile, combine apple cider vinegar, honey, maple syrup, and Dijon mustard in a saucepan and boil until the mixture is reduced to a syrupy glaze, about 10 minutes. Drizzle the glaze over the caramelized vegetables. Finish with a sprinkling of kosher salt and cracked black pepper and the reserved 1 teaspoon rosemary.

Baked Brussels Sprouts with Lemon and Goat Cheese

15

October

Serves 6

I'd heard about this tavern on a small island off Hvar in Croatia located in a remote village and nestled in a vineyard. To get there, we anchored our sailboat in a cove, took the dinghy to a rocky beach, and then followed a mile-long trail through the pine forest. The tavern was run by two brothers, one who cooked and one who served. They were the entire staff, but there were only a dozen tables. We had grilled fresh fish of some kind (of course) but also these incredible brussels sprouts roasted over olive wood embers, coated with lemon and olive oil, then served with dollops of locally produced goat cheese. My recipe is an ode to that simple dish, and looks superb in a cast iron skillet served alongside a roasted chicken or steak.

- 2 tablespoons extra-virgin olive oil
- 1 pound brussels sprouts, halved or quartered if large
- 6 ounces (¾ cup) plain unsweetened yogurt
- 4 ounces (½ cup) goat cheese
- ¼ cup buttermilk (or substitute goat milk)
- zest of 1 lemon
- 2 tablespoons lemon juice
- 2 cloves garlic, minced
- 1 teaspoon kosher salt, plus more to taste
- 3 dashes hot sauce (Tabasco)
- ⅓ cup grated Parmesan cheese
- ¼ cup raw slivered almonds
- 2 tablespoons chopped basil
- 2 tablespoons chopped mint
- 2 tablespoons chopped parsley
- freshly ground black pepper

Heat oven to 400 degrees.

Heat the olive oil in a 12-inch oven-safe skillet over medium-high heat for 1 minute. Add the brussels sprouts and cook undisturbed for 2 minutes, then shake the pan to redistribute the sprouts and cook for 2 more minutes so that the sprouts' surfaces brown and start to crisp. Transfer the skillet to the oven and roast the brussels sprouts for about 10 minutes.

Meanwhile, combine the yogurt, goat cheese, buttermilk, lemon zest, lemon juice, garlic, salt, and hot sauce in a medium bowl and pulse with an immersion blender until smooth.

Remove the brussels sprouts from the oven. Turn the broiler to high and pour the yogurt mixture onto the sprouts, stirring to combine. Sprinkle with Parmesan cheese and almonds. Return to the oven and broil for 2–3 minutes, or until the cheese has melted. Remove pan from oven and top with the chopped basil, mint, and parsley. Finish with freshly ground black pepper and kosher salt to taste.

Maple Roasted Butternut Squash with Sage Browned Butter

Serves 2

This combination reminds me of the ubiquitous butternut squash ravioli with sage browned butter sauce served at many fine Italian restaurants. What's great about this dish is that you don't need to go to the trouble of making the ravioli. It's delicious paired with roasted chicken.

1 butternut squash, halved, seeds removed

2 tablespoons extra-virgin olive oil

1 teaspoon kosher salt

½ teaspoon black pepper

2 tablespoons maple syrup

2 tablespoons unsalted butter

4–6 sage leaves

2 ounces prosciutto

¼ cup walnuts

Heat oven to 400 degrees. Rub inside of each squash half with olive oil and season with salt and pepper. Place on a large sheet pan and roast cut side down for 45 minutes, until the squash begins to soften.

Remove the squash from the oven and flip over. Add half of the maple syrup, butter, sage leaves, and prosciutto to each squash cavity. Scatter the walnuts on the baking dish and return to the oven. Bake for another 10 minutes, until the squash is tender. Transfer to a serving platter and top the cooked squash with the toasted walnuts.

Braised Red Cabbage with Apples

October 17

Serves 6

I came to red cabbage late in life. I do remember my grandmother making sauerkraut, canning pickles, and cooking fruit preserves, but that sort of home cooking went out of style as more convenience and processed foods were introduced to grocery store shelves in the seventies. It was only five years ago that I started my own garden, and only three years ago that I was forced to do something with the cabbages I impulsively grew. It was then that I learned the art of fermentation.

Today cabbage is one of my favorite fall vegetables. I serve this side with pork roast, loin, or chops.

- olive oil (for stovetop version)
- 1 large head red cabbage
- 1 large onion, sliced
- 1 cup grated apple (about 2 apples grated on a box grater; any apples will do)
- ⅓ cup apple cider
- ¼ cup apple cider vinegar
- 1 teaspoon cumin
- ½ teaspoon ground cloves
- ½ teaspoon caraway seeds, crushed with a rolling pin, or substitute ground caraway
- 1 bay leaf
- 2 teaspoons kosher salt
- 1 teaspoon black pepper

Slow Cooker Instructions

Add all ingredients to the slow cooker and stir well to mix. Turn the slow cooker to low and cook for 4 hours. Remove the lid and cook 30–60 minutes more; the liquid will start to evaporate, but keep an eye on it so the cabbage doesn't dry out. Season with salt and pepper to taste.

Stovetop Instructions

Heat 1 tablespoon olive oil in a very large skillet over medium-high heat. Add cabbage, onions, and apples and cook to wilt the vegetables, about 3 minutes. Add apple cider, apple cider vinegar, cumin, cloves, caraway, and bay leaf; reduce heat to low and continue cooking for 45 minutes, until the cabbage is soft and stewed. If the pan gets too dry, add ¼ cup water. Season with salt and pepper to taste.

Double Potato Gratin with Apples and Onions

Serves 12

I have always loved potato and sweet potato gratins. Who doesn't savor potatoes in cream, butter, and spices? This recipe takes that classic approach and doubles the fun: both regular and sweet potatoes, apple and maple syrup for extra sweetness, and sage and thyme for a duet of herbs. I've made it many times to get the balance exactly right, and I think this one goes in the "Wow!" category of culinary delights. Note: don't make the mistake of substituting watery milk or half-and-half for heavy cream. This is not intended to be a low-calorie dish.

- **2 tablespoons butter**
- **2 medium onions, halved and thinly sliced**
- **2 medium apples, grated on a box grater**
- **2 cups heavy cream**
- **2 tablespoons maple syrup**
- **2 teaspoons finely chopped fresh sage**
- **2 teaspoons fresh thyme**
- **2 teaspoons kosher salt**
- **1 teaspoon black pepper**
- **2 medium sweet potatoes, peeled and thinly sliced (about ⅛ inch)**
- **3 medium Yukon gold potatoes, thinly sliced (about ⅛ inch); reserve slices in water so they don't brown**

Melt butter in a heavy-bottomed pan over medium-low heat. Add the onions and cook, stirring occasionally, until the onions are caramelized with a golden color, about 15 minutes. Stir in the apples and cook 5 minutes more, until the mixture is caramelized and well combined.

Heat oven to 400 degrees. Grease a 9x12–inch or 2-quart baking dish and add the onion mixture to the bottom.

In a large bowl, combine the cream, maple syrup, sage, thyme, salt, and pepper.

In another large bowl, combine the sweet potato slices with half the cream mixture, tossing to coat. In a separate large bowl, combine the Yukon gold potato slices with remaining cream mixture, tossing to coat. Separate any slices that are sticking together to get the cream mixture in between them.

Alternating slices of potatoes and sweet potatoes, organize into a neat stack and lay them in the prepared baking dish with their edges aligned vertically until the dish is full. Pour any remaining cream mixture from the two bowls over the top.

Cover the baking dish tightly with foil and transfer to the oven. Bake for 45 minutes. Remove the foil and continue baking until the top is pale golden brown, about 30 minutes longer. Remove from the oven, let rest for 10 minutes, and serve.

19

October

Skillet Shells with Sausage, Ricotta, and Greens

Serves 6

My first experience with kale was as a waitress: we were expected to garnish each plate that came from the kitchen with a crinkly green leaf. For some unknown reason, all breakfast dishes were served with a kale leaf and a slice of orange. Some customers ate the pulp of the orange, but the kale was uniformly left untouched. Back then, most people probably thought kale was inedible.

Then, at the restaurant Joan's in the Park in St. Paul, I ordered a kale Caesar salad, and my world turned upside down. Now I love kale wilted in salads, sautéed with garlic, cooked with scrambled eggs, and simmered in soups. The kale in this recipe adds color and hardiness to a rib-sticking one-skillet pasta dish. My repertoire of leafy greens has expanded over time; you can swap spinach, beet greens, Swiss chard, or even collards for the kale. If you have a jar of roasted red peppers or sun-dried tomatoes on hand, you could add those too.

- 1 pound medium pasta shells or large rigatoni
- 2 tablespoons extra-virgin olive oil
- 1 pound hot Italian sausage, casings removed
- 6 cloves garlic, coarsely chopped
- 1 tablespoon dried oregano
- 2 teaspoons lemon zest
- 2 teaspoons kosher salt
- 1 teaspoon black pepper
- 1 teaspoon chopped fresh sage or ½ teaspoon ground dried
- ½ teaspoon crushed red pepper flakes
- 1 bunch lacinato kale, chopped
- 1 bunch baby spinach, chopped
- ½ pint (2 cups) ricotta cheese
- 1 cup heavy cream
- ⅓ cup Parmesan cheese

Heat oven to 350 degrees. Boil the shells until very al dente, about 7 minutes. Reserve 1 cup pasta water. Drain the pasta and set aside.

Meanwhile, heat a large, deep cast iron skillet over medium-high heat. Add olive oil and brown the sausage. Add garlic, oregano, lemon zest, salt, pepper, sage, red pepper flakes, and chopped kale to the sausage and cook, stirring, about 3 minutes. If the kale seems tough, cover the skillet to steam the leaves. Stir in spinach, ricotta, cream, and 1 cup pasta water and simmer until slightly thickened, about 2 minutes. Stir in the shells and remove from heat.

Cover skillet with foil and bake in the middle of the oven for 30 minutes. Remove skillet from oven and turn on broiler. Remove foil and sprinkle pasta with Parmesan cheese. Broil for 5 minutes, until the cheese is browned in spots and the casserole is bubbly.

21

October

Sheet Pan Shawarma Two Ways

Serves 6

Vegetarians and meat eaters alike can have the best of both worlds with this versatile method that utilizes two sheet pans with the same seasoning profiles. The finished dish can go in pita pockets like a sandwich, or you could serve it on a bed of tzatziki or in a bowl of plain yogurt dressed up with garlic and lemon juice.

Sheet Pan One
- **6 boneless chicken thighs**
- **1 red bell pepper, cut into quarter-inch strips**
- **½ large red onion, cut into quarter-inch slices**
- **1 tablespoon extra-virgin olive oil**

Sheet Pan Two
- **1 head cauliflower, broken up into florets**
- **1 red bell pepper, cut into quarter-inch strips**
- **½ large red onion, cut into quarter-inch slices**
- **1 (14.5-ounce) can chickpeas, drained and rinsed, then patted dry**
- **1 tablespoon extra-virgin olive oil**

Chicken Marinade
- **zest and juice of 1 lemon**
- **¼ cup extra-virgin olive oil**
- **¼ cup plain unsweetened yogurt**
- **6 cloves garlic, minced**
- **2 teaspoons black pepper**
- **1 teaspoon kosher salt**

Seasoning Blend
- **2 tablespoons za'atar**
- **2 tablespoons garlic powder**
- **2 tablespoons smoked paprika**
- **1 tablespoon plus 1 teaspoon kosher salt**
- **1 teaspoon cayenne pepper**
- **1 teaspoon turmeric**
- **1 teaspoon cumin**
- **1 teaspoon cinnamon**
- **dash nutmeg**

Tahini Sauce
- **½ cup tahini**
- **2 cloves garlic, minced or grated**
- **2 tablespoons lemon juice**
- **1 tablespoon harissa paste**
- **1½ teaspoons kosher salt**

Assembly
- **pita or naan bread or rice**
- **sliced lemons**
- **sliced cucumbers**
- **cilantro or mint sprigs**

Combine marinade ingredients in a plastic bag and marinate the chicken for at least 1 hour or overnight.

Heat oven to 425 degrees. Combine ingredients for the seasoning blend and divide in half for each sheet pan.

Prepare Sheet Pan One
Line a sheet pan with parchment paper or a silicone mat. Remove chicken from the marinade and arrange on the prepared sheet pan.

Meanwhile, prepare the vegetables. In a medium bowl, toss the red peppers and onions with oil and one-quarter of the seasonings. Sprinkle the other one-quarter of the seasoning on the chicken and add the vegetables to the sheet pan.

Prepare Sheet Pan Two
Line a sheet pan with parchment paper or a silicone mat. In a large bowl, combine vegetables and chickpeas with oil. Toss with remaining half of seasoning, then transfer vegetables to the prepared sheet pan.

Place both sheet pans in the oven for 40 minutes, rotating pan positions halfway through cooking.

For the Tahini Sauce
Whisk together sauce ingredients in a small bowl. Check the consistency of the sauce, as the thickness of store-bought tahini varies greatly. If the sauce is too thick, add 1 tablespoon of water at a time until sauce will drizzle easily over chicken and vegetables. Let sit for a minute or two to let the garlic mellow.

To Serve
Prepare one serving platter for the chicken and vegetables and a second platter for the cauliflower, chickpeas, and vegetables. Serve with naan, pita bread, or rice and the tahini sauce. Garnish the platters with sliced lemons, sliced cucumbers, and cilantro or mint as desired.

23

October

Roast Chicken with Autumn Vegetables

Serves 6

There's a time in the fall when you must make the difficult decision to either turn on the furnace or tough it out for another week. My husband, Kurt, wants the heat, but often I just can't bring myself to embrace the arrival of winter. To ease into it, I like to slow cook something in our oven that does double duty warming the house. This is my fall comfort food dish for just those occasions.

Compound Butter
½ cup (1 stick) butter, at room temperature

2 teaspoons chopped fresh rosemary

2 teaspoons chopped fresh thyme

zest of 1 lemon (reserve juice for the sauce)

1 teaspoon kosher salt

1 teaspoon black pepper

3 large cloves garlic, minced

Chicken
1 (4–5 pound) roasting chicken, patted dry

2 teaspoons kosher salt

1 teaspoon black pepper

3–5 sprigs rosemary

3–5 sprigs thyme

1 lemon, quartered

Vegetables
12 fingerling potatoes, halved if large

12 baby carrots, halved lengthwise

2 large parsnips, peeled and cut into 1-inch pieces

1 large onion, peeled and cut into 1½-inch chunks

3 tablespoons extra-virgin olive oil

1 teaspoon chopped fresh rosemary

1 teaspoon chopped fresh thyme

1 teaspoon kosher salt

1 teaspoon black pepper

Sauce
chicken juices

reserved juice from 1 lemon

1 tablespoon honey

fresh rosemary or thyme, for garnish

25
October

Heat oven to 400 degrees. In a small bowl, combine the compound butter ingredients, stirring until smooth.

Sprinkle the cavity of the chicken with salt and pepper. Place the rosemary, thyme, and quartered lemon in the cavity. Place the chicken in a large roasting pan. Loosen the skin over the entire chicken breast, starting at the neck, and rub the butter mixture over the outside and under the skin, being careful not to tear the skin.

In a large bowl, toss together the vegetables, oil, rosemary, thyme, salt, and pepper. Arrange the vegetables in the roasting pan around the chicken and bake for 1½ hours or until the chicken temperature is 165 degrees at the thigh and wing joint.

Place chicken on a platter surrounded by the vegetables. Strain any juices from the pan into a glass measuring cup and add the reserved lemon juice and honey, stirring to combine. Serve juices alongside chicken or pour over the vegetables on the platter before serving. Garnish the platter with fresh rosemary or thyme.

Short Rib Bolognese

Serves 6

My mother used to make a kind of spaghetti Bolognese with ground beef, olive oil, canned tomato sauce, onions, garlic, and red wine. Of course, my sisters and I just called it spaghetti and ate every last strand of pasta with the sauce. This recipe is similar to Mom's. By slow cooking the short ribs and pulling the meat off the bones, you get a sassy and saucy meat pile atop your favorite starch. Polenta or pasta is my chosen way to enjoy all the sauce from this delicious dish, though my husband, Kurt, always wants mashed potatoes. The only thing that bothers me about this recipe is that short ribs used to be less expensive than ground beef. Then again, I remember when a cup of coffee was fifty cents and you would get free refills.

- **2 pounds meaty short ribs**
- **kosher salt**
- **black pepper**
- **3 tablespoons extra-virgin olive oil**
- **1 medium onion, chopped**
- **2 carrots, chopped**
- **2 ribs celery, chopped**
- **1 (12-ounce) can beer or 2 cups red wine, divided**
- **4 cloves garlic, minced**
- **2 teaspoons fresh thyme leaves**
- **1½ teaspoons smoked paprika**
- **1 (6-ounce) can tomato paste**
- **1 (14-ounce) can chopped tomatoes**
- **1 (28-ounce) can crushed tomatoes**
- **pasta, polenta, or potatoes for serving**

Season short ribs generously with salt and pepper, and let sit on the counter for 30 minutes. Meanwhile, heat oven to 350 degrees.

Add olive oil to a Dutch oven over medium-high heat and brown the short ribs on all sides. Don't rush them; you want them to be good and crusty all over. Set ribs aside; drain excess fat from the pan, leaving behind about 1 tablespoon. Add the onions, carrots, and celery and cook, stirring, for about 5 minutes. Add half the beer or wine and scrape up any browned bits. Stir in the garlic, thyme leaves, smoked paprika, 2 teaspoons kosher salt, and 1 teaspoon black pepper. Let most of the liquid evaporate before adding the tomato paste, then cook for 2 minutes more. Add the chopped tomatoes, crushed tomatoes, and remaining wine or beer, and give the sauce a good stir. Add the ribs to the Dutch oven and cook, covered, for 2 hours.

Once the meat is tender and falling off the bone, take the short ribs out of the sauce and shred the meat. Discard the bones, return meat to the sauce, and stir. If sauce is thin, return pan to the oven, uncovered, and cook to reduce excess liquid.

Taste and adjust the seasonings. Serve over your favorite pasta (pappardelle, ziti, farfalle) or polenta or mashed potatoes.

Mom's Meatloaf

October

Serves 8

My mom had a special meatloaf pan that was pulled from the cupboard at least twice a month. This was no repurposed bread loaf pan, but a genuine Corningware Nature's Bounty pan with images of carrots, tomatoes, and mushrooms stenciled on the side. You can find this same pan on Etsy now for $28. Mom's recipe was a classic one that she zhuzhed up with barbecue sauce and spices. As a kid, my favorite part was the topping of ketchup that I tried to scoop up with each bite. My second favorite part was slices the next day on white toast slathered with mayonnaise. I think my older sister still has that pan.

- 1 large egg, beaten
- ¾ cup whole milk
- 1 cup dried breadcrumbs
- ⅓ cup finely chopped onion
- ¼ cup chopped celery
- 1 carrot, grated on a box grater and chopped fine
- 2 tablespoons chopped parsley
- 1 tablespoon Worcestershire sauce
- 1 teaspoon kosher salt
- ½ teaspoon black pepper
- 1 pound ground beef
- ½ pound ground pork
- 3 tablespoons ketchup
- 1 teaspoon yellow mustard
- 2 tablespoons barbecue sauce

Heat oven to 350 degrees.

In a large bowl, combine beaten egg, milk, and breadcrumbs and let the breadcrumbs soak up the milk. Add the onions, celery, carrots, parsley, Worcestershire sauce, salt, pepper, and meats. Mix with your hands and form into a 4x8–inch loaf on top of a 9x13–inch broiler pan. Bake for 1 hour or until the internal temperature reads 160 degrees on a meat thermometer.

Remove the loaf from the oven. Stir together the ketchup, mustard, and barbecue sauce, and spread it on the loaf. Bake for 10 more minutes, until the glaze is glossy.

Pork Chop and Scalloped Potato Casserole

Serves 4

You know we like a good, hearty meal in the Midwest — meat and potatoes, as they say. This delicious pork chop and potato casserole is a two-for-one, with creamy potatoes as a built-in accompaniment. The recipe is adapted from *The New Basics Cookbook* by Julee Rosso and Sheila Lukins. *New Basics* and *The Joy of Cooking* were my two essentials as I learned to cook in my twenties. You can use a traditional casserole dish or, my choice, a large cast iron skillet. Put that skillet in the middle of the table and dig in!

3–4 cups peeled and thinly sliced russet potatoes

2 cups heavy cream

2 cloves garlic, grated on a microplane

¼ cup stone-ground or Dijon mustard

6 boneless pork loin chops

1½ teaspoons kosher salt, divided

1 teaspoon black pepper

2 tablespoons unsalted butter

¼ cup chicken broth

1 tablespoon lemon juice

1 cup thinly sliced sweet onion

1 tablespoon fresh thyme leaves, divided

1 tablespoon chopped parsley

Heat oven to 350 degrees. Fill a large pot with water and bring to a boil. Drop in the russet potatoes and cook for 3 minutes. Drain the potatoes and spread out on paper towels to dry.

In a medium bowl, whisk together the cream, garlic, and mustard; set aside.

Next, season the pork chops with 1 teaspoon salt and ½ teaspoon pepper.

Melt the butter in a skillet over medium-high heat. When the butter starts to pop and splatter, carefully add the pork chops to the pan. Brown them for 2 minutes on each side; then set aside. Add the chicken broth and lemon juice to the skillet and simmer for 30 seconds, scraping up any browned bits. Add this accumulated liquid to cream mixture.

In an 8x12–inch baking dish or 12-inch cast iron skillet, layer half the potatoes and half the onions and sprinkle with the remaining ½ teaspoon salt and ½ teaspoon pepper and half the thyme leaves. Lay the pork chops on top of the potatoes and onions, then layer the remaining potatoes and onions on top. Pour the cream mixture over the dish. Sprinkle with the remaining fresh thyme and all the parsley. Bake uncovered for 1 hour and 15 minutes; place a sheet pan underneath to catch any drips. If the top starts to brown too fast, cover loosely with aluminum foil while casserole finishes cooking.

29 October

Pumpkin Dark Chocolate Snack Cake

Serves 10

Pumpkin and dark chocolate go together like peas and carrots. This snack cake is moist and chocolatey, the perfect after-school treat or accompaniment to a cup of hot coffee on a Sunday morning when the autumn leaves are falling.

- 2⅓ cups all-purpose flour
- 2 tablespoons pumpkin pie spice
- 1 teaspoon kosher salt
- 1 teaspoon baking soda
- 1 cup (2 sticks) butter, at room temperature
- 1 cup packed brown sugar
- 1 cup granulated sugar
- 2 large eggs
- 2 teaspoons vanilla extract
- 1 (15-ounce) can pumpkin puree (not pie filling)
- 1 (10-ounce) package dark chocolate pieces

Heat oven to 350 degrees. Grease the bottom and sides of a 9x13-inch pan.

In a medium bowl, whisk together flour, pumpkin pie spice, salt, and baking soda.

In the bowl of a stand mixer, combine the butter and sugars on medium speed until smooth, then mix in the eggs, vanilla, and pumpkin puree. The mixture may look lumpy or curdled. Add the dry mixture and combine at low speed. Mix in the dark chocolate pieces by hand with a wooden spoon.

Pour batter into prepared pan. Bake for 35–40 minutes, until a toothpick inserted into the center comes out clean.

Pumpkin Muffins

Makes 12

One of my favorite bread baskets has to be at Burntside Lodge in Ely, Minnesota. In addition to a sourdough roll and a crisp grainy cracker, they serve a mini pumpkin muffin with rosemary, cranberry, and salted butter. This recipe is my attempt to re-create their delicious muffin.

1⅔ cups all-purpose flour

1½ teaspoons pumpkin pie spice

1 teaspoon baking soda

½ teaspoon kosher salt

½ teaspoon cinnamon

½ teaspoon ground ginger

¼ teaspoon nutmeg

2 large eggs

⅔ cup granulated sugar

½ cup packed brown sugar

⅓ cup vegetable oil

¼ cup applesauce

1 cup pumpkin puree (not pie filling)

¼ cup whole milk

Heat oven to 375 degrees. Spray muffin tins with cooking spray or prepare with paper liners.

In a large bowl, whisk together flour, pumpkin pie spice, baking soda, salt, cinnamon, ginger, and nutmeg.

In a medium bowl, whisk together eggs and sugars until combined. Add oil and applesauce and whisk until combined. Add pumpkin puree and milk and whisk until combined. Pour the wet mixture into the dry mixture and stir gently until just combined.

Divide batter evenly among the muffin cups. Bake for 18–20 minutes, until a toothpick inserted into a muffin comes out clean. Allow to cool for 5 minutes in the pan, then transfer to a wire rack to cool completely.

October

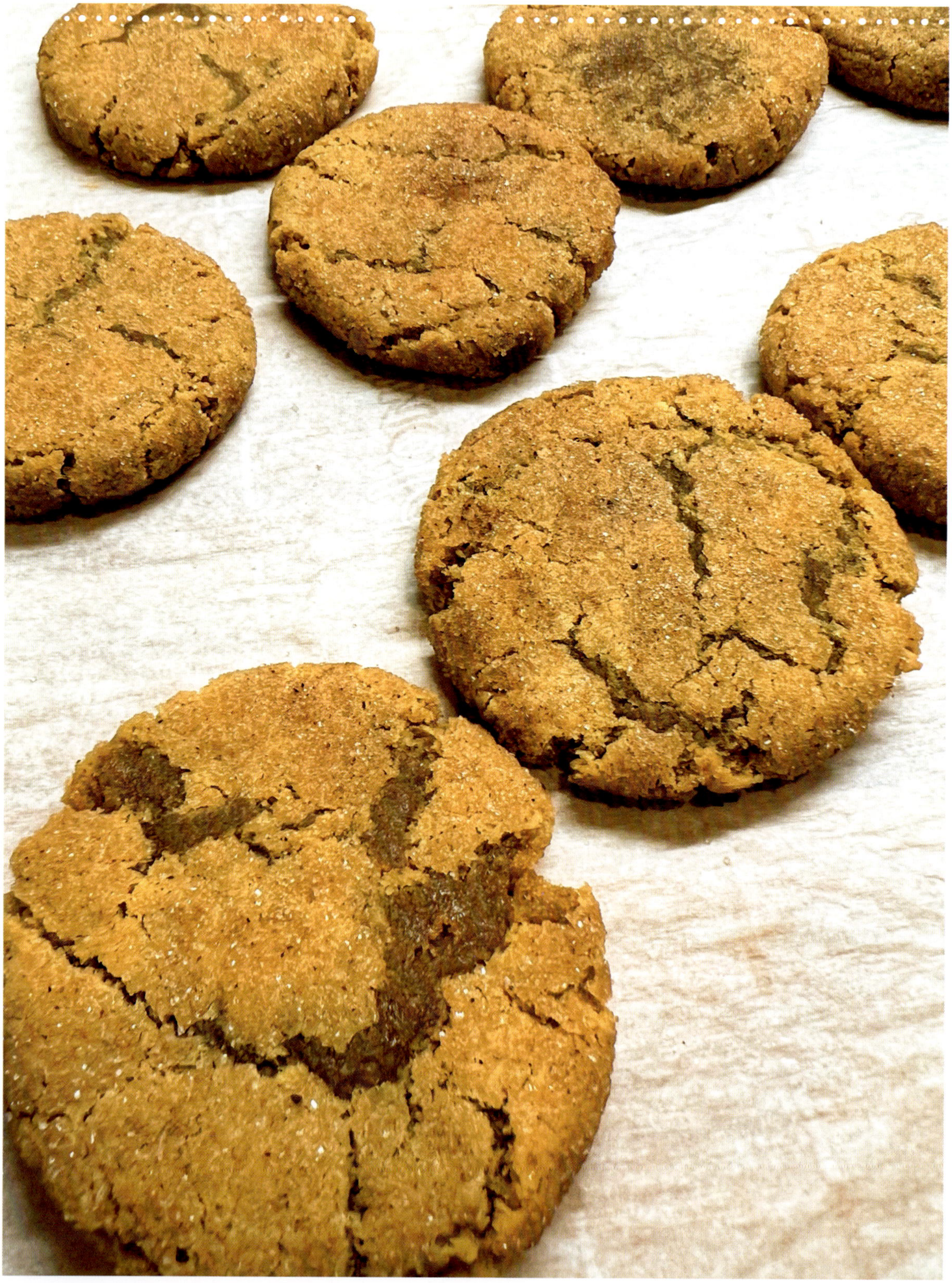

Pumpkin Snickerdoodle Cookies

October

Makes 2 dozen cookies

The addition of pumpkin to this traditional recipe gives the sweet cinnamon cookie a touch of savory plus extra chewiness. I knew I had a winning recipe on my hands when I set them out to cool one Saturday morning and my husband, Kurt, consumed the entire tray while reading his book.

½ cup (1 stick) unsalted butter

⅔ cup pumpkin puree (not pie filling)

1 tablespoon molasses

½ cup granulated sugar

½ cup packed brown sugar

2 large egg yolks

2 teaspoons vanilla extract

1⅔ cups all-purpose flour

2 teaspoons confectioners' sugar

1½ teaspoons pumpkin pie spice

1 teaspoon kosher salt

½ teaspoon baking soda

For Rolling

¼ cup granulated sugar

1 teaspoon cinnamon

Heat oven to 350 degrees and line 2 baking sheet pans with parchment paper.

Brown the butter in a pot on the stove for about 4 minutes over medium-high heat. While it cooks, it will foam, sputter, and eventually darken to a golden brown with flecks in it that smell nutty. When this happens, take it off the heat right away — it's easy for those flecks to start turning black and burn, in which case you need to start again. Pour the browned butter into a bowl and allow to cool to room temperature.

Place pumpkin in a dish towel, cheesecloth, or paper towel and squeeze as much moisture out of it as you can. The pumpkin will have lots of moisture, so you will need to do this step a few times. When it is ready, it will feel like play dough and barely make an imprint of moisture on a paper towel.

In a large bowl, whisk cooled browned butter and molasses, then whisk in the ½ cup granulated sugar and brown sugar until the mixture looks like sand. Add egg yolks, vanilla, and pumpkin puree, stirring to combine. Stir in flour, confectioners' sugar, pumpkin pie spice, salt, and baking soda until combined. Refrigerate dough for 30 minutes.

Meanwhile, combine the ¼ cup granulated sugar and cinnamon in a small bowl.

Scoop the dough into 1½ tablespoon–size balls and roll in the cinnamon sugar. Place balls on prepared baking sheets 3 inches apart. Bake for 10 minutes.

When the cookies are done, they will be puffy. Immediately after removing them from the oven, flatten by pressing with a spatula or the back of a spoon until you smush out the air.

NOTE: Thanks to Minnesota baker and cookbook author Sarah Kieffer for teaching me the smush technique.

Salted Caramel Apple Bars

Makes 16 bars

When was the last time you had a caramel apple? I remember the first time I had one. I must have been around eight years old. My mom came back from the SuperValu grocery store one afternoon with a caramel apple–making kit called Wrapples for us. I remember that I peeled off the caramel from the waxed paper sheets with sticky fingers and left the apple untouched. I now know that's a sin. In later years, my mom shopped at Byerlys, and their caramel apples were and still are the gold standard in my opinion.

These bars are an ode to those caramel apples. I like to make the caramel in a pressure cooker (Instant Pot), but you can substitute store-bought if you are crunched for time. There is no separating the caramel from the apples with these tasty treats!

Caramel
1 (14-ounce) can sweetened condensed milk

½ teaspoon vanilla extract

1 teaspoon coarse flaky salt (Maldon)

Crust
½ cup (1 stick) unsalted butter, melted

1 cup all-purpose flour

¼ cup granulated sugar

1 teaspoon vanilla extract

¼ teaspoon kosher salt

Filling
2 large apples, peeled, cored, and chopped into quarter- to half-inch pieces

¼ cup packed brown sugar

2 tablespoons all-purpose flour

2 tablespoons granulated sugar

1 teaspoon cinnamon

½ teaspoon allspice

¼ teaspoon ground ginger

Topping
½ cup granola (store-bought is fine)

⅓ cup packed brown sugar

¼ cup all-purpose flour

¼ teaspoon cinnamon

¼ cup unsalted butter, cold, cubed into pea-size pieces

October

For the Caramel
Peel the label off the can of sweetened condensed milk and remove the lid. Securely cover the can with a square of aluminum foil folded around the top; the foil should extend two-thirds of the way down the can. Place the can on the metal trivet in an Instant Pot. Add approximately 8 cups of water around the can so the can is halfway submerged. Secure the lid and cook on Manual for 40 minutes. Quick release when done and carefully remove the can from the pot (it will be hot). Remove the foil and allow the can to cool for 20 minutes.

Carefully stir vanilla into the can. Stir for about 2 minutes, until the caramel absorbs the vanilla and has a creamy versus lumpy consistency. Pour into a container or a ramekin and top with coarse flaky salt. Store any leftover caramel in a mason jar in the refrigerator for up to 6 weeks.

For the Crust
Heat oven to 300 degrees. Line the bottom and sides of an 8-inch square baking pan with parchment paper, leaving about an inch of overhang on all sides.

In a medium bowl, stir together the melted butter, flour, granulated sugar, vanilla, and salt until combined. Press the mixture evenly into the prepared baking pan. Bake for 15 minutes, then remove from the oven and set aside. Increase oven temperature to 350 degrees.

For the Filling
In a medium bowl, mix the chopped apples, brown sugar, flour, granulated sugar, cinnamon, allspice, ginger, and salted caramel (retain some caramel for drizzling if you like). Evenly spread the filling over the crust.

For the Topping
In a medium bowl, mix the granola, brown sugar, flour, and cinnamon. Mix in the chilled butter with your fingers until the mixture resembles coarse crumbs. Sprinkle mixture evenly over the filling layer.

Bake for 35 minutes or until the top layer is golden brown. Cool for 30 minutes on the counter, then freeze overnight.

Pull bars out of the freezer, use a fork to drizzle additional caramel as a garnish (optional), and top with coarse kosher salt or salt flakes. Cut into bars and store in the refrigerator.

Apple Donut Cake

Makes 12 squares

We have a photo of my daughter, Ellie, at the age of five or so, sitting on top of an antique tractor at Emma Krumbee's apple orchard, scarecrows lining the field behind her. We'd go there every fall to do the kid thing and pick a half bushel of Honeycrisps right off the trees. Ellie loved a messy, sugary apple donut, and the orchard made them fresh daily. This is my grown-up version of the apple donut in cake form.

Apples in Minnesota are big business. Since the University of Minnesota started its apple program in 1878, twenty-nine apple varieties have been released. Honeycrisp is my favorite, but these bars will work well with a Granny Smith or any apples from the nearest orchard.

Cake

- ½ cup whole milk
- ⅓ cup vegetable oil
- ¼ cup full-fat plain yogurt
- 1 large egg
- 1 teaspoon vanilla extract
- 1 teaspoon lemon zest
- 2 teaspoons lemon juice
- ⅔ cup packed brown sugar
- 1 cup all-purpose flour
- ½ cup whole wheat flour
- 2 teaspoons baking powder
- 1 teaspoon kosher salt
- ½ teaspoon nutmeg
- 2 medium or 3 small apples, peeled, cored, and thinly sliced into half moons

Topping

- 3 tablespoons granulated sugar
- 1 teaspoon cinnamon
- pinch kosher salt

Heat oven to 350 degrees. Grease an 8-inch square baking pan with cooking spray.

In a large bowl, whisk the milk, vegetable oil, yogurt, egg, vanilla, lemon zest, lemon juice, and brown sugar until smooth. Add the flours, baking powder, salt, and nutmeg, then stir to combine. Stir in the apples.

Pour the batter into the prepared pan. Combine topping ingredients and sprinkle over the batter. Bake for 25–30 minutes, until a toothpick inserted in the center comes out clean.

Tarte Tatin

Serves 12

This is my mother-in-law Dolores's favorite fall recipe to make when apples are in season. I've been lucky to enjoy lots of tarte tatin over the years, always beautifully made in the specialty Le Creuset pan that was a wedding gift from her sister Janice. If you don't have a tarte tatin pan like Dolores, you can use a cast iron skillet.

With only four ingredients and using puff pastry as a substitute for the classic pie crust, you can easily make this delicious dish. The type of apple you use matters: they should be firm and hold their shape and texture through the baking process. I recommend Granny Smith, Cortland, or Braeburn apples, but feel free to use your favorite. The fruit, baked in butter and sugar, caramelizes on the bottom of the pan. When flipped for serving, the apples are exposed with the luscious caramel covering the dessert like frosting. Serve with ice cream.

¾ cup granulated sugar

1 teaspoon vanilla extract

4 tablespoons unsalted butter, 2 tablespoons cut into quarter-inch bits

2 pounds apples (see note above), peeled, cored, and quartered

1 sheet frozen puff pastry, thawed

Heat oven to 375 degrees.

In a 10-inch cast iron skillet or tarte tatin pan, combine the sugar and vanilla. Heat the pan over medium heat, stirring until the sugar is dissolved. Continue cooking, without stirring, for 5 minutes or until the mixture is dark amber in color. Remove from heat. Add 2 tablespoons butter to the skillet and swirl until the butter has melted. Let cool for 10 minutes, then start building your base.

Arrange apples in the skillet so the rounded side is down. Form concentric circles with apples overlapping each other. Keep the pieces close together so that they support one another, standing upright. They will look like the petals of a flower and need to be packed tight. Dot with remaining 2 tablespoons butter pieces.

Place the puff pastry over the top, tucking the sides around the apples. Bake for 35 minutes or until the crust is golden brown and crisp and the pan juices are bubbling. Let cool in the pan for 30–45 minutes for the caramel to set, then carefully invert onto a rimmed plate to serve.

November

THANKSGIVING MEMORIES

November

I grew up in one of those homes with a formal dining room used roughly three times a year: Thanksgiving, Christmas, and Easter. Otherwise, it was off-limits for us kids. The chairs had yellow velvet cushions that were like a magnet to our grubby little hands. The table would be set with heirloom silver, crystal, and (very nonabsorbent) polyester napkins. Thanksgiving included the giant Butterball turkey, mashed potatoes, gravy, reanimated Green Giant frozen peas, Ocean Spray jellied cranberry sauce, soft white buns, green bean casserole topped with Durkee fried onions, and of course stuffing. It was Pepperidge Farm sage stuffing made from the very simple recipe right on the package, with none of the options like mushrooms or dried fruit. And of course the pumpkin pie was made from the recipe on the Libby's can.

Highlights one year included a guest who was a vegetarian. My mother was not informed before the guest arrived, and so the person ate only peas, green bean casserole, mashed potatoes without gravy, and those soft buns. We thought she was pretty, with long brunette hair and bright red lipstick on lips that never touched the food. She acted cheerful and repeatedly said she was fine, just fine. We were told she was a friend of my grandpa's who'd recently relocated from California. Later in life, it occurred to me that she might have been my grandfather's lady friend who may have been an escort for older men.

Another year, my mother brought home an elaborate centerpiece: a cardboard turkey. I believe she bought it at the local Byerlys supermarket. The thing stood over a foot tall and had a printed cardboard head and legs, then a body that filled out with an elaborate crepe paper circle like one of those foldout 3D greeting cards. We were not allowed to touch it until after Thanksgiving dinner was over, and then we played with it for hours, folding the body in and out, then decorating it with our bracelets, necklaces, and earrings until my sister accidentally spilled a Coke on the delicate crepe paper. It dissolved like the Wicked Witch when she was doused with water. I hated my sister for that — among other things at that time.

Fast-forward twenty years. Kurt and I put our daughter, Ellie, in the ski racing program at Hyland Hills Ski Area, where I'd learned to ski. Kids sports had already become somewhat absurd in their intensity. Other parents had their kids in hockey or basketball, once one-season sports that turned into six-month seasons with almost mandatory summer camps. We thought ski racing might be different, a sport all of us could enjoy as a family for the rest of our lives. This turned out to be true, but the ski race season kept expanding — summer training on glaciers near Portland, preseason dry-land training, then ski racing camp in Colorado every Thanksgiving.

Few things are more demoralizing than eating in a hotel restaurant for a holiday. We tried that and were depressed. Our Colorado hotel room had a small kitchen with a two-burner stove, no oven, and a microwave. On the deck was a gas Weber grill. The next year we knew to prepare, and we made the best of it. We slow cooked a stuffed chicken over indirect heat on the grill and made mashed potatoes and peas on the stovetop. Have you ever made a pie on the grill? I did. I made the crust from scratch using a convenient wine bottle to roll out the pastry. For the filling I followed the recipe on the Libby's can, and I put the whole thing on the grill where the chicken had been, the indirect heat from just a single burner on the opposite side. One trick was to plug up the back grill vent with aluminum foil, so the covered barbecue acted like an oven. It's fun to improvise a meal like that.

Fast-forward another five years. My daughter's ski racing career is over (concussions, ankle surgery, torn ACL — why do we do this to our children?), and we're back to serving Thanksgiving dinner in our home at a dining room table that gets much more use than my parents' table ever did. I have the heirloom silverware from my mother, who passed away from breast cancer when Ellie was still skiing. We have the silver platters, serving dishes, and gravy boat from Kurt's mother, who's still kicking as I write this. Kurt's mother joins us now; so does my sister, whom I no longer fight with, her daughter, and whoever else needs a home for the holiday. We've had as many as fifteen, which necessitated a kids' table for us kids.

The menu hasn't changed much, though Kurt tried. For two years he made stuffing — drying out cubes of sourdough in the oven, mixing in fresh sage, adding onions, celery, sautéed ground liver and heart from the turkey, broth from the boiled neck, mushrooms, and chopped dates. That second year, after the pie was served, and after we'd maybe had too much wine, there was an intervention. All of us sat in the living room and invited in Kurt, who by then was watching a college football game. He took a chair in the center, all of us silent. Saddles of sweat appeared beneath his armpits. "We have something to discuss," I said. "OK," he said nervously, like he'd been caught searching the trash for uneaten donuts.

Ellie interjected, getting right to the point. "We want our Pepperidge Farm stuffing back."

One sister said, "We grew up with Pepperidge Farm. My mother made it that way."

"I don't like fruit in my dinner," another sister, the non-adventurous one, said.

I tried to buffer the onslaught of criticism. "I like your stuffing, but it's not for everyone."

Kurt looked stunned for a moment. But he is a humorist at heart. He said, "I suppose you want frozen peas too." Almost in unison, we all said, "Yes!"

So, there it is: we've come full circle, back to where it all began — Butterball, Ocean Spray, Green Giant peas, Libby's pumpkin pie, and Pepperidge Farm stuffing. Sometimes a good thing comes in a package. Thankfully, other things don't — otherwise, I wouldn't have a very interesting cookbook.

41

November

Cranberry French 75

Serves 1

I was the first in my family to marry, and I inherited the two crystal champagne glasses my mom and dad used to celebrate their wedding. They married in Waupaca, Wisconsin, and honeymooned in the Wisconsin Dells. Both talked about a Friday dinner in the Dells at the Del-Bar supper club. The Del-Bar dates back to 1943 and was known for its charbroiled steaks and Friday night cod fish fry. Like all great Wisconsin supper clubs, its decor was kitschy, with stuffed fish and deer heads on the wall, along with old beer signs and photos of its owners and friends. You can still get a charbroiled steak or fish fry there today. On our thirtieth wedding anniversary I pulled out those crystal glasses and made this hybrid French 75 champagne cocktail. The champagne makes me think of my parents, now both deceased, and the cranberries are pure Wisconsin.

So how did French Champagne end up with British gin? Apparently, British soldiers fighting in France during World War I mixed up this cocktail in spent 75 mm artillery shell casings. The casings were about seven inches tall and three inches in diameter, making them the perfect cocktail shaker.

For each made-to-order cocktail
1½ ounces gin

1 ounce cranberry simple syrup (recipe follows)

½ ounce freshly squeezed lemon juice

extra-fine sugar for glass rim

3 ounces sparkling white wine

rosemary sprig, for garnish

orange peel, for garnish

Add the gin, cranberry simple syrup, lemon juice, and a handful of ice to a cocktail shaker. Shake vigorously, about 30 seconds. Pour into flute or coupe glass lined with extra-fine sugar. Top with sparkling wine. Garnish with a fresh rosemary sprig and a curl of orange peel.

To make a batch cocktail for 10 servings
Stir together 2 cups gin, 1 cup cranberry simple syrup, and ⅔ cup lemon juice and store in the refrigerator for up to 24 hours. When you're ready to serve, gently pour in one 750-milliliter bottle of sparkling wine. Float cranberries and a few sprigs of fresh rosemary in the bowl for garnishes.

Cranberry Simple Syrup

2 cups cranberries

1 cup water

1 cup granulated sugar

1 cinnamon stick

1 teaspoon freshly grated orange zest

2 dashes orange bitters

In a small saucepan over medium-high heat, stir together the cranberries, water, sugar, cinnamon stick, and orange zest. Bring to a boil, stirring occasionally to dissolve the sugar. Reduce heat and simmer for 10 minutes. Turn off the heat, and allow the mixture to steep for another 10 minutes. Stir in the bitters.

Strain the syrup through a fine-mesh sieve into a bowl. Store the cranberry simple syrup in an airtight container in the refrigerator for up to several weeks.

Pomegranate Old-Fashioned

Serves 1

Old-fashioneds have become very trendy in recent years. This variation with pomegranate and maple syrup feels downright autumnal.

1 tablespoon pomegranate seeds

2 ounces pomegranate juice

¼ teaspoon maple syrup

4 dashes orange bitters

2 ounces bourbon

orange slice, for garnish

In a cocktail shaker, muddle the pomegranate seeds, pomegranate juice, maple syrup, and orange bitters. Add bourbon and shake to combine. Pour over a rocks glass with ice and garnish with an orange slice.

Thanksgiving Punch

Serves 8

One way to make holiday entertaining easy is to prepare batch cocktails ahead of time. Then all you have to do is put ice in a glass and pour, or allow guests to assemble the drink themselves. You can also make punch and serve it in a punch bowl with ice alongside glasses or punch cups for self-service. If there are teetotalers or kids present, you can set out the alcohol separately with a shot glass for people to mix their own. This punch is excellent with rum, but you could also use vodka.

Punch bowls have gone out of fashion, and I often see beautiful cut crystal ones with matching cups at thrift stores. I am all for bringing back fancy dishes!

- 1 orange, sliced
- 1 cup cranberries
- ½ cup pomegranate seeds, plus more for garnish
- 2 cups cranberry juice
- 2 cups orange juice
- 2 cups blood orange soda (Lorina in the bottle or Sanpellegrino in the can)
- 1 cup light or dark rum, vodka, or gin or 1 bottle sparkling wine, optional (or 1 ounce per glass for a family-friendly nonalcoholic punch presentation)
- rosemary sprigs, for garnish

Add the orange slices, cranberries, and pomegranate seeds to a large pitcher or punch bowl. Pour in cranberry juice, orange juice, and blood orange soda. Add alcohol or sparkling wine, if using. Serve in glasses over ice and garnish with fresh rosemary sprigs and pomegranate seeds.

Roasted Carrot Hummus

Serves 6

Hummus is having a moment lately, and rightly so, as it's delicious. You can buy it premade with various flavors, but it's easy to make yourself, and it's vegan. You can serve it with pita chips, bread, crackers, or vegetables or slather it on a sandwich. When I made this version for a retirement dinner recently, three of the six guests asked for the recipe before they left. The key to a super-smooth texture is adding very cold ice water, one tablespoon at a time, until you get the consistency you like.

1½ pounds carrots, trimmed and peeled

1 tablespoon extra-virgin olive oil

1 teaspoon kosher salt

2 cloves garlic, roughly chopped

1 (14.5-ounce) can chickpeas, rinsed and drained

zest and juice of 1 lemon

¾ cup tahini

1 teaspoon black pepper

1 teaspoon smoked paprika

ice water

2 tablespoons coarsely chopped parsley, for garnish

1 tablespoon chopped pistachios, for garnish

Heat oven to 400 degrees and line a sheet pan with parchment paper.

Cut any thick carrots in half lengthwise, then slice all carrots crosswise into 2- to 3-inch pieces and place them on the prepared pan. Add the olive oil and salt and toss to coat. Spread out carrots evenly on the sheet pan and roast until very tender and starting to brown, about 1 hour.

Transfer the carrots to a food processor. Add garlic, chickpeas, lemon zest and juice, tahini, pepper, and paprika. Process to combine, adding 1 tablespoon ice-cold water at a time if needed, until the mixture is almost completely smooth. Taste the dip and add more lemon juice and/or salt if needed.

Transfer the dip to a small bowl, drizzle with more oil, and top with parsley and chopped pistachios.

Butternut Squash Soup with Crispy Prosciutto Croutons

Serves 6

There are so many variations of squash soup, but adding apple really amps up the sweetness and makes it something special. At home I make lots of soup and store the leftovers in variously sized mason jars. One-quart jars of soup become a quick meal with a salad, sandwich, cheese board, or hearty bread. Soups for lunches or gifts to friends are stored in pint (two-cup) mason jars that can be easily microwaved at the office or for a quick solo dinner on a busy weeknight. You might say I have become what my friend Jen calls a jar hoarder, or "joarder."

When using jars for freezing, be sure to leave 1½ inches of headspace or room at the top so they don't crack when the soup freezes and expands.

3 cups vegetable or chicken broth

4 cloves garlic, minced

3 carrots, peeled and roughly chopped

1 Granny Smith apple, cored and roughly chopped

1 medium (about 4 pounds) butternut squash, peeled and cut into cubes

1 onion, roughly chopped

2 sprigs sage leaves, plus more for garnish

1 teaspoon kosher salt

½ teaspoon black pepper

¼ teaspoon smoked paprika

pinch nutmeg

⅔ cup unsweetened full-fat coconut milk

4–6 slices prosciutto

Add broth, garlic, carrot, apple, butternut squash, onion, sage, salt, pepper, paprika, and nutmeg to a slow cooker. Stir to combine. Cook for 6–8 hours on low or 3–4 hours on high, until the squash is completely tender and mashes easily with a fork. Remove and discard the sage. Stir in the coconut milk.

Use an immersion blender to puree the soup until smooth. Or transfer the soup in two batches into a stand blender like a Vitamix and puree until smooth, being extremely careful not to fill the blender too full of hot liquid (see tip page 10).

Heat oven to 400 degrees. Line a sheet pan with parchment paper.

Lay prosciutto slices flat on the prepared pan and bake for 12 minutes or until browned (watch carefully; it browns very quickly in the last couple of minutes and will be smoky). Cool until crispy, then break into shards.

Taste the soup and season with additional salt or pepper. Ladle into bowls, then garnish with crispy prosciutto and sage leaves if desired.

Thanksgiving Leftovers Turkey Wild Rice Soup

Serves 6-8

My first exposure to wild rice was in the soup at Byerlys supermarket, which was my mom's happy place. What's not to love about a fancy grocery store that has carpet and a chandelier? Mom liked their diner-style restaurant. My three sisters and I took turns getting chosen to go grocery shopping, and if you were that week's favorite kid, chances were you'd get treated to a cup of the delicious and creamy wild rice and ham soup.

After the Thanksgiving holiday, I use homemade turkey stock and leftover meat to make this soup. For Christmas I often gift family and friends frozen soup from the Thanksgiving turkey. Of course, you could also substitute chicken and chicken broth.

1 tablespoon butter

1 tablespoon extra-virgin olive oil

1 medium onion, chopped

6 medium carrots, peeled and chopped

4 ribs celery, chopped

3 cloves garlic, minced

1 cup uncooked wild rice

2 tablespoons all-purpose flour

6 cups turkey or chicken broth

2 cups cooked turkey or chicken

8 ounces white mushrooms, sliced

2 teaspoons kosher salt

1 teaspoon black pepper

1 teaspoon dried thyme

1 teaspoon dried sage

2 cups heavy cream

Add the butter and oil to a large soup pot over medium-high heat. Add the onion, carrots, and celery. Cook for 7 minutes, stirring occasionally. Stir in the garlic, wild rice, and flour. Cook for 2 minutes, stirring to disperse the flour evenly among the vegetables. Add the broth. Increase the heat to high and bring the soup to a boil. Loosely cover the pot and reduce the heat to medium-low to gently boil for 30 minutes.

Add the turkey or chicken and mushrooms to the soup and simmer with the lid slightly ajar for another 15 minutes or until the rice is cooked through. Wild rice will maintain a chew but should not be hard. Stir in salt, pepper, thyme, and sage and taste the soup, adjusting seasonings if necessary. Stir in the cream, ladle into bowls, and enjoy.

47

November

Mom's Chili Mac

Serves 10

My mom was a stay-at-home mom. When we'd get off the school bus at 3 p.m., Mom would have the eight-inch black-and-white TV on the kitchen counter next to the ironing board, and she'd be watching *All My Children*, *One Life to Live*, and *General Hospital* while ironing sheets, pants, shirts, and even my dad's underwear. On the stove she might have her chili cooking away. My best friend, Renee, would come home with me after school, and chili days, in her words, "were the best." Mom's chili was unusual because it was full of elbow macaroni. We'd grab a bowl of my mom's chili for that tide-you-over after-school meal between lunch and dinner. We'd dip saltines into the chili topped with cheese and sour cream. Only when I was an adult did I realize not everyone puts elbow macaroni in their chili.

1 tablespoon extra-virgin olive oil

2 cups diced onion

4 ribs celery, diced

1 cup diced red bell pepper

2 pounds ground beef

2 cloves garlic, minced

1 (28-ounce) can crushed tomatoes

1 (15-ounce) can tomato sauce

2 (14-ounce) cans kidney beans

1 (10.75-ounce) can condensed tomato soup

2 cups beef broth

1 cup water

8 ounces uncooked elbow macaroni

2 tablespoons chili powder

1 teaspoon cumin

1 teaspoon smoked paprika

2 teaspoons kosher salt

1 teaspoon black pepper

2 cups shredded cheddar cheese, divided

Heat the oil in a large Dutch oven over medium heat. Cook the onions, celery, and red pepper for about 5 minutes to soften. Add the beef and cook until browned, about 8–10 minutes. When the beef is cooked through, add the garlic and cook for 2 minutes before stirring in tomatoes, tomato sauce, kidney beans, tomato soup, beef broth, water, macaroni, and spices.

Cover and cook for 22–25 minutes, until the macaroni is al dente. Taste and add more salt or pepper if needed. Remove from heat and stir in 1 cup of cheese. Prepare individual bowls and top with the remaining cheese.

Asian Pear Spinach Salad with Maple Pecans and Ginger Vinaigrette

November

Serves 8-10

This salad looks great on a Thanksgiving table. I realize the notion of having salad on the Thanksgiving table is controversial. My cohost Stephanie March and I debated this topic on our radio show, *Weekly Dish*, with most commenters feeling it was an unnecessary filler on a holiday full of fatty, creamy, delicious indulgences. I, however, am always going to be pro salad. In my opinion, making fresh vegetables and fruit available as a palate cleanser is a great idea.

In this salad I like to use Asian pear, which eats like a crisp apple. You can serve the nuts on the side and even add prosciutto crumbles (see page 46) for some crunchy protein.

Vinaigrette
- 2 small shallots, minced or grated
- 1 tablespoon minced or grated ginger
- ⅔ cup extra-virgin olive oil
- ⅓ cup rice vinegar
- ¼ cup plus 2 tablespoons apple cider
- 1 teaspoon kosher salt
- 1 teaspoon black pepper
- ¼ teaspoon cinnamon

Maple Pecans
- 2 cups whole pecans
- ¼ cup maple syrup
- 1 teaspoon kosher salt

Salad
- 14 ounces baby spinach
- 2 Asian pears

For the Vinaigrette
Shake all ingredients in a mason jar until smooth and emulsified.

For the Maple Pecans
Spread out nuts in a cast iron skillet. Over medium heat, toast until light brown, about 3 minutes, stirring occasionally. Add maple syrup and stir to coat. The syrup will bubble in the hot pan and stick to the nuts. Stirring continuously, quickly sprinkle in the salt while the nuts are caramelizing. Do not let the nuts burn: this entire process takes less than a minute.

For the Salad
Rinse and dry the greens; thinly slice the pears by cutting in half to get a flat surface and then cutting into slivers.

Just before serving, toss the spinach with the vinaigrette. Assemble the salad on individual plates; arrange the pear slices in a flower shape in the center of the greens and sprinkle with the maple pecans.

Or, if you're serving this buffet-style, toss the spinach with the vinaigrette and pecans and place in a salad bowl or on a large serving platter. Top with the pear slices arranged in flower shapes.

Kale, Pomegranate, and Apple Salad with Roasted Pumpkin Seeds

Serves 4–6

Kale is the workhorse of the Ely Hilltop Garden, as you may recall if you have the first volume of *True North Cabin Cookbook*. It grows in cold weather and bad weather and is often the last of the leafy greens to survive the chilly nights. This salad has bitter, sweet, toasty, crunchy, and salty flavors — all the hallmarks of a beautiful salad in the year's coldest months.

Salad

1 cup pomegranate seeds

2 Honeycrisp apples, diced into half-inch chunks

½ cup crumbled feta cheese

2 bunches lacinato kale, torn into bite-size pieces

⅓ cup pumpkin seeds

Vinaigrette

⅓ cup extra-virgin olive oil

juice of 1 lemon

1 tablespoon Dijon mustard

1 teaspoon pomegranate molasses (or substitute maple syrup)

1 teaspoon honey

1 teaspoon kosher salt

½ teaspoon black pepper

In a large bowl toss together pomegranate seeds, apple pieces, crumbled feta, and kale. In a cast iron skillet over medium heat, toast pumpkin seeds for 10–15 minutes, until they start to brown, shaking every few minutes. Once they start to smell nutty, watch carefully as they will toast quickly. Add the toasted seeds to the salad bowl.

Combine the vinaigrette ingredients in a mason jar and shake vigorously until combined. Pour over salad and toss well to combine.

Sesame Almond Chicken Salad

Serves 4

In high school I worked as a server at Dayton's Boundary Waters Restaurant. A favorite on the menu was their famous chicken salad, which instead of the usual mayo had an Asian flavor profile with sesame oil, soy sauce, and tons of crunchy vegetables like cabbage, carrots, and radishes. Inspired by that combination, this light winter salad offers an antidote to weeks of holiday indulgences.

Dressing

- 2 cloves garlic, minced or grated
- 3 tablespoons minced or grated ginger
- ¼ cup rice vinegar
- 3 tablespoons sesame oil
- 3 tablespoons extra-virgin olive oil
- 3 tablespoons soy sauce
- 2 tablespoons honey
- 2 tablespoons tahini

Salad

- 2 pounds uncooked chicken tenders (or use pulled rotisserie chicken)
- ¼ cup sesame seeds
- ⅓ cup slivered raw almonds
- 4 cups shredded green cabbage
- 2 cups shredded red cabbage
- 1 head romaine lettuce, rinsed, cored, and thinly sliced
- 1 cup shredded daikon or red radish (use a box grater)
- ½ cup diced green onion, plus more for garnish
- 1 yellow bell pepper, cut into thin strips
- ¾ cup chopped cilantro, plus more for garnish

In a medium bowl, whisk together dressing ingredients. Use ¼ cup of dressing to marinate the chicken tenders for 30 minutes.

Toast the sesame seeds in a dry medium skillet until they smell nutty, about 3 minutes; watch carefully, as they burn quickly. Repeat with the sliced almonds, toasting them as well.

Grill the chicken tenders until cooked through (165 degrees). Alternatively, cook the chicken tenders in a skillet over medium-high heat until they reach 165 degrees, or bake chicken tenders at 350 degrees for about 20–25 minutes, until they reach 165 degrees.

Toss prepared vegetables and cilantro with the remaining dressing. Top the salad with the cooked chicken, toasted sesame seeds and almonds, and reserved cilantro and green onions.

November

Cranberry Wild Rice Salad with Candied Pecans and Bitter Greens

Serves 10

I adore wild rice, Minnesota's state grain. The traditional harvest of seeds from this aquatic grass is accomplished in partnership, with one person pushing or paddling and the other using sticks to knock the ripe rice into the canoe. Most commercial wild rice is harvested by machine, but rice harvested by hand has a drier and nuttier texture, and it cooks much faster. Wild rice flavors are bold and hold up really well with strong bitter greens like radicchio and kale.

Wild Rice

1 cup uncooked wild rice

1 teaspoon kosher salt

4 cups water

Candied Pecans

¼ cup plus 2 tablespoons brown sugar

1 teaspoon cinnamon

1 teaspoon kosher salt

⅛ teaspoon cayenne pepper

2 cups whole or halved pecans

Cranberry Salad Dressing

1 (14-ounce) can whole-berry cranberry sauce

zest and juice of 1 lemon

1 clove garlic, minced or grated

⅔ cup extra-virgin olive oil

2 teaspoons Dijon mustard

1 teaspoon kosher salt

Salad

2 heads radicchio, cored and cut into ribbons

1 bunch lacinato kale, cut into ribbons

⅓ cup chopped parsley

⅓ cup chopped mint

⅓ cup dried cranberries

November

For the Wild Rice
Combine wild rice, salt, and water in a saucepan or pot and bring to a boil. Reduce to a simmer, cover, and let cook for about 40 minutes. Remove from heat, drain rice in a colander, and allow to cool.

For the Candied Pecans
Line a baking sheet with parchment paper or a silicone baking mat.

Add brown sugar, cinnamon, salt, and cayenne to a medium skillet set over medium heat and cook, stirring often, until the brown sugar melts into a bubbling sauce, about 1 minute. Add the pecans, stirring to coat. Cook, stirring constantly, until the pecans look candied (or shiny) and smell nutty, 2–3 minutes; watch closely so they do not burn. Pour the nuts onto the prepared baking sheet to cool. Break into bite-size pieces.

For the Cranberry Salad Dressing
Place all ingredients in a 1-quart mason jar and shake to combine.

Assembly
Add wild rice, greens, herbs, and cranberries to a large bowl and toss to combine. Drizzle on the dressing, toss, and taste, adjusting salt and pepper as needed. Serve topped with candied pecans.

Roasted Parmesan Delicata Squash

Serves 8

Delicata squash are those elongated yellow ribbed ones with green stripes. When I was growing up, they sat in my mother's autumn centerpiece until just before Christmas, when they were replaced with something involving candles and holly. I didn't learn until later in life that they are quite good to eat.

The hardest part of this recipe is cutting the firm squash into slices. Otherwise, you just season to taste and throw it in the oven. The Parmesan cheese and fresh thyme add a savory note to the sweet and creamy squash.

2 delicata squash

⅓ cup freshly grated Parmesan cheese

1 tablespoon finely chopped fresh thyme

1 tablespoon extra-virgin olive oil

1 teaspoon kosher salt

½ teaspoon black pepper

Heat oven to 425 degrees. Line a sheet pan with parchment paper or a silicone mat.

Slice the squash in half lengthwise and scoop out the seeds with a spoon. Cut the halves into quarter-inch-thick slices (half circles). Place in a large bowl.

In a small bowl, combine the Parmesan and thyme.

Drizzle the olive oil, salt, and pepper over the squash slices, tossing well to coat. Lay the slices flat on the prepared pan and sprinkle with the Parmesan mixture. Bake in the center of the oven for 25 minutes, until soft and golden brown.

Roasted Brussels Sprouts with Pomegranate Seeds

Serves 6

I'll never forget the night my friend KC came over for a dinner party and was stunned that I was cooking brussels sprouts. He remembered his childhood years when his mother boiled them, and the result was a pile of bitter slime. He wasn't allowed to leave the table until he cleaned his plate, and the brussels sprouts were definitely a sticking point for him. He explained those details after he tasted this recipe and finally understood the joys of well-prepared brussels sprouts.

I like to serve this side with a table full of rich dishes like prime rib, mashed potatoes, and creamed vegetables. The pomegranate seeds add the perfect pop of fresh acid to stimulate your palate amid all the comfort foods.

- **2 pounds brussels sprouts, trimmed and halved**
- **2 tablespoons extra-virgin olive oil**
- **1 teaspoon kosher salt**
- **½ teaspoon black pepper**
- **1 cup pomegranate seeds**
- **¼ cup roughly chopped walnuts**
- **¼ cup chopped mint**

Vinaigrette
- **3 tablespoons extra-virgin olive oil**
- **2 tablespoons balsamic vinegar**
- **2 tablespoons honey**

Heat oven to 425 degrees and line a sheet pan with parchment paper.

Place the halved brussels sprouts on the prepared pan. Drizzle with olive oil and season with salt and pepper. Bake for 25–30 minutes, until the sprouts are fully cooked and the edges are crispy. Set aside.

Prepare the vinaigrette by whisking together all the ingredients in a large bowl until well combined. Add the roasted brussels sprouts to the vinaigrette and toss with the pomegranate seeds, walnuts, and mint. Serve immediately.

November

Wild Rice Stuffing

Serves 10

Wild rice is as Minnesotan as the Vikings. In the fall, I love to make this dressing to stuff a chicken, half of an acorn squash, or a thick-cut pork chop. You can also bake the stuffing in a covered casserole dish with some heavy cream. The rice absorbs the cream, making for a decadent side dish.

- **2 cups uncooked wild rice**
- **4 cups chicken broth**
- **1 tablespoon extra-virgin olive oil**
- **1 tablespoon butter**
- **1 cup chopped onion**
- **1 cup apple chopped into quarter-inch pieces**
- **4 ribs celery, chopped**
- **1 teaspoon kosher salt**
- **½ teaspoon black pepper**
- **2 cloves garlic, minced or grated**
- **⅓ cup dried cranberries**
- **2 tablespoons roughly chopped fresh sage**
- **2 teaspoons fresh thyme leaves**
- **⅓ cup heavy cream, optional**

Heat oven to 350 degrees.

Rinse the rice and place it in a 4-quart casserole dish with the broth. Cover with the lid or a piece of aluminum foil and bake in the oven for 1 hour. Remove from the oven, fluff rice with a fork, and let rest to absorb any remaining liquid while you prepare the stuffing.

Heat olive oil and butter in a saucepan. Add in the onion, apple, celery, salt, and pepper and cook until softened, 5–7 minutes, stirring occasionally. Stir in garlic and cook for 30 seconds. Season with additional salt and pepper to taste.

Transfer mixture to a large bowl, add the rice, and stir in the cranberries, sage, and thyme. Stuff poultry for roasting or transfer mixture to a casserole dish with heavy cream and bake for 20 minutes to warm through.

Pan-Seared Ribeye Steaks with Shallot Cream Sauce

November

Serves 4

My husband has never met a steak he didn't like. Kurt could eat a steak every day. His favorite is New York strip; my favorite is ribeye. When Kurt is charged with making dinner, his go-to meals are pizzas, ribs, or steak — and his steak meal is always accompanied by creamy fettuccine alfredo. This recipe brings all that together with an easy shallot cream sauce to top the steak. I highly recommend doubling the sauce and serving half over fettuccine or spaghetti noodles or even sautéed mushrooms. It's a divine, steaky side.

3 tablespoons butter, divided

3 large shallots, finely chopped

1 tablespoon tomato paste

2 cups beef broth

1½ cups dry white wine

1 cup heavy cream

4 (10- to 12-ounce) ribeye steaks

salt and pepper

1 tablespoon chopped parsley

Melt 1 tablespoon butter in a medium saucepan over medium-high heat. Add shallots and cook, stirring, for 2 minutes. Stir in tomato paste and cook for 1 minute more. Stir in broth and wine; boil until reduced to 1 cup, about 15 minutes. Add cream and boil until sauce coats the back of a spoon, about 7 minutes.

Sprinkle steaks with salt and pepper on both sides. Melt 1 tablespoon butter in each of 2 heavy large skillets over medium-high heat. Add 2 steaks to each skillet and cook until medium-rare, about 4 minutes per side. Transfer to a platter and tent with foil to rest and keep warm.

Add half of the cream sauce to each skillet. Bring to a boil, scraping up any browned bits. Transfer steaks to serving plates, pour sauce over steaks, and garnish with chopped parsley.

Cranberry Orange Sauce

Serves 10

I feel like you can tell a lot about a family by the type of cranberries they serve at their holiday table. Are you an Ocean Spray aficionado who cranks open both sides of the can and slides the can-shaped gelatin onto the serving dish? Or are you a purist who makes homemade cranberry sauce, flavoring it with cloves, oranges, cinnamon, and nutmeg and scooping it onto a crystal dish? Our family does both: we have true-blue traditionalists and finicky foodies. Husband Kurt likes the sucking sound of sliding the canned cranberry sauce onto a plate; he slices it into disks. I make sauce from scratch. We are food-inclusive, and everyone is welcome!

⅔ cup water

½ cup granulated sugar

¼ cup honey

zest and ¼ cup juice from 1 large orange

1 cinnamon stick

12 ounces fresh or frozen cranberries

In a saucepan, combine water, sugar, honey, orange zest and juice, and cinnamon stick. Bring to a simmer over medium heat, stirring to dissolve the sugar. Add cranberries and bring to a boil. Adjust the heat to keep mixture at a low boil and cook for 10 minutes, uncovered, stirring occasionally. The cranberries will burst, and the sauce will begin to thicken. Remove from heat, discard the cinnamon stick, and cool to room temperature (the sauce will continue to thicken), then refrigerate until ready to serve.

TIP: Any cranberry leftovers? Try using them for a tasty cocktail. Heat up the sauce to make it more viscous, then add your favorite vodka or gin. Mix vigorously in a martini shaker, pour into a tall glass with ice, and top with tonic.

Pecan Bars

Serves 12

These bars are an excellent alternative to pecan pie if you'd rather not go to the trouble. You get all the nutty, caramelly, buttery goodness of pecan pie with an easy press-in crust that requires no dough rolling. In Minnesota, bars are a potluck staple — easier to pull together than cookies.

Crust
- ¾ cup (1½ sticks) unsalted butter, at room temperature
- ⅓ cup granulated sugar
- 1¾ cups all-purpose flour

Filling
- 1½ cups corn syrup (light or dark)
- ⅔ cup packed brown sugar
- 4 large eggs
- 1 tablespoon vanilla extract
- ⅓ cup all-purpose flour
- 1 teaspoon kosher salt
- 1½ cups coarsely chopped pecans, plus 70 or so whole pecans for finishing
- 1 teaspoon kosher salt or sea salt flakes (Maldon), for finishing

Heat oven to 350 degrees. Line a 9×13–inch baking dish with parchment paper.

For the crust, in a stand mixer, combine the butter and granulated sugar on medium speed, then mix in flour until combined. The mixture will feel dry and crumbly. Transfer the mixture to the prepared pan and press to evenly distribute. Bake for 18–20 minutes, until golden brown.

Meanwhile, for the filling, in a large bowl, whisk together the corn syrup, brown sugar, eggs, and vanilla until smooth. Add in the flour and salt and mix until combined. Stir in the chopped pecans.

When the crust is done baking, remove from the oven and top with the filling mixture. Arrange whole pecans in rows on top of the filling, then sprinkle with kosher salt or sea salt flakes (Maldon). Bake for 30–35 minutes, until the center is set.

Let cool for 15 minutes, then refrigerate until cooled completely. Cut into bars and serve.

November

Pumpkin Pudding, aka Crustless Pumpkin Pie

Serves 8

For years I was uncomfortable with making pie crusts and would use the store-bought variety. You can definitely tell the difference. The store-bought crusts look too uniform, aren't flaky like hand-rolled ones, and taste like the cook held back the butter. And for someone who writes cookbooks, presenting a pie with a store-bought crust is downright embarrassing. To avoid learning the art of crust making, I made this crustless pie for an appearance on *The Jason Show*, my appeal to people like me. I've since taken a pie-making class and perfected my crust, but this Pumpkin Pudding is still in the rotation each fall.

¾ cup granulated sugar

1 teaspoon salt

1 teaspoon ground ginger

½ teaspoon cinnamon

½ teaspoon pumpkin pie spice

½ teaspoon ground cloves

2 large eggs

1 teaspoon vanilla extract

1 (15-ounce) can pumpkin puree (not pie filling)

1 (15-ounce) can evaporated milk

1 cup whipped cream sweetened with 2 tablespoons confectioners' sugar, for garnish

8 gingersnaps, ground into coarse crumbs, for garnish

Heat oven to 350 degrees.

Mix the sugar, salt, ginger, cinnamon, pumpkin pie spice, and cloves in a medium bowl.

In a large bowl, beat the eggs; add the vanilla, pumpkin puree, and sugar and spice mixture, whisking to blend. Add the evaporated milk and whisk to combine all the ingredients.

Pour about ¼ cup of the mixture into each of 8 (4-ounce) ramekins. Bake for 35 minutes or until the pudding has set and a knife inserted in the center comes out clean.

Cool completely before serving. Serve with whipped cream and crushed gingersnaps on top.

Pumpkin Bars with Cream Cheese Frosting

November

Serves 18–24

These bars are full of the good things that go into making a pumpkin pie, then topped with decadent cream cheese frosting. Everyone loves to see these bars on the potluck table.

Pumpkin Bars

4 large eggs, at room temperature

1⅔ cups granulated sugar

1 cup canola oil

1 (15-ounce) can pumpkin puree (not pie filling)

2 cups all-purpose flour

3 teaspoons pumpkin pie spice

2 teaspoons baking powder

1 teaspoon baking soda

1 teaspoon kosher salt

Cream Cheese Frosting

6 ounces cream cheese, at room temperature

2 cups confectioners' sugar

4 tablespoons butter, at room temperature

1 teaspoon vanilla extract

1–2 tablespoons whole milk

For the Pumpkin Bars

Heat oven to 350 degrees.

In a large bowl, whisk the eggs, sugar, oil, and pumpkin until well blended. In a medium bowl, combine the flour, pumpkin pie spice, baking powder, baking soda, and salt. Gradually add the dry mixture into the wet mixture and mix well. Pour the batter into an ungreased 10x15–inch baking pan. Bake for 25–30 minutes, or until set. Cool completely.

For the Cream Cheese Frosting

In a medium bowl, beat the cream cheese, confectioners' sugar, butter, and vanilla with a hand mixer. If the ingredients are soft enough, you could even do this with a wooden spoon and some elbow grease. Add enough milk to achieve spreading consistency. Spread over the cooled bars. Store the frosted bars in the refrigerator.

Pumpkin Cheesecake

Serves 12

This recipe is adapted from one my friend Vanessa Drews made on a Halloween episode of my TV show, *Taste Buds with Stephanie*. Vanessa owns Cheesecake Funk in Minneapolis, where she makes fantastic, over-the-top cheesecakes piled high with whipped cream. When Vanessa worked at Paisley Park, she made cheesecakes for friends, family, and late-night revelers at Prince's recording studio. Prince became a big fan and championed her baking prowess. Vanessa is a phenomenal cheesecake maker who leads her business with heart and perseverance.

Crust
14 ounces old-fashioned gingersnap cookies
½ cup (1 stick) unsalted butter

Cheesecake
2 pounds full-fat cream cheese, at room temperature
2 cups granulated sugar
4 large eggs
1 (14-ounce) can pumpkin puree (not pie filling)
1 teaspoon pumpkin pie spice
1 teaspoon vanilla extract

Cinnamon Whipped Topping
2 cups heavy cream
1 cup granulated sugar
1 tablespoon confectioners' sugar
1 teaspoon vanilla extract
½ teaspoon cinnamon

For the Crust

Heat oven to 325 degrees. Line a 9-inch springform pan with parchment paper.

In a food processor, process the gingersnap cookies until the crunching noise subsides and the mixture resembles sand. Transfer the crumbs to a medium bowl.

Add butter to a saucepan over medium heat. Begin stirring to move the butter around as it melts. Once melted, the butter will begin to foam and sizzle around the edges. Keep stirring. The butter will turn golden brown in about 5–8 minutes from when you start. The foam will slightly subside, and the milk solids on the bottom of the pan will toast. It will smell intensely buttery, nutty, and rich. There are only a few seconds between browned butter and burnt butter, so keep your eye on the pan the entire time. Don't walk away, and don't stop stirring!

Add the browned butter to the bowl with the gingersnap crumbs and mix with a fork. Press the crust mixture into the prepared springform pan and pat firmly. Bake for 2–3 minutes; remove pan from oven and set aside.

November

For the Cheesecake
In the bowl of a stand mixer, combine the cream cheese with the sugar and blend for about 1 minute, until light and fluffy. Add the eggs, pumpkin puree, pumpkin pie spice, and vanilla and blend for 30 seconds, being careful not to overmix.

Spray the inside of the pan above the crust with cooking spray. Pour the filling into the crust and bake for 50 minutes.

Refrigerate the cheesecake overnight.

For the Cinnamon Whipped Topping
Blend all the ingredients on high until you make whipped cream; be careful not to over-whip. Dollop the whipped cream on top of the cooled cheesecake and spread to the edges of the cake.

December

THE CHRISTMAS EVE PARTY

December

What is now our annual Christmas Eve party began in 1968, the year I was born. It started with four families that had moved to Minneapolis the year before: the Jacobs from Boston, the Reids from Cleveland, the McKhanns from Hartford, and my husband's family, the Johnsons, from San Francisco. The Johnsons hosted the party at their home near Lake Harriet. As my mother-in-law, Dolores, tells it, the first meal was a Swedish smorgasbord with Swedish meatballs, cucumber salad, herring salad, and lefse. Appetizers included pickled herring and two non-Swedish dishes: stalks of celery smeared with Roka Blue Cheese Spread (Kraft still makes it) and beef tartare — chopped fillet with capers, cornichons, and thin melba toasts. The Jacobs were Jewish, and the McKhanns and Reids were both of Scottish descent. Only Kurt's father, Richard, was remotely Swedish (half Norwegian). I guess you'd call it a theme party — costumes optional.

Legend has it that it became a tradition for the kids to assemble in the Johnsons' basement to play table tennis and smoke dope. The tradition required one or two of the dads to descend into the basement to either catch their kids smoking dope or join in the fun. Half the participants at dinner were stoned. The Johnsons moved downtown into the 510 Groveland apartments sometime in the mid-seventies, and the party shifted up the block to the Reids' very large Victorian home. That's when I entered the scene, twenty years after that first party.

I was the fresh college girl whom Kurt had brought back from his role managing nightclubs. The first time I met Dr. Jacob, who was Kurt's best friend's father, was right after Kurt and I moved in together in Loring Park. I had excruciating back pain, a fever, and no health insurance. Kurt walked me the few blocks to Greenway Gables, where Dr. Jacob lived, to see if he could help. He prescribed antibiotics for my first urinary tract infection. How embarrassing!

Over the years, the party has evolved as people moved on or passed on, new people have scored invitations, and the menu has changed — but not much. Nieves Field joined us in the late nineties after moving with her husband, Fred, from Mexico City. The connection was somewhat convoluted. Dr. Jacob's wife, Lila, had grown up a Vanderbilt in New York City. Her biological father was Fred Vanderbilt Field, but after divorcing Lila's mother he had moved on to other relationships. He was driven from the country by the Communist witch hunts of Senator Joseph McCarthy. There he met Lila's new stepmother, Nieves. Nieves was born in 1922, grew up in Mexico City, trained to be a dancer, and then became a model for Diego Rivera. Her back can be seen in the painting *Nude with Calla Lilies*. When I met her, she looked beautiful in a traditional Mexican dress, her hair tied up with strings of multicolored ribbons. Each Christmas Eve she brought a dish of cauliflower fritters, tortas de coliflor. The cauliflower in her dish was cut into florets, coated in an egg wash batter, deep-fried, then covered in a spicy red tomato sauce. I loved that dish. After Nieves died, Kurt tried to re-create the dish for Christmas Eve but could never get it right — too greasy or the wrong flavor profile. The dish has now been permanently retired to the Christmas Eve Hall of Fame. So has the pink beet and herring salad.

The party has moved down a generation and now resides at our home. Our friends Myles (son of Dr. Jacob) and Sue passed us the hosting torch. And so the party continues to evolve. When I joined the gathering, I craved simple potatoes. For years and generations, they'd ignored the starch the Swedish meatball gravy demanded. My second year at the party I made, essentially, au gratin potatoes, slices arranged in a baking dish with butter, cream, and herbs. They were delicious and a welcome addition to the spread. My only complaint was that instead of just calling them au gratin potatoes, Dolores thought she needed to Swedish them up by adding anchovies and making Jansson's temptation.

The tradition continues. Dolores and a few of her generation still arrive every year; members of the original families, the Reids, McKhanns, Jacobs, and Johnsons, still participate; and now we're moving into generation four, with small children once more running through the house and keeping the party lively. I'm guessing in a few years when they're in their teens they may be the new generation down in the basement smoking pot or eating THC gummies or whatever trend fits late 2020s Minnesota.

December

Homemade Irish Cream

Makes 1½ quarts or 3 pints

My friend Lisa made her own Irish cream in corked vintage bottles that she passed out at one of our annual holiday cookie exchanges. I was hooked on the boozy chocolate milkshake and decided to make my own for housewarming gifts throughout the holiday season. Cute bottles of this rich blend make great party favors or holiday gifts. They last for four weeks in the refrigerator. I like mine on a holiday morning with coffee, or any weekend evening served with a couple of ice cubes. It's also delicious over ice cream or chocolate cake.

3 tablespoons cocoa powder

1 tablespoon granulated sugar

1 tablespoon instant coffee granules

1 teaspoon vanilla extract

⅓ cup cold press coffee or brewed coffee cooled to room temperature, divided

3 cups heavy cream

1 (14-ounce) can sweetened condensed milk

2½ cups Irish whiskey

Combine cocoa powder, sugar, instant coffee, vanilla, and 1 tablespoon cold press coffee and whisk with a fork until smooth, pressing out any cocoa powder lumps. Then add the rest of the coffee, stirring until incorporated.

Place the cocoa mixture, cream, and sweetened condensed milk in a blender that can hold 6 cups of liquid (I use my Vitamix) and mix on low speed for 30 seconds. With the blender still on low, slowly add the whiskey through the feed tube and whirl mixture for a few more seconds.

Transfer the Irish cream into glass bottles with tight-fitting lids and store in the refrigerator for up to 4 weeks. Shake well before use. Enjoy on the rocks or serve over ice cream.

Cranberry Old-Fashioned

Serves 1

Old-fashioneds are the state drink of Wisconsin, where my family is from. My grandma would drink them and allow us to steal the boozy cherries from her empty rocks glass. Her version was made with brandy instead of whiskey and tended toward the sweet side.

During our cold northern winters, there's something so homey and nostalgic about the old-fashioned, whether you are enjoying it at a supper club or at a ski lodge. This version, with a festive rosemary and cranberry garnish, will warm you right up.

1 cup granulated sugar

1½ cups water

1 cup fresh or frozen cranberries

3 ounces whiskey

2 shakes orange bitters

garnishes: orange peel, fresh cranberries, rosemary sprig

In a saucepan, bring sugar, water, and cranberries to a boil. Cook for 4–5 minutes, stirring occasionally, until the cranberries start to pop and release their liquid. Strain syrup through a fine mesh sieve and cool completely.

Stir the whiskey, 1.5 ounces cranberry simple syrup, and bitters in a serving glass with ice. Garnish with orange peel, fresh cranberries, and rosemary.

December

Eggnog

Serves 10

Eggnog is always served at our Christmas Eve party, which has been going strong for more than five decades (see pages 65–66). Over the years, the punch bowl has rotated from person to person, and our daughter, Ellie, has now been assigned to make the special beverage. One eggnog essential: nutmeg freshly grated on top.

6 large eggs, yolks and whites separated

⅓ cup plus 1 tablespoon granulated sugar

2 cups whole milk

1 cup heavy cream

½ cup bourbon

1 teaspoon vanilla extract

1 teaspoon freshly grated nutmeg, plus more for garnish

In the bowl of a stand mixer, beat together the egg yolks and ⅓ cup sugar until the yolks lighten in color and the sugar is completely dissolved. Add the milk, cream, bourbon, vanilla, and nutmeg, stirring to combine. Transfer the mixture to a punch bowl and set aside. Wash the bowl.

Place the egg whites in the bowl of the stand mixer and beat to soft peaks. With the mixer still running, gradually add the remaining 1 tablespoon sugar and beat until stiff peaks form. Gently fold the egg whites into the mixture in the punch bowl.

Chill and serve topped with freshly grated nutmeg.

Spiced Nuts

Makes 3 cups

One of my favorite things about Europe is when you order a drink it's always served with something to snack on. Often it's a dish of candied or spiced mixed nuts. Other times it's a bowl of olives and breadsticks. In Italy it can feel like a meal with cheese, meatballs, potato chips, and olives. This recipe is great to serve with cocktails. I also use these to elevate a winter salad or to send home with guests in little cellophane party favor bags. I'm sure there are a million other uses.

2 tablespoons brown sugar

3 tablespoons maple syrup

2 tablespoons water

1 tablespoon chopped fresh rosemary

2 teaspoons kosher salt

1 teaspoon cinnamon

½ teaspoon cayenne pepper

3 cups unsalted mixed nuts

Heat oven to 350 degrees and line a baking sheet with parchment paper or a silicone baking mat.

Combine the brown sugar, maple syrup, water, chopped rosemary, salt, cinnamon, and cayenne in a small bowl. Stir to combine. Pour the mixture over the nuts, stirring to coat evenly, then spread them out on the prepared baking sheet.

Bake, stirring every 5 minutes, until the sugar caramelizes and coats the nuts, about 20 minutes. Remove from the oven and continue to stir every 5 minutes until the nuts have cooled and the sugar hardens, about 20 minutes.

Serve, or put in cellophane bags and tie them with a ribbon for gifting.

December

Baked Party Brie

Serves 10-12

This dish first crossed my path when I worked at *Twin Cities Reader*, an alternative weekly newspaper, and my friend and colleague Nikki made it for a potluck. We both worked in the classifieds department. People would come in and pay for their "Personals" ads, the precursor to Match or Tinder. We'd help them rewrite their ads to make them more compelling. They paid by the word, so we made the ads longer, which was more profitable for the company — and ultimately more likely to make a dream date a reality.

1 (16-ounce) wheel Brie

1 (3-ounce) package sun-dried tomatoes, chopped

½ cup balsamic vinegar

¼ cup extra-virgin olive oil

2 cloves garlic, minced or grated

2 tablespoons unsalted butter

½ cup sliced almonds

crackers for serving

Cut the top skin off the Brie and discard; set the cheese on a serving plate.

Place the sun-dried tomatoes, vinegar, olive oil, and garlic in a microwave-safe dish. Microwave for 45 seconds, then set aside.

Melt butter in a small skillet over medium heat. Add the almonds and cook, stirring, until slightly brown, about 5 minutes. Remove from heat.

Drain the oil and vinegar from the sun-dried tomatoes and pour the remaining sun-dried tomatoes over the Brie. Top with the toasted almonds. Microwave 1 minute.

Serve with water crackers or whole grain crackers.

Gruyère Puff Pastry with Sun-Dried Tomatoes

December

Serves 4-6 as an appetizer

I first made this dish when filming a holiday cooking episode that would serve as the pilot for my TV show, *Taste Buds with Stephanie*. It's a real crowd-pleaser, looks great on the plate, and tastes divine.

¼ cup balsamic vinegar

15–20 sun-dried tomato halves

1 clove garlic, minced or grated

1 sheet frozen puff pastry, thawed

1 pound Gruyère cheese, cut into half-inch cubes (about 2½ cups)

1 tablespoon chopped fresh rosemary

1 large egg, beaten

coarse salt, for sprinkling

Heat oven to 425 degrees. Line a baking sheet with parchment paper.

Mix the balsamic vinegar with the sun-dried tomato halves and microwave for 1 minute to soften the tomatoes. Add garlic, stir, and set aside for 10 minutes.

Drain the tomatoes, reserving 1 tablespoon of vinegar (you can use the remaining vinegar for salad dressing).

Lay the thawed puff pastry flat on the prepared baking sheet and flatten with a rolling pin to smooth out the seams. Pile the cubes of cheese in the center of the puff pastry, leaving 3–4 inches around each border. Tuck the tomatoes among the cheese cubes and sprinkle with the rosemary. Fold the corners of the pastry up over the cheese and tomatoes, bringing the edges together like an envelope. You do not need to seal the dough. Brush the pastry with beaten egg and sprinkle lightly with salt.

Bake for 25–30 minutes or until the pastry is deep golden brown and the cheese is bubbly.

Beth's Chex Party Mix

Makes 28 (2-cup) servings

My sister Beth makes Chex mix each year as a gift to us. It is both a blessing and a curse: I love it and look forward to it, but I always eat too much. At some point I figured out I could freeze the mix, so after the New Year, when it's time to get rid of all the holiday dribs and drabs, I freeze whatever Chex mix is left over. Then I bring it back out when we all gather at the cabin on Burntside Lake in August. Crispy, crunchy, salty, and delicious, this recipe is highly addictive: you have been warned.

1 (12-ounce) box Rice Chex

1 (12-ounce) box Corn Chex

1 (12-ounce) box Wheat Chex

1 (12-ounce) box Cheerios

1 (12-ounce) bag pretzel sticks

2 pounds roasted salted cashews

1 pound roasted salted almonds

1 pound dry roasted peanuts

1 cup (2 sticks) unsalted butter

1 cup (2 sticks) margarine (I Can't Believe It's Not Butter)

1 tablespoon garlic salt

1 tablespoon celery salt

1 tablespoon onion powder

¼ cup plus 2 tablespoons Worcestershire sauce

Heat oven to 225 degrees.

Mix the cereals, pretzels, and nuts in an unscented garbage bag. Pour into large roasting pans: this will probably take 2 baking sessions using 2 large roasting pans.

Melt the butter and margarine and stir in the seasonings. Pour the mixture over the dry ingredients, stirring to evenly coat. Cover the roasting pans tightly with aluminum foil and bake for 1 hour. Remove the aluminum foil, stir, and bake, uncovered, for 1 more hour.

Ham Hock and Split Pea Soup

December — 75

Serves 10

This is the December soup that everyone in Minnesota needs when peppered with freezing rain or *ferskederzzle*. I first heard this word as a teenager when listening to WLOL's morning DJs, John Hines and Bob Berglund. *Ferskederzzle* is the combination of freezing rain and drizzle that we get in the months of November and December before the full-on snow season sets in. The cold rain is bone-chilling, and the only cure is soup.

3 tablespoons extra-virgin olive oil

2 cups chopped onion

1 cup chopped celery

1 cup diced carrots

2 teaspoons kosher salt

3 cloves garlic, minced or grated

2 tablespoons concentrated chicken soup base (Better than Bouillon)

2 cups yellow split peas

1 meaty ham bone (or substitute 1 bone-in ham steak or 1 smoked turkey leg or 2 cups cubed ham)

12 cups chicken broth

2 teaspoons black pepper

1 teaspoon cayenne pepper

2 tablespoons finely chopped parsley, plus more for garnish

grated Parmesan cheese, for garnish

Heat oil in a large Dutch oven over medium heat. Add onion, celery, carrots, and salt. Cook until soft, about 5 minutes, stirring occasionally. Add garlic and cook 2 minutes more. Stir in chicken soup base to coat vegetables. Stir in split peas and ham bone, then add chicken broth, black pepper, cayenne, and parsley. Bring to a boil, then reduce to a simmer and cover. Cook about 2 hours, or until the ham is falling off the bone.

Remove bone and use two forks to shred the ham, then stir meat back into the soup. Sprinkle with fresh parsley or grated Parmesan cheese to serve.

Beef Barley Soup

Serves 8

My mother would make this soup the day after Christmas with leftovers from the prime rib roast. One trick is to add leftover gravy to the soup, which makes for a richer consistency and keeps your gravy from going to waste. Depending on how much gravy you have left, you may need to thin it with some broth.

2 tablespoons extra-virgin olive oil

1 medium onion, chopped

2 carrots, peeled and chopped

2 ribs celery, chopped

2 tablespoons concentrated beef soup base (Better than Bouillon)

3 cloves garlic, minced

10 cups broth (beef, chicken, or vegetable)

leftover beef ribs from a prime rib roast, plus more meat as desired

leaves from 2 sprigs thyme

leaves from 2 sprigs rosemary

3 tablespoons kosher salt, plus more to taste

freshly ground black pepper

1½ cups pearled barley

¼ cup chopped parsley, for garnish

Heat the oil in a large pot over medium heat. Add onions, carrots, and celery, and cook for 5 minutes, stirring occasionally. Stir in beef soup base and garlic and cook for 1 minute more. Add 1 cup of broth and scrape up any browned bits that have accumulated in the pot. Nestle the beef ribs among the vegetables and cover with the remaining broth. Add thyme and rosemary leaves, salt, and pepper. Bring the mixture to a boil and cover with a lid. Reduce heat and simmer for 1½ hours.

Remove ribs and set aside to cool. Cut meat off ribs and chop into bite-size pieces. Add back to the pot with the barley and any optional pieces of leftover prime rib roast. Simmer for another hour, until the barley is tender. Season with more salt and pepper to taste and sprinkle with chopped parsley.

Christmas Eve Cheesy Artichokes

Serves 12

At our annual Christmas Eve gathering with my husband Kurt's friends and family we were initially assigned the artichokes, probably because they are easy to make so we couldn't screw them up too badly. It was a way for us newbies to get involved in the potluck, and now it's our specialty.

- **6 (9-ounce) packages frozen artichoke hearts, thawed (Birds Eye; or substitute canned or jarred)**
- **1 pound cream cheese, at room temperature**
- **2 cups shredded Parmesan cheese**
- **1 cup (2 sticks) unsalted butter**
- **1 cup chopped chives (or substitute green onions)**
- **1 teaspoon kosher salt**
- **½ teaspoon black pepper**

Heat oven to 375 degrees. Place artichokes in a shallow baking dish.

In a stand mixer fitted with the paddle attachment, mix cream cheese, Parmesan, butter, chives, salt, and pepper. Dollop the cream cheese mixture over the artichokes. Bake for 20 minutes, until bubbly, a bit brown on top, and heated through.

TIP: If you have leftovers from this dish, chop them up and place the mixture in a shallow vessel that you can freeze. When you want an easy and delicious hot dip (think New Year's Eve), top with a fresh layer of Parmesan cheese and bake until warmed through. Serve with crackers, vegetables, or bread.

December

Scalloped Potatoes with Gruyère Cheese

Serves 8-10

I was first invited to the Johnson annual Christmas Eve Swedish gathering in 1989 (see page 65). I remember the food being dreadful. I recall steak tartare, cold beet salad with horseradish cream, Swedish meatballs, pickled herring, and a fried cauliflower dish in red sauce alongside artichoke hearts, lingonberries, lefse, rolls, and cookies. At the time, I wasn't very adventurous with my food choices. I recall three meatballs rolling around on my plate accompanied by three rolls contributed by my friend Sue. This was not the plate of the foodie I would become years later. One thing I wondered: *If this is a Swedish smorgasbord, where are the potatoes?* Potatoes were Swedish, right? I vowed to bring potatoes the following year, and I did. These are the potatoes I introduced to the gathering. The two large casserole dishes I made that first year were practically licked clean. Success!

4 tablespoons butter, at room temperature, divided

2 pounds (about 5 medium) russet potatoes, peeled and sliced ⅛-inch thick

kosher salt and cracked black pepper

2 cups (about 8 ounces) grated Gruyère cheese, divided

¾ cup (about 2 ounces) grated Parmesan cheese, divided

3 cups half-and-half

1 tablespoon chopped chives, green onions, or parsley, for garnish

Heat oven to 350 degrees. Grease a 9x13–inch baking dish with 2 tablespoons butter.

In a large pot, bring to boiling enough water to cover the potato slices; add potatoes and parboil for 8 minutes. Drain in a colander.

Layer the bottom of the prepared baking dish with a third of the potato slices. Sprinkle the layer with salt and pepper. Layer on ⅔ cup of the Gruyère cheese, then ¼ cup Parmesan cheese. Repeat for another 2 layers. Top the casserole with the half-and-half and dot the potatoes with the remaining 2 tablespoons butter. Bake the casserole on the middle rack of the oven for 1 hour and 15 minutes, until the potatoes are soft and cooked through. If the top is browning too quickly, cover with aluminum foil. Top with chives, green onions, or parsley, plus a fresh crack of pepper and sprinkle of salt before serving.

Creamed Corn

Serves 6 as a side dish

Creamed corn was not my favorite dish as a kid. I hated the texture and wondered why anyone was ruining good corn. Now I absolutely love it, and I feel it really works on a potluck table.

Speaking of corn, one of the most fun episodes to record for *Taste Buds with Stephanie* was at the Minnesota State Fair with Melissa Peterman of *Reba* and *Young Sheldon* fame. Of course, many Minnesotans will recall that Melissa made her film debut as "Hooker #2" in the locally beloved, Oscar-winning Coen brothers movie *Fargo*. We visited many iconic state fair spots for the show, including the Hamline Church Dining Hall, the Giant Slide, and the corn roast stand, where we munched on ears of corn. It was a hilarious, fun day that had me smiling from ear to ear (see what I did there?).

8 tablespoons unsalted butter, divided

3 tablespoons grated white onion (use a microplane or the large holes of a box grater)

3 tablespoons all-purpose flour

1 teaspoon kosher salt

½ teaspoon black pepper

1½ cups whole milk

1 large egg, beaten

2 cups canned whole-kernel corn; reserve 3 tablespoons of the liquid

⅓ cup heavy cream

30 saltine crackers, crushed (Ritz crackers are yummy too)

Heat oven to 350 degrees. Grease a 6-cup gratin or 9-inch square baking dish.

Melt 6 tablespoons butter in a large skillet over medium heat. Add onion and stir to coat. Cook for 2–3 minutes, until the onion is tender and fully incorporated with the butter. Add the flour and cook, stirring, for 2 minutes. Season with the salt and pepper. Slowly add the whole milk, a half cup at a time, whisking constantly until incorporated. When the texture is smooth, remove from heat and add the beaten egg, corn and reserved liquid, and heavy cream, stirring until well combined. Pour into prepared dish and top with crushed crackers. Dot generously with remaining 2 tablespoons butter and bake for 30 minutes. Let rest for 5 minutes before serving.

December

Lila's Swedish Meatballs with Gravy

Serves 10

For years, these meatballs were Lila Jacob's job every Christmas Eve. The meatballs are always the star of the Christmas Eve dinner. I remember Lila's extra-large green Dutch oven with the meatballs piled high and surrounded by a creamy gravy. Each meatball was browned to perfection, with craggy, crispy bits that caught the scrumptious gravy. Lila made the meatballs until well into her eighties, when my husband, Kurt, and I took over the task. I still use her recipe, but I take a shortcut by baking them in the oven instead of browning them in a skillet. Three pounds of ground meat feeds about ten adults, so you can double, triple, or even quadruple this recipe. Baking the meatballs is the way to go when making multiple batches.

Meatballs

⅔ cup plain ground breadcrumbs (or panko)

¼ cup whole milk

1 large egg, beaten

2 tablespoons ricotta cheese

1½ teaspoons kosher salt

1 teaspoon allspice

1 teaspoon cardamom

½ teaspoon ground ginger

½ teaspoon nutmeg

1 teaspoon dried dill

½ cup fresh dill, cut with scissors

1 large onion, grated on a box grater

1 pound ground beef (80–85% fat)

1 pound pork

1 pound veal

Gravy

4 tablespoons butter

2 tablespoons all-purpose flour

1½ cups beef broth

1 cup heavy cream

1 teaspoon browning and seasoning sauce (Kitchen Bouquet), optional

salt and pepper, to taste

For the Meatballs

Heat oven to 450 degrees. Line a sheet pan with parchment.

In a large bowl, soak the breadcrumbs in the milk. To the soaked breadcrumbs, add the beaten egg, ricotta, dried spices, fresh dill, onion, and ground meat and mix with your hands until all the ingredients are combined. Shape the mixture into balls using a 1½–tablespoon scoop and place on the prepared sheet pan. Bake for 10–13 minutes or until browned. Remove the meatballs from the baking sheet.

For the Gravy

Place a Dutch oven over medium heat. Scrape into the pan any browned bits from the baking sheet along with the fat from the meat. Add the butter. When the butter has melted, add the flour and stir, scraping up all the browned bits, until the fat is well incorporated. Add the broth and stir until everything is incorporated; then add the cream. Whisking continuously, bring the gravy to a boil, cooking until it coats the back of a spoon. Stir in seasoning sauce, if using; add salt and pepper to taste. Serve with meatballs.

December

Reverse-Seared Prime Rib with Horseradish Cream

Serves 4-10, depending on the size of your roast

Prime rib is our traditional Christmas Day meal. There has been much debate on my radio show, *Weekly Dish*, about how to cook the perfect roast. Do you first sear it in a hot skillet, then roast it in the oven until the internal temperature reaches 130 degrees for the perfect medium-rare? Or do you cook it low and slow at 250 degrees and then sear it during the last half hour of cooking? After much trial and error among husband Kurt, his mom, and my radio partner, Stephanie March, the low and slow method with the reverse sear takes the cake. The result is crispy skin and no gray meat.

Roast
- 1 (3- to 12-pound) standing rib roast
- 2 tablespoons kosher salt
- 1 tablespoon black pepper

Horseradish Cream
- 1 cup sour cream
- ¼ cup prepared horseradish
- 2 tablespoons mayonnaise
- 1 tablespoon finely chopped chives
- 1 tablespoon lemon juice
- 1 teaspoon kosher salt
- pinch black pepper

Heat oven to 250 degrees.

Season the roast generously with kosher salt and black pepper. Place roast with fat cap up on a roasting rack set in a large roasting pan. Place the roast in the oven and cook until the center registers 120–125 degrees on an instant-read thermometer for rare, 130 degrees for medium-rare, or 135 degrees for medium to medium-well. Depending on how large your roast is, this will take about 3½ hours.

Remove the roast from the oven, tent it with foil, then let it rest for 30 minutes. Increase oven temperature to at least 500 degrees (higher if possible).

Meanwhile, combine the horseradish cream ingredients, stirring well.

Remove the foil and place the roast back in the oven for 6–10 minutes to crisp the exterior. Remove from the oven, carve, and serve immediately accompanied by the horseradish cream.

Popovers with Honey Butter

Serves 6

I worked as a server at Dayton's Boundary Waters Restaurant during high school. Servers wore white pants, white aprons, and a white dress shirt, and I was always covered in contrasting food stains. People came for shopping but stayed for the restaurant's fresh-baked popovers. This recipe is adapted from the one the internet thinks we used during that time.

Honey Butter

- ½ cup (1 stick) unsalted butter, at room temperature
- ¼ cup honey
- ½ teaspoon kosher salt

Popovers

- 5 large eggs
- 1⅔ cups whole milk
- 5 tablespoons unsalted butter, melted and cooled
- 1⅔ cups all-purpose flour
- ½ teaspoon kosher salt

For the Honey Butter

Mix ingredients in a bowl until smooth. Set aside.

For the Popovers

Heat oven to 400 degrees. Lightly coat popover pans or deep muffin tins with nonstick cooking spray and heat the pans in the oven for at least 15 minutes.

In a large bowl, use an electric mixer on medium speed to beat the eggs until frothy. Add the milk and melted butter and mix well. Add the flour and salt and mix until just combined. Carefully divide the batter among the preheated pans, filling each cup just under half full. Bake for 30–40 minutes, until puffy and well browned (do not open the oven during this span if you can help it). Finished popovers should pull away from the pan easily and feel light to the touch. Remove from the oven and serve warm with honey butter.

Aebleskivers

Serves 10–12

I grew up with my dad making aebleskivers on special Saturday mornings. He was quite the expert, scooping the batter into the very hot and well-oiled pan. An aebleskiver pan, available at specialty cookware stores or online, is made of cast iron and has seven little cups that make seven perfect donuts the size of golf balls. There is a trick to these. The cups need to be well oiled, so the puffed batter doesn't stick, and then you need to turn the donuts delicately with a toothpick or, in my father's case, a knitting needle or a chopstick. My dad had it down, and now my brothers, Alex and Jack, have taken over the tradition for their families and mine. They call them baseball pancakes. Alex made the aebleskivers pictured here.

2 cups all-purpose flour

1 teaspoon baking powder

1 teaspoon baking soda

1 teaspoon kosher salt

2 large eggs

2 tablespoons granulated sugar

2 cups buttermilk

1 tablespoon vegetable shortening, melted, plus more for the pan

syrup or jam for serving

In one bowl, whisk together flour, baking powder, baking soda, and salt. In a separate bowl, beat eggs slightly, then stir in sugar and buttermilk. Stir in melted shortening, then mix in the dry ingredients.

Put 1 teaspoon shortening in each hole of the aebleskiver pan. Heat the pan on the stove over medium heat for 4 minutes. When the pan is good and hot, fill each hole halfway with batter. When the bottom is browned, after about 3 minutes, turn the aebleskiver with a knitting needle, toothpick, or fork, flipping the dough ball inside the cup to brown the other side, another 3 minutes. Remove finished aebleskivers to a plate. Add more shortening to the pan as needed to finish the batter. Serve with syrup or jam.

Eggnog Croissant Christmas Casserole

December

Serves 8

I usually make this casserole with the leftover Christmas Eve eggnog (see page 70), but I also use refrigerated eggnog from the grocery store. I assemble it Christmas morning, bake it while we open presents, and serve it later that day. You can change up the recipe by adding leftover Christmas Eve popovers (see page 83), blueberries and lemon zest, or diced apples and crushed toasted pecans.

8 large eggs

1⅓ cups eggnog

1 teaspoon vanilla extract

½ teaspoon pumpkin pie spice

10 croissants, each torn into 4–5 pieces

1 (4-ounce) log honey-flavored goat cheese, cut into 10 pieces

maple syrup and freshly grated nutmeg for serving

Heat oven to 400 degrees. Grease a 9x13–inch baking pan.

In a large bowl, whisk the eggs, eggnog, vanilla, and pumpkin pie spice.

Layer the torn croissants to cover the bottom of the prepared pan. Pour the egg mixture over the croissants until all the bread is covered. Tuck the pieces of goat cheese into pockets of the croissants. Cover the baking dish with aluminum foil and bake for 30 minutes. Remove the foil and cook for another 10 minutes, until the bread turns golden brown. Remove from the oven and serve with maple syrup and freshly grated nutmeg.

Savory Sausage Breakfast Bread Pudding

Serves 8

This is a great breakfast dish for Christmas morning. You can prep it before the little ones wake up and let it sit until you're ready to bake. With a winning combination of sausage, eggs, and cheese, this casserole is like a breakfast sandwich in a perfectly cut square.

- 2 tablespoons extra-virgin olive oil
- 1 pound pork breakfast sausage
- 1 medium onion, chopped
- 2 tablespoons finely chopped fresh rosemary
- 4 cups cubed crusty sandwich bread
- 1 cup shredded cheese (any combination of Parmesan, mozzarella, Gruyère, or Swiss), divided
- 6 large eggs, lightly beaten
- 1 cup heavy cream
- 1 cup 2% milk
- 4 dashes hot sauce (Tabasco)
- 1 teaspoon kosher salt
- 1 teaspoon black pepper

Heat oven to 375 degrees. Grease a 2-quart baking dish.

Heat the olive oil in a large skillet over medium heat and brown the sausage. Add the onions and rosemary and cook until softened, about 10 minutes.

In a large bowl, toss bread cubes with sausage mixture and half the cheese. Transfer the mixture to the prepared baking dish.

Whisk together the eggs, cream, milk, hot sauce, salt, and pepper and pour over the bread mixture. Sprinkle the remaining cheese over the top. Bake for 45–50 minutes, until a toothpick inserted in the center comes out clean.

Cranberry Orange Bread

Makes 1 large loaf, 3 mini loaves, or 1 dozen muffins

I started making this bread to give as hostess gifts throughout the holidays. One year, I made it for my cookie exchange, giving each family a mini loaf along with a blueberry-lemon and lemon–poppy seed version. This recipe makes three mini loaves or one large loaf. The ones I gift are wrapped in waxed paper or plastic food wrap and tied with green ribbon. These breads also look great in cardboard loaf pans wrapped in cellophane.

- 1 cup granulated sugar
- zest of 1 large orange, plus 1 tablespoon orange juice
- 1½ cups all-purpose flour
- ½ teaspoon kosher salt
- 1 teaspoon baking powder
- ½ cup (1 stick) unsalted butter, melted and cooled
- ½ cup plain unsweetened yogurt
- ¼ cup whole milk
- 2 large eggs, lightly beaten
- ½ teaspoon vanilla extract
- 1 cup chopped fresh or frozen cranberries

Heat oven to 350 degrees and grease a 5x9–inch loaf pan, mini loaf pans, or muffin tins.

Add the sugar and orange zest to a large bowl and stir until the sugar starts to turn a bit orange and is fragrant. Mix in the flour, salt, and baking powder.

In a separate bowl, whisk together the cooled melted butter, yogurt, milk, eggs, orange juice, and vanilla. Add the wet ingredients to the dry ingredients and stir until just combined. Fold in the cranberries and then transfer the batter to the prepared pan(s).

Bake until a toothpick inserted into the center comes out clean, about 1 hour and 10 minutes for a traditional loaf pan, or about 35 minutes for mini loaf pans or 20 minutes for muffins. Remove the bread from the oven and allow it to cool on a wire rack for 20–30 minutes. Run a knife along the edges of the pan, then invert to remove loaf or muffins from the pan to cool completely.

December

87

Mom's Toffee Bars

Makes 24 bars

My mom was known for three holiday cookies: roll-out sour cream sugar cookies, pecan tea cakes, and these toffee bars. I didn't love these as a kid. I remember comparing the chocolate to Hershey's, and the German chocolate used here is decidedly more bitter. Over the years, these bars grew on me. I learned to like the salty base and the crunch of the pecans as I settled into the not-so-sweet chocolate topping. When I make these now, I often sprinkle a layer of crispy Maldon salt flakes over the top of the nuts and chocolate. As a kid, I definitely didn't like salt on my chocolate, but now I find it enhances the flavor.

- 1 cup (2 sticks) unsalted butter, at room temperature
- 1 cup packed brown sugar
- 1 large egg yolk, beaten
- 1 teaspoon vanilla extract
- 2 cups all-purpose flour
- ½ teaspoon kosher salt
- 8 ounces German sweet baking chocolate (Baker's)
- 1½ cups chopped pecans
- sea salt flakes (Maldon), optional

Heat oven to 350 degrees. Grease a shallow 10x15-inch pan with baking spray.

In a large bowl, mix together butter, brown sugar, well-beaten egg yolk, and vanilla and mix well. Stir in flour and salt until well combined. Spread the batter in the prepared pan and press with your fingertips. Bake for 20 minutes; the bars will be fairly blond in color.

Break chocolate into pieces and place in a microwave-safe bowl. Heat on high in 30-second increments, stirring after each, until melted. Spread the chocolate over the bars while warm. Sprinkle with the nuts and sea salt flakes, if using. Let the bars set until the chocolate is firm but not fully cool. Cut into 2-inch square bars.

Easiest Roll-Out Sugar Cookies

December

Makes 3 dozen cookies

My mother made beautiful frosted and decorated cookies. Her sour cream cookie dough was so sticky that she used a cloth-sleeved rolling pin to roll out the dough. Mixing, rolling, and baking the cookies took one day. The next day we would invite friends over to speed up the job of decorating six to eight dozen cookies. My mom was a wizard with frosting and a handful of toothpicks, making decorated snowmen and snow angels.

This recipe is the exact opposite of my mom's. I could never get the texture of the cookies right or roll them thin enough. This dough is forgiving, requires no chilling, and can be rolled as thin as you like. Most importantly, the cookies come out almost as good as my mom's, and the taste is, well, maybe better. Sorry, Mom.

Cookies

1 cup (2 sticks) unsalted butter, at room temperature

1 cup granulated sugar

½ teaspoon vanilla extract

½ teaspoon almond extract

1 large egg

3 cups all-purpose flour

2 teaspoons baking powder

1 teaspoon kosher salt

Frosting

2 pounds confectioners' sugar

½ cup (1 stick) unsalted butter, at room temperature

1 teaspoon vanilla extract

2 tablespoons whole milk

food coloring, optional

For the Cookies

Heat oven to 350 degrees. Line baking sheets with parchment paper.

In a stand mixer fitted with the paddle attachment, beat butter and sugar until smooth. Add the extracts and egg and mix to combine.

In a medium bowl, combine flour, baking powder, and salt. Add dry ingredients to the butter and sugar mixture and mix until the dough is crumbly but starting to come together.

Dump the dough onto a lightly floured work surface or parchment paper. Knead the dough by hand. Divide the dough into workable batches, then roll out to about ¼ to ⅛ inch thick (thicker for children's cookies) and cut into shapes with cookie cutters. Transfer the shapes to the prepared baking sheets. Bake for 9–10 minutes. Let cool on the baking sheet until firm enough to transfer to a wire rack.

For the Frosting

In a large bowl, beat confectioners' sugar, butter, and vanilla with an electric mixer until smooth. Add milk a little at a time to reach desired consistency. Stir in food coloring (if using) to reach the desired color. Decorate cookies and allow the frosting to set, ideally overnight.

Cherries in the Snow

Serves 12–16

This was my mom's annual Christmas dessert and my father's favorite. It's a little strange, with its meringue crust topped with canned cherries and a marshmallow cream cheese whipped cream. Mom would bake and chill this at least a day ahead, so dessert taunted us every time we opened the refrigerator.

Crust
6 large egg whites
½ teaspoon cream of tartar
¼ teaspoon kosher salt
1¾ cups granulated sugar

Filling
6 ounces cream cheese, at room temperature
1 cup granulated sugar
1 teaspoon vanilla extract
2 cups heavy cream, chilled
2 cups miniature marshmallows

Topping
1 (21-ounce) can cherry pie filling

For the Crust

Heat oven to 400 degrees. Grease a 9x13-inch pan.

Beat egg whites until they reach soft peaks. Continue beating and add cream of tartar and salt and then slowly add sugar, 1 tablespoon at a time. Beat until stiff and glossy, about 15 minutes. Spread the meringue on the bottom of the pan and put it in the oven. Turn off the oven; leave pan in the oven with the door closed overnight, or for at least 12 hours.

For the Filling

Mix cream cheese, sugar, and vanilla. Set aside.

Beat cream in a chilled bowl until stiff. Fold whipped cream and marshmallows into the cream cheese mixture. Spread over meringue and refrigerate for at least 12 hours.

Cut into bars and serve, topped with cherry pie filling.

Ginger Molasses Cookies

December

Makes 2 dozen cookies

This recipe invites you to use those adorable Christmas cookie stamps. I have a set from my mother-in-law, Dolores, that was handed down by her mother. I also have one from Nordic Ware, the Minnesota company responsible for bringing us the Bundt pan.

- 3¾ cups all-purpose flour
- 1 tablespoon ground ginger
- 1 tablespoon cinnamon
- 2 teaspoons ground cloves
- ½ teaspoon nutmeg
- 1 teaspoon kosher salt
- 1 cup (2 sticks) unsalted butter, at room temperature
- 1 cup granulated sugar, plus more for rolling
- 1 large egg
- ½ cup molasses
- 1 tablespoon orange zest
- 1 tablespoon orange juice

In a medium bowl, sift together the flour, spices, and salt.

In a stand mixer fitted with the paddle attachment, beat the butter and sugar on medium speed until light and creamy, about 3 minutes. Scrape the sides of the bowl with a rubber spatula. Add the egg, molasses, orange zest, and orange juice, and mix until combined. Scrape down the sides of the bowl, and with the mixer on low, add the flour mixture and blend thoroughly. Refrigerate dough for at least 2 hours or up to 2 days.

Heat oven to 350 degrees. Use a cookie scoop to shape the dough into golf ball–size balls. Roll into smooth balls in your hands and then roll in sugar before placing on a cookie sheet. You should be able to fit 3 cookies in a row. Press each dough ball with a cookie stamp until you begin to see dough along the edges. Bake for 10–14 minutes.

Cookie Exchange Salted Caramels

Makes about 5 dozen caramels

Each year, for the past three decades, my girlfriends and I have a cookie exchange. The vague rules are that you make a dozen cookies for each person and an extra dozen for eating at the exchange. But inevitably store-bought cookies show up. I've brought cranberry orange breads (page 87), easy roll-out cookies (page 89), and these salted caramels. They get individually wrapped in waxed paper and tied in a cellophane bag with a sparkly ribbon.

1 cup (2 sticks) unsalted butter

4 cups granulated sugar

2 cups light corn syrup

1 (12-ounce) can evaporated milk

2 cups heavy cream

1½ teaspoons vanilla extract

1 tablespoon sea salt flakes (Maldon)

Line a 9x13–inch pan with parchment paper and fold over the sides, leaving at least 2 inches all around so you can lift the caramels out of the pan.

Place a large, heavy-bottomed saucepan over medium heat. Add butter, sugar, and corn syrup and stir until the mixture begins to boil, about 5–10 minutes.

Gradually add the evaporated milk and heavy cream, 1 cup at a time, very slowly, stirring constantly. You want to make sure the mixture maintains a steady heat and constant boil; it takes time to dribble in the liquid, and it may bubble up. Be patient.

Stir the mixture constantly, scraping the sides occasionally, until it reaches a firm ball stage, about 240–245 degrees on a candy thermometer, then remove from heat. Stir in the vanilla. Pour caramel into the prepared pan and sprinkle with sea salt flakes. Refrigerate overnight until cooled and hardened.

Cut caramels into 1x2–inch pieces, wrap in waxed paper, and roll the ends.

December

January

AMATEUR NIGHT

My first memory of New Year's Eve involves my sister, Laura, who took care of us while our parents went out to a party. I remember our one goal was to stay up until midnight, when we could celebrate by banging together pots and pans and wearing sparkly paper hats. We ate Totino's Pizza Rolls and watched Wolfman Jack on a music countdown show.

A decade later I worked New Year's Eve at the Heartthrob Nightclub in St. Paul. We called it Amateur Night, the first of three throughout the year. Kurt and I met at the Heartthrob. He was a seasoned manager, but as a cocktail waitress in the trenches, I already knew the significance of working Amateur Nights. New Year's Eve brought out a segment of the population who wanted to get really smashed for that special occasion, unlike the nightclub regulars who mostly knew how to pace their drinking — how to have a good time without falling on the dance floor or collecting a DUI on their way home.

The next Amateur Night was St. Patrick's Day. In St. Paul with its significant Irish population, St. Paddy's Day was an excuse for all otherwise responsible people to drink from about 10 a.m., as the parades wrapped up, to closing time, which at the time was 1 a.m. I'd coached Kurt, a newbie from Las Vegas, on the fine art of hosting the debauchery: take out all the tables and chairs, remove all the glassware and stock up on plastic cups, put trash cans randomly throughout the club, have cattle troughs filled with cans of beer every twenty feet staffed by a cocktail waitress and a bouncer, and open the doors at 9 a.m. for the pre-party parade goers. We'd all work sixteen-hour shifts and make crazy money.

I remember Kurt's first St. Paddy's Day. I saw a kid pass out on the floor. Kurt saw him too and went to call a paramedic. By the time he was back, the kid's friends had lifted him high above their heads and, like Flea from Red Hot Chili Peppers, passed him above the crowd to the exit and then out. The third

Amateur Night of the year was the evening before Thanksgiving, when every college student was back home and wanting to reconnect with high school friends away from the nervous supervision of their parents. And all these college kids had bulletproof IDs. More ridiculous behavior.

Needless to say, since our nightclub days, Kurt and I *do not* go out on Amateur Nights. We're parents now, with extended families and grown-up friends. Thanksgiving night is spent prepping food for the next day while our daughter goes out on the town. On St. Patrick's Day we lock the doors, close the curtains, and stay off the streets. The week after, we go shopping for the unsold corned beef brisket, stocking up for less than two dollars per pound. Slow cooked in the oven, corned beef brisket becomes melt-in-your-mouth tender (see page 165). It's an easy way to feed lots of summer cabin guests.

New Year's Eve usually is spent with friends, often out in the country somewhere — Ely, or at our friend's farmhouse in Wisconsin; a place that's safe. Now we enjoy making elaborate and delicious dinners. One year we splurged and made roast tenderloin with a creamy tarragon lobster pasta from the original *Silver Palate Cookbook*. Last year it was lamb osso buco slow cooked with shallots, carrots, garlic, celery, and red wine, served with couscous flavored with black olives and mint.

For Kurt and me, New Year's Eve is also a time to reflect on goals we made for the previous year and to set new ones. Personal goals are a mixed bag of hopes and wants. Of course you want everyone to be healthy and the world to be a safer place. Those are the fundamental goals of life, but in truth we don't have much control over them. Sadly, what is rewarding are those materialistic and vain goals — the raise at work, completing another cookbook, losing a few pounds. You make those, and it's like, *Yeah, I did it!* Ultimately, I win some and I lose some.

My one very immediate goal last New Year's Eve was simply to stay up until midnight and bang some pots and pans. Dinner ended at 9 p.m., we played cards until 10:30, and then Kurt put on a record, something cosmic by Frank Zappa that made my drowsy eyes flutter and my head nod. I didn't make it. Maybe next year.

97

January

Beth's Spinach Dip

Serves 8

In my childhood years, my sister Beth would make this recipe while we planned our New Year's Eve of banging pots and pans and watching the Times Square countdown on television. I remember being surprised that I liked a dish made with spinach and water chestnuts. Spinach and water chestnuts? Yuck! But this creamy dip was served in a hollowed-out bread bowl, great for dipping in hunks of torn bread chunks, and the chestnuts gave it a tasty crunch. Over the years I've reduced the cream cheese, subbing mayo and sour cream, which ultimately may not be lighter but gives the dip a tangy flavor that I love.

- 1 cup sour cream
- 1 cup mayonnaise
- 3 green onions, chopped
- 2 teaspoons chopped parsley
- 1 teaspoon kosher salt
- 1 teaspoon garlic powder
- ½ teaspoon black pepper
- ½ teaspoon onion powder
- ½ teaspoon dried thyme
- ½ teaspoon dried oregano
- 1 (10-ounce) package frozen chopped spinach, thawed and squeezed dry in a paper towel
- 1 (8-ounce) can sliced water chestnuts
- for serving: bread bowl, vegetables, tortilla chips, or pumpernickel rye crisps

Mix dip ingredients together in a large bowl. Refrigerate for a couple of hours before serving.

Hollow out a round bread loaf; place the dip inside and the bread hunks alongside. Or serve dip with cut vegetables, tortilla chips, or pumpernickel rye crisps.

Artichoke Dip

Serves 6

The first time I had a hot artichoke dip was at the Loring Pasta Bar in Minneapolis. The restaurant was known for its artistic shabby chic decor and delicious artichoke dip. It seems soldiers returning to America from World War II had grown accustomed to the Mediterranean flavors of artichokes and liked to make the dip to eat in front of their living room televisions. This dish is always a crowd-pleaser. Adding goat cheese gives it a fluffier texture and tangier taste.

- 2 (14-ounce) cans artichoke hearts, drained and chopped into quarters
- 8 ounces cream cheese
- 4 ounces goat cheese
- 1 cup grated Parmesan cheese, divided
- ¼ cup mayonnaise
- ¼ cup chopped chives (or substitute the green parts of scallions)
- 1 teaspoon kosher salt
- 1 teaspoon black pepper
- 3 dashes hot sauce (Tabasco)
- ¼ cup toasted breadcrumbs (or substitute panko)
- crackers for serving

Heat oven to 350 degrees.

Put artichokes, cream cheese, goat cheese, ¾ cup Parmesan, mayonnaise, chives, salt, pepper, and hot sauce in a food processor and pulse until blended. Mix until well combined, but leave some texture. Spread into a pie pan or a small casserole dish. Top with breadcrumbs and remaining ¼ cup Parmesan. Bake for 25 minutes, until warm all the way through and bubbly on top. Serve with water crackers or Triscuits.

Thai Chicken Rice Soup

Serves 6

My daughter, Ellie, and her partner, Kate, once cooked this soup for me. I loved it so much I begged for the recipe. I am including it here so you can love it too.

Few things in life are more rewarding than your child cooking for you. Naturally, along the way I spoke with Ellie about food and exposed her to a wide range of dishes. But I didn't teach her how to cook. I think she observed and then figured it out herself using cookbooks and YouTube. When she came back with her own spin on the dishes she grew up with, I was overwhelmed. Now she introduces me to new dishes, preparations, and flavors. Here's one of hers with my own spin: I added rice.

- 1 tablespoon coconut oil (refined or unrefined)
- 1 medium onion, thinly sliced
- 2 cloves garlic, chopped
- 1 red jalapeño (green is fine too), thinly sliced
- 3-inch knob ginger
- 1 lemongrass stalk, cut into 2-inch-long pieces
- 1 tablespoon red curry paste
- 6 cups chicken broth
- 1 (13.5-ounce) can unsweetened full-fat coconut milk
- 2 medium chicken breasts, cut into bite-size pieces
- 1 cup jasmine rice
- 1 red bell pepper, sliced into thin strips
- 3 tablespoons lime juice
- 2 tablespoons fish sauce
- 3 green onions, green and white parts, thinly sliced
- ¼ cup chopped cilantro

Heat the coconut oil in a large pot over medium heat. Add the onion, garlic, half the jalapeño slices, ginger, lemongrass, and red curry paste and cook, stirring frequently, for about 5 minutes, until the onions are softened. Add the chicken broth and bring to a boil. Reduce the heat and simmer, uncovered, for 20 minutes.

Strain out and discard the aromatics (onions, garlic, jalapeño, ginger, and lemongrass). To strained broth add coconut milk, chicken, and rice; simmer about 10 minutes, until chicken is cooked through and rice is tender. Stir in red pepper, lime juice, and fish sauce. Cook for 2 minutes more, then ladle into serving bowls and top with sliced green onions, fresh cilantro, and remaining jalapeño slices.

Italian Sausage Soup

Serves 4

I'm known as the soup queen on *The Jason Show*, where I make weekly TV appearances. Between the Instant Pot and the slow cooker, I have more than thirty soup recipes on my website, stephaniesdish.com. There's something comforting and warming about eating soup in a Minnesota fall or winter. I always have a mason jar (or ten!) of soup in my freezer, and I bring them to neighbors, to coworkers, or as hostess and housewarming gifts, labeled with brown tags tied with garden string.

- 1 pound bulk hot Italian sausage
- 1 cup chopped onion
- 3 cloves garlic, minced or grated
- 5 cups beef broth
- 1 cup water
- 1 (28-ounce) can diced tomatoes
- 1 (8-ounce) can tomato sauce
- 2 cups sliced zucchini
- 1 cup sliced carrots
- 1 medium red bell pepper, diced
- 1 tablespoon kosher salt
- 2 teaspoons black pepper
- 1 teaspoon dried basil
- 1 teaspoon dried oregano
- 1 (18-ounce) package refrigerated cheese tortellini
- 1 (5-ounce) bag baby spinach
- garnishes: ¼ cup grated Parmesan cheese; ¼ cup basil, cut into strips

In a large pot, brown the sausage with the onion and garlic. Drain off the fat. Stir in broth, water, tomatoes, tomato sauce, zucchini, carrots, bell pepper, salt, pepper, dried basil, and oregano and bring to a boil. Simmer for about 30 minutes. Add the tortellini and the spinach, and cook for 8 minutes, until the spinach is wilted, the tortellini are cooked through, and the carrots are tender. Serve with Parmesan cheese and fresh basil to sprinkle on top.

Arugula Clementine Salad with Dried Cherries

Serves 4

After all the holiday indulgences, in January more salads tend to make their way to my plate. This time of year requires a bit of work to make salads shine because the list of fresh ingredients is more limited. Dried fruits and roasted vegetables, a variety of seeds, and various cheeses or grains can all liven up a winter salad. When I worked at Dayton's Boundary Waters Restaurant, I particularly loved a walnut oil–based dressing served with a roasted chicken salad. Don't be afraid to experiment with different types of oils or even flavored olive oil when making winter salads.

Vinaigrette

2 tablespoons champagne or salad vinegar

2 tablespoons clementine juice from about 2 clementines

1 teaspoon honey

½ teaspoon kosher salt

½ teaspoon Dijon mustard

¼ cup walnut oil

Salad

1 (5-ounce) bag arugula

2 green onions (green and white parts), sliced

1 medium avocado, halved, pitted, and diced

2 clementines, broken into sections

½ cup dried cherries

2 tablespoons freshly grated Parmesan cheese

In a large bowl, whisk together the vinegar, juice, honey, salt, and mustard. While whisking, slowly drizzle in the walnut oil to emulsify the dressing. Add in the salad components and toss to combine.

Spinach Salad with Instant Pot Jammy Eggs and Bacon Vinaigrette

Serves 2

I love a soft-boiled egg, and nothing prepares them better than the Instant Pot. You can cook eighteen eggs in the pot at a time, and they all come out perfectly and so easy to peel. Four minutes on the Manual setting and a quick release and you have a jammy soft egg. When broken into, the beautiful yolk runs all over the spinach leaves, mixing with the tart vinaigrette and giving you the perfect, flavorful bite.

Salad

- **2 large eggs**
- **1 medium shallot, thinly sliced**
- **¼ cup white vinegar**
- **1 teaspoon granulated sugar**
- **2 small bunches baby spinach, torn into bite-size pieces**
- **4 slices bacon, cut into quarter-inch strips and pan-fried; reserve 1 teaspoon fat for the dressing**

Dressing

- **1 clove garlic, minced or grated**
- **3 tablespoons extra-virgin olive oil**
- **3 tablespoons apple cider vinegar**
- **2 teaspoons lemon juice**
- **2 teaspoons Dijon mustard**
- **1 teaspoon mayonnaise**
- **1 teaspoon brown sugar**
- **1 teaspoon bacon fat**
- **pinch kosher salt**
- **freshly ground black pepper**

To prepare soft-boiled eggs in an Instant Pot: set the eggs on a trivet and cook for 4 minutes on the Manual setting with a quick release. Cool the eggs in ice water for 5 minutes, then peel. To prepare soft-boiled eggs on the stovetop: in a small pot bring an inch of water to boiling. Add the eggs and cook for 6 minutes. Cool the eggs in ice water, then peel.

Place shallots in a bowl and cover with vinegar, sugar, and ¼ cup hot water. Let soak for at least 30 minutes, then drain.

Add dressing ingredients to a mason jar and shake until emulsified.

Toss spinach with the dressing. Top each salad with shallots, bacon, and eggs, split lengthwise.

Broiled Scallops à la Simpson's with Oven-Baked Lemon Risotto

Serves 4

When I was little, my sisters and I would go to our grandma's house for two weeks every summer. Grandma lived on Main Street in Waupaca, Wisconsin. It was a small town, and we could walk to the beach, Dairy Queen, the library, and the dime store that sold little glass ceramic animals I bought with my allowance. All family celebrations were held at either the country club or Simpson's Supper Club, which is still there today. Our favorite menu item was the broiled seafood platter with shrimp, haddock, and scallops. This is my version of Simpson's broiled scallops with a simple oven-baked lemon risotto on the side.

Risotto

1½ cups arborio rice

4 cups chicken broth

½ cup diced yellow onion

1 clove garlic, minced or grated

3 tablespoons butter, cut into 6 chunks

1 teaspoon kosher salt

1 teaspoon black pepper

zest of 1 lemon

3 tablespoons lemon juice

⅓ cup Parmesan cheese

3 tablespoons chopped fresh dill

1 tablespoon chopped parsley

Scallops

½ cup all-purpose flour

1 teaspoon paprika

½ teaspoon seasoned salt (Lawry's)

½ teaspoon black pepper

pinch sugar

4 tablespoons unsalted butter

¼ cup dry white wine

¼ cup lemon juice

16 large Dayboat scallops, patted dry

lemon slices for serving

For the Risotto

Heat oven to 350 degrees.

In a 10-inch oven-safe skillet or pot with a lid, combine the rice, broth, onion, garlic, and butter. Cover the pot with aluminum foil to seal in the juices and place the lid on top. Bake for 45 minutes. Remove the pot from the oven and start the broiler for the scallops.

Add salt, pepper, lemon zest, 3 tablespoons lemon juice, and Parmesan to the rice pot and vigorously stir for 3 minutes, combining all the ingredients and blending the risotto until creamy. If the mixture seems dry, add additional broth or cream, a few tablespoons at a time, to reach desired consistency and creaminess. Cover the pot and let rest until the scallops are done.

Right before serving, stir the dill and parsley into the rice.

For the Scallops

Mix all dry ingredients in a plastic bag.

Melt butter in a baking dish under the broiler. Stir in the wine and ¼ cup lemon juice.

Toss scallops in dry ingredients, shaking until coated. Put scallops in the buttered baking dish and spoon a teaspoon of butter over each scallop. Broil for 4–6 minutes, until cooked through and no longer opaque. Serve the scallops alongside the risotto with fresh lemon slices. Spoon the broiled butter over the scallops and drizzle over the risotto.

January

Cheesy Sausage Lasagna

Serves 12

Everyone needs a good lasagna recipe, and this one is mine. It comes in handy for a Sunday family dinner or when you need to bring food to a new neighbor or a new parent. One of my favorite Hansen Hacks is to buy inexpensive baking pans at thrift stores — most have stacks on their shelves. Deliver the lasagna with a note that the pan is nonreturnable. It holds up better than a disposable foil pan and won't end up in the recycling bin.

12 lasagna noodles

2 tablespoons extra-virgin olive oil

1 medium white onion, diced

1 pound ground sausage

5 cloves garlic, minced or grated

2 cups finely chopped kale or spinach

½ cup finely chopped mushrooms

5 cups tomato sauce, divided

1 (15-ounce) container ricotta cheese

4 ounces goat cheese, at room temperature

3 cups shredded mozzarella cheese

2 teaspoons kosher salt

1 teaspoon black pepper

1 teaspoon dried herbs (oregano, basil, or Italian seasoning)

Heat oven to 350 degrees. Grease a 9x13–inch baking pan.

Soak lasagna noodles in hot tap water for 20 minutes, or use oven-ready noodles.

Heat olive oil in a large skillet over medium heat and add onion and sausage. Cook until onion is tender and sausage is no longer pink, about 5–7 minutes. Add garlic, greens, and mushrooms and cook until wilted. Stir in 3 cups tomato sauce.

In a medium bowl, mix ricotta and goat cheese until combined.

Spread 1 cup tomato sauce on the bottom of the prepared pan. Cover with 4 lasagna noodles. Top with 1 cup of the meat mixture. Sprinkle with ½ cup mozzarella, then dollop ½ cup of ricotta cheese mixture on top. Repeat with noodles, meat mixture, mozzarella, and ricotta mixture for 2 more layers. Top with remaining 1 cup sauce and finish with remaining 1½ cups mozzarella cheese. Sprinkle with salt, pepper, and seasoning. Bake, uncovered, for 1 hour. If the top is browning too quickly, cover with aluminum foil. Let stand for 30 minutes before serving.

Heavenly Chicken and Rice

Serves 2-4

The first time I made this dish my friend called it "heavenly chicken and rice," and the name stuck. Who doesn't love chicken, rice, and cream? This one-skillet chicken dish is perfect for two but can be scaled up for a large family or a dinner party. If you're not a mushroom lover, substitute zucchini or yellow squash. Either way, it will be fantastic.

2 tablespoons extra-virgin olive oil

½ cup all-purpose flour

1 teaspoon kosher salt, plus more for garnish

1 teaspoon black pepper, plus more for garnish

4 skin-on boneless chicken thighs

3 tablespoons butter

½ cup chopped yellow onion

1 cup sliced mushrooms

2 cloves garlic, minced or grated

2 teaspoons chopped fresh rosemary

1 teaspoon dried sage

1½ cups long-grain rice

3 cups chicken broth

1 cup heavy cream

juice and zest of ½ lemon

1 tablespoon chopped parsley

Heat oven to 350 degrees.

Heat the olive oil in a 10- or 12-inch cast iron skillet set over high heat.

Mix flour, salt, and pepper in a plastic zip-top bag. Add the chicken thighs to the bag and toss to coat. Add the chicken to the pan, skin side down, and brown for about 8 minutes. Flip and cook the other side for 4 minutes more. Place the cooked thighs on a plate and set aside.

Add butter to the pan and cook onion and mushrooms for 4 minutes, scraping up any browned bits. Add the garlic, rosemary, sage, rice, broth, cream, and lemon juice. Nestle the browned chicken thighs in the pan, cover with foil, and bake for 40 minutes. Remove from oven and let stand for 5 minutes. Garnish with lemon zest, chopped parsley, and a sprinkle of kosher salt and cracked black pepper.

107

January

Stuffed Chicken Breasts

Serves 6

When Kurt and I first met, he did all the cooking. I couldn't cook anything except chili, grilled cheese, and scrambled eggs. One of the first dishes he made for me was chicken breasts stuffed with sun-dried tomatoes, onions, and basil. In a skillet, he made a heavy cream sauce flavored with Dijon mustard and garlic. The chicken was covered in the sauce and served on top of white rice. I was so excited to have a boyfriend who cooked. But that would be the only time Kurt made that dish for me. Even today, when I ask him to make it, he says, "Why, when everything you cook is so good?" He has a way with flattery!

Here's my twist on his dish.

Chicken and Stuffing
- **1½ teaspoons extra-virgin olive oil**
- **1 tablespoon unsalted butter**
- **3 cups finely diced onion**
- **1½ teaspoons chopped garlic**
- **2 tablespoons diced sun-dried tomatoes**
- **1 cup heavy cream**
- **2 tablespoons lemon juice**
- **2 teaspoons black pepper**
- **1 teaspoon kosher salt**
- **1 cup breadcrumbs, finely ground (or substitute panko)**
- **1 cup grated Gruyère cheese**
- **¼ cup grated Parmesan cheese**
- **2 tablespoons chopped fresh basil**
- **6 small to medium boneless, skinless chicken breasts**

Rice
- **1 cup jasmine rice**
- **2¼ cups chicken broth**
- **4 tablespoons unsalted butter**
- **2 teaspoons kosher salt**
- **1 teaspoon lemon juice**

For the Chicken and Stuffing

Set a skillet over medium-high heat. When hot, add oil and butter. Add onion and cook, stirring, until soft, about 3 minutes. Add garlic and sun-dried tomatoes and cook for 3 minutes, stirring occasionally. Stir in cream, lemon juice, pepper, and salt and simmer for about 5 minutes. Remove from heat; taste and adjust seasoning if needed. Stir in the breadcrumbs until the mixture has the consistency of cookie dough. Stir in the cheeses and the basil; place the pan in the freezer for 15 minutes to cool while preparing the chicken breasts.

Heat oven to 350 degrees.

Using a rolling pin or a meat mallet, pound each chicken breast to quarter-inch thickness. Set ¼ cup of the cooled stuffing in the center of each chicken breast. Roll up chicken breasts, tucking in the sides. Secure with toothpicks if desired and set aside to prepare the rice.

For the Rice
Grease a 2½-quart baking dish and pour rice into the prepared baking dish.

In a saucepan set over medium heat, stir together broth, butter, salt, and lemon juice and bring to boiling. Pour the boiling mixture over the rice.

Place rolled chicken breasts, seam side down, on top of the rice. Season with salt and pepper and bake, covered, for 35 minutes or until the internal temperature reaches 165 degrees. Heat the broiler, uncover the dish, and broil for 5 minutes, until the chicken breasts are browned and any remaining liquid has evaporated from the rice. Let rest for 5 minutes before serving.

Apple Cider–Braised Lamb Shanks with Parmesan Risotto

Serves 4

I love this dish because it reminds me of my dad, who loved slow-braised meats like osso buco or a meaty lamb shank. However, he hated rice. Apparently, in a traumatic fraternity initiation, he was forced to eat Spanish rice for a week. If I were to make this dish for him now, I'd substitute mashed potatoes for the creamy risotto.

This braise heats up your house — perfect for when the temperatures outside are dipping below zero.

Lamb Shanks

- 4 lamb shanks
- 1 teaspoon kosher salt
- ½ teaspoon black pepper
- ¼ cup tomato paste
- 2 tablespoons finely chopped fresh rosemary
- 2 tablespoons fresh thyme leaves
- zest and juice of 1 lemon
- ½ teaspoon cinnamon
- ¼ teaspoon nutmeg
- 3 cloves garlic, minced or grated
- 1 tablespoon extra-virgin olive oil
- 1 medium onion, sliced
- 1 Granny Smith apple, sliced
- 1 bay leaf
- 2 cups apple cider
- 1 cup beef broth

Parmesan Risotto

- 1 tablespoon extra-virgin olive oil
- ½ medium onion, diced
- 1 clove garlic, minced or grated
- 2 cups arborio rice
- ½ cup dry white table wine
- 5 cups chicken broth
- ¼ cup heavy cream
- ½ cup grated Parmesan cheese, plus more for garnish
- 1 teaspoon kosher salt
- ½ teaspoon coarse black pepper

For the Lamb Shanks

Heat oven to 325 degrees. Season lamb shanks generously with salt and pepper.

In a small bowl, combine tomato paste, rosemary, thyme, lemon zest, cinnamon, nutmeg, and garlic; stir thoroughly to make a paste. Rub paste liberally over each lamb shank.

Heat oil in a large pot or Dutch oven over medium-high heat. When the oil is hot, place lamb shanks in the pot and brown on all sides. Add onions, apple slices, and bay leaf. Pour cider and broth over the top of the shanks and gently stir. Bring to a boil; stir in lemon juice. Cover the pot with aluminum foil to seal in the juices and place the lid on top. Bake for 2½ hours, turning shanks every 30 minutes or so.

For the Parmesan Risotto

Heat the olive oil in a large pot over medium-low heat. Add the onions and cook for 8–10 minutes or until lightly browned and translucent. Add the garlic and cook for about 45 seconds, until fragrant. Add the rice and toast for 3–4 minutes, stirring constantly. Pour in the wine and stir, scraping up any browned bits, until all of the liquid has been absorbed. Add ½ cup chicken broth, stirring constantly until it has been absorbed; repeat with remaining broth until the rice is cooked to al dente. Stir in the cream, Parmesan cheese, salt, and pepper, and cook for 2–3 more minutes.

Serve shanks on a bed of risotto with pan juices and an extra sprinkle of cheese.

Lentil and Sausage Stew with Spinach and Lemon

Serves 4

I made this dish a few years back when a friend was stranded at my house during a snowstorm. He and my husband had to shovel the driveway at least three times throughout the evening, and they were exhausted when they were done. Gazing at my pantry, I was trying to think what I could do with lentils that would be hearty and warming for the hard-working men. This meaty stew was the perfect solution.

The lemon zest and juice added right before serving really brightens this hearty stew, making it that much more delicious.

1 pound bulk pork sausage

3 carrots, cut into half-inch chunks

1 medium onion, finely chopped

1 red bell pepper, chopped

4 cloves garlic, minced or grated

1 (6-ounce) can tomato paste

1 cup dried lentils

4 cups chicken broth

1 bay leaf

1 teaspoon cumin

2 teaspoons kosher salt

1 teaspoon black pepper

2 cups baby spinach

zest and juice of 1 lemon

rice or bread for serving

In a large Dutch oven over medium-high heat, cook the sausage, carrots, onion, and red pepper until sausage is cooked through and crumbled. Stir in garlic and tomato paste and cook for 2 minutes more. Stir in lentils, broth, bay leaf, and cumin and bring to a boil. Reduce heat and simmer, covered, until the lentils are tender, about 15 minutes. Stir in salt, pepper, spinach, lemon juice, and lemon zest and cover to cook 3 minutes more or until spinach is wilted. Taste and adjust seasonings. Remove the bay leaf and serve with rice or crusty bread.

Mom's Oven Barbecue Spare Ribs

Serves 6

It goes without saying that I'd much prefer slow-cooked ribs on the barbecue. But there you are in the middle of winter, access to the outdoor Weber nonexistent, and yet you're still wishing for spare ribs. This recipe was my mother's solution, and I remember coming home from school to find the whole house filled with the wonderful smell of barbecued meat. She'd always serve a vegetable and starch with dinner — with her ribs, I remember mashed potatoes and simmered Birds Eye corn — accompanied by two percent milk poured into little Dixie cups. I still crave this fall-off-the-bone winter spare ribs solution, and I like to serve it with slaw and a baked potato.

2 (3- to 4-pound) racks pork spare ribs (plan on 4–6 ribs per person)

1 large onion, chopped

1 (15-ounce) can tomato sauce

1 cup water

¾ cup ketchup

¼ cup Worcestershire sauce

3 tablespoons apple cider vinegar

2 teaspoons chili powder

½ teaspoon hot sauce (Tabasco)

Heat oven to 450 degrees. Place ribs in a shallow pan, meat side up, and roast for 30 minutes.

Combine the remaining ingredients in a medium saucepan and bring to a boil. Cook for 10 minutes, until the sauce starts to thicken.

Reduce oven temperature to 350 degrees. Pour sauce over ribs and continue baking, basting every 15 minutes, for 1 hour and 15 minutes. If the sauce gets too thick or the pan becomes dry, add ⅓ cup water.

Old-School Beef Stroganoff

Serves 6

My stepmom, Kathy, gave me this recipe to include in the book because it was favored by my father, who was a basic meat-and-potatoes kind of guy. The addition of mushrooms and garlic was a departure from basic, but he loved it. My father preferred stroganoff served over mashed potatoes, but I'm more inclined toward egg noodles or wild rice.

2 pounds round steak, cut into thin strips

1 onion, sliced

3 cups beef broth, divided

½ cup water

2 teaspoons kosher salt

1 teaspoon black pepper

2 tablespoons unsalted butter

3 pounds mushrooms, sliced

3 cloves garlic, minced or grated

2 tablespoons concentrated beef soup base (Better than Bouillon)

1 tablespoon browning and seasoning sauce (Kitchen Bouquet)

½ cup whole milk

¼ cup all-purpose flour

1 (16-ounce) container sour cream

wild rice, egg noodles, or mashed potatoes for serving

Heat oven to 325 degrees.

Combine the steak, onion, ½ cup beef broth, water, salt, and pepper in a Dutch oven. Cover and bake for 2 hours.

Meanwhile, melt butter in a large saucepan over medium heat until foaming. Add mushrooms and cook for 7 minutes. Add garlic, beef soup base, and seasoning sauce and cook for 3 minutes more. Stir in remaining 2½ cups broth.

In a small bowl, whisk together milk and flour until well combined. Add to the mushroom mixture and cook, stirring, until thickened, about 5 minutes. Set aside while the meat is cooking.

Add the mushroom mixture to the meat in the Dutch oven, stirring to combine. Cook on the stovetop until heated through. Stir in sour cream and gently heat for serving. Serve over wild rice, egg noodles, or mashed potatoes.

Thai Pork Noodle Goulash

January 115

Serves 4

Southeast Asian or Thai cooking doesn't necessarily bring to mind goulash, but I got the idea for this dish after cooking with James Beard Award–winning chef Christina Nguyen from Hola Arepa and Hai in Minneapolis. We recorded a *Taste Buds with Stephanie* episode where she made a turmeric dill fish bowl with spring rolls while I made a turmeric shrimp noodle bowl. As I was putting that dish together, I thought it would be fun to mash up Thai ingredients with my usual go-to for a goulash egg noodle. It's super delicious!

- 2 tablespoons extra-virgin olive oil
- 2 medium carrots, peeled and cut into half-moons
- 1 small onion, thinly sliced
- 1 medium zucchini, diced
- 1 tablespoon chopped ginger
- 1 tablespoon lemongrass (see tip)
- 1 pound ground pork
- 1 (13-ounce) can unsweetened full-fat coconut milk
- 3 tablespoons lime juice
- 1 tablespoon Thai red curry paste
- 2 teaspoons chili sauce (Sriracha)
- 6 ounces egg noodles cooked according to package instructions
- ½ cup chopped basil leaves
- 2 teaspoons kosher salt
- 1 teaspoon black pepper

Heat the olive oil in a large, deep skillet over medium heat. Add the carrots and onions and cook, stirring, until the onions are translucent, about 4 minutes. Add the zucchini, ginger, and lemongrass and cook, stirring, until fragrant, about 2 minutes. Add the ground pork and cook, breaking up the meat, until no pink remains, about 3 minutes. Reduce heat to medium and add the coconut milk. Stir in lime juice, red curry paste, and chili sauce and turn off heat. Add the noodles and toss until thoroughly coated. Stir in basil, season with salt and pepper, and serve.

TIP: Lemongrass paste is sold in tubes in the produce section.

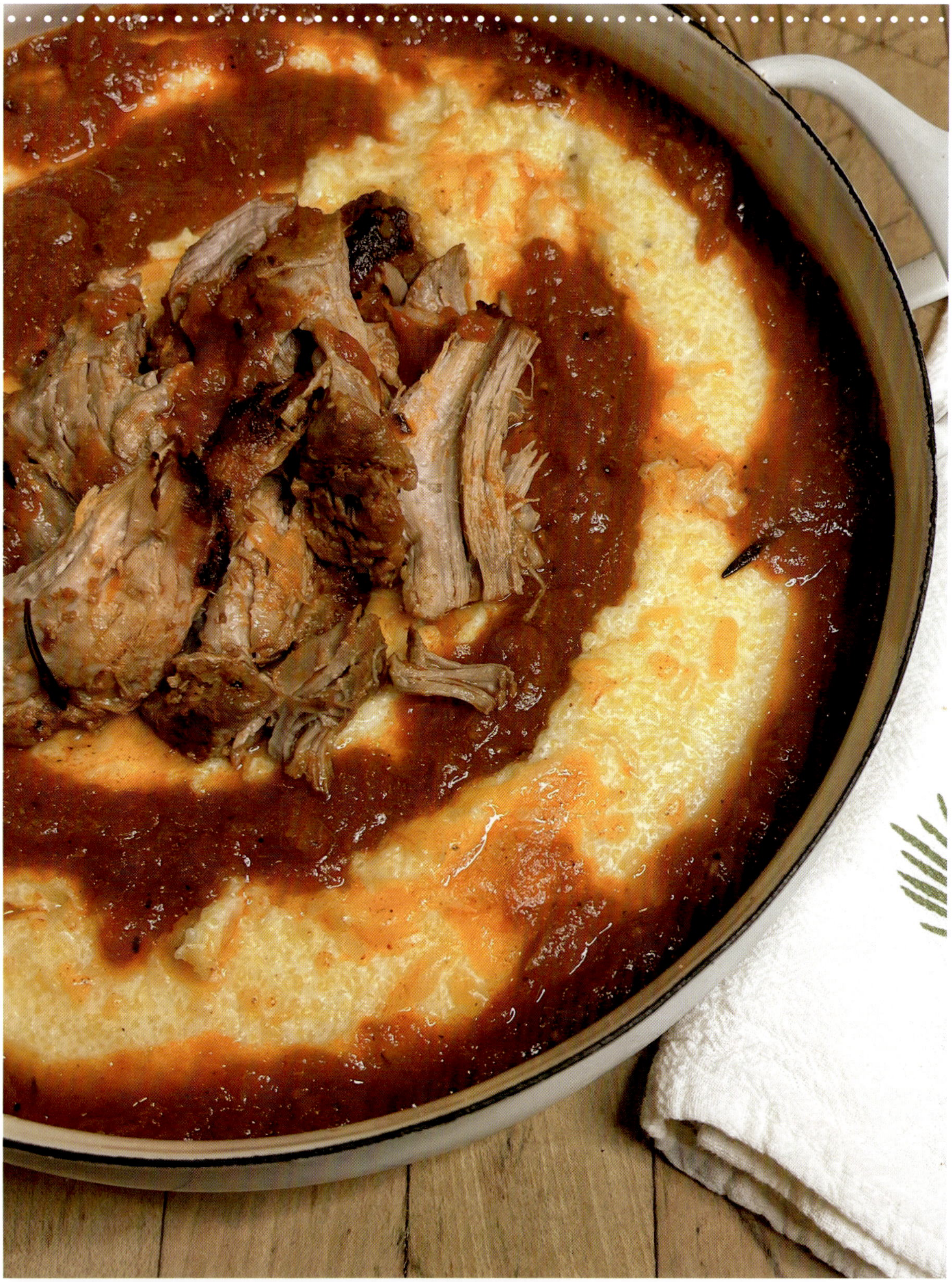

Pork Shoulder Ragu with Cheesy Polenta

January

Serves 6

I absolutely love stewed meat, whether prepared in a slow cooker during the holy month of "Crocktober" or in a Dutch oven in mid-January, when the snow is piled up outside the cabin door. This pork shoulder ragu cooks low and slow all day and is served atop a heap of cheesy polenta. This is stick-to-your-ribs comfort food.

Pork Ragu

1 (3-pound) pork shoulder roast

2 teaspoons kosher salt

1 teaspoon black pepper

2 tablespoons extra-virgin olive oil

2 cups finely chopped onion

4 cloves garlic, minced or grated

1 (6-ounce) can tomato paste

2 cups chicken or vegetable broth

1 (28-ounce) can crushed tomatoes

2 sprigs rosemary, chopped

leaves from 2 sprigs thyme

1 bay leaf

Polenta

3 cups water

2 teaspoons kosher salt

1 cup polenta (coarse cornmeal)

½ cup heavy cream

⅓ cup shredded cheddar cheese

For the Pork Ragu

Heat oven to 300 degrees.

Season pork all over with salt and pepper. Heat olive oil in a large Dutch oven over high heat and brown the pork shoulder on all sides, about 10–12 minutes. Transfer to a platter and discard pan drippings.

Add the onion to the pot and cook until translucent, about 5 minutes. Add the garlic and cook for 2 minutes more. Add the tomato paste and cook, stirring, for about 5 minutes, until the paste starts to turn from red to brown. Stir in broth and crushed tomatoes. Add pork with any accumulated juices to the pot, nestling the pork in the sauce to cover. Add the chopped rosemary, fresh thyme leaves, and bay leaf. Transfer to the oven and braise pork, covered, for 3 hours. Uncover the pot and braise for 30 minutes more, allowing the sauce to concentrate and thicken.

When meat is fall-off-the-bone tender, scoop it out of the pot and set aside to cool. Discard any woody herb stems and bay leaf. Skim off any visible fat. Blend the sauce with an immersion blender or stand blender (be careful to vent so hot liquid doesn't splash; see tip page 10). Pull the pork into big chunks, discard any fat, and set aside.

For the Polenta

In a medium saucepan, bring water and salt to boiling. Add polenta and reduce heat to low. Cook for about 5 minutes, stirring constantly, until the water is absorbed. Add the cream and stir until combined. Remove from heat.

Scoop polenta into a large bowl or onto a platter and sprinkle with the cheese. Place pieces of pork on top of the polenta and drizzle the ragu around the dish. Serve extra sauce alongside.

Swedish Meatloaf with Brown Gravy

Serves 8

I love meatloaf. The love started with my mom's meatloaf and grew over the years. This version has all the flavors of Swedish meatballs but none of the hassle of rolling and browning the individual nuggets. Cook this on a broiler pan with a slotted rack as instructed: the fat that drains off is key to making the rich and delicious gravy.

Meatloaf

1 tablespoon extra-virgin olive oil

4 tablespoons unsalted butter

1 medium onion, grated on a box grater

1 small zucchini, peeled with a vegetable peeler and grated on a box grater

1 large egg

¼ cup whole milk

2 tablespoons ricotta cheese

1 cup dried breadcrumbs or panko

½ cup chopped fresh dill

1 tablespoon dried dill

2 teaspoons kosher salt

2 teaspoons black pepper

½ teaspoon nutmeg

1 pound ground beef

1 pound ground veal

3 strips bacon, cut in half

Gravy

2 tablespoons unsalted butter

2 tablespoons all-purpose flour

1½ cups beef broth or stock

1 teaspoon Worcestershire sauce

1 teaspoon soy sauce

1 teaspoon kosher salt, plus more to taste

½ teaspoon black pepper, plus more to taste

½ teaspoon nutmeg

¼ cup sour cream

January

For the Meatloaf

Heat oven to 350 degrees.

Heat olive oil and butter in a large skillet over medium heat. Add onions and zucchini and cook, stirring, for 10 minutes, until the onions are lightly browned. Remove from heat and set aside for 10 minutes to cool.

In a large mixing bowl, whisk together egg, milk, ricotta, and breadcrumbs. Stir in dill, salt, pepper, and nutmeg. Add onion and zucchini mixture and ground beef and veal. Use your hands to mix well, incorporating the meat with the seasonings and vegetables.

Line a broiler pan with heavy-duty foil. Use a fork to poke holes in the foil to allow liquid to drain into the broiler pan. Form the meat mixture into a loaf about 10 inches long, 4 inches wide, and 4 inches high. Lay bacon strips over the loaf.

Bake for about 1 hour and 10 minutes or until the bacon strips are crispy and the internal temperature is 155 degrees. Place the loaf on a platter to sit for 5–10 minutes (the temperature will continue to rise to reach 165 degrees) while making the gravy.

For the Gravy

Reserve any juices from the broiler pan and the foil; pour into the bottom of the broiler pan. Melt the butter in the broiler pan and whisk in the flour. Continue whisking over medium heat for a couple of minutes while the mixture goes from pasty to nice and brown. Slowly whisk in the broth, Worcestershire sauce, soy sauce, salt, pepper, and nutmeg. Cook, whisking constantly, until gravy comes to a boil and has thickened a bit. If the gravy is too thick, add more broth. Remove from heat and let sit for a minute or two to cool, then stir in the sour cream. Season with salt and pepper.

Cabbage Almond Pasta with Toasted Breadcrumbs

Serves 2

I think cabbage is replacing cauliflower as the new "it" vegetable. I've lately seen cabbage wilted, salted, grilled, and made into wedge salads, and I am digging all of it. I harvested twelve heads of cabbage one fall at the Ely Hilltop Garden, thinking I'd be making sauerkraut. I ended up preparing most of it using a variety of "it" recipes and making only a few jars of kraut.

Adding cabbage to pasta creates a buttery, melty texture enhanced by crunchy almonds and toasty, nutty breadcrumbs. Make this a comfy weeknight meal or a side dish for roasted chicken or grilled pork tenderloin.

- ¼ cup extra-virgin olive oil
- 4 tablespoons unsalted butter, divided
- 2 leeks, rinsed, white and tender green parts thinly sliced
- 2 pounds green cabbage, finely sliced
- 1 teaspoon kosher salt
- 3 teaspoons black pepper, divided, plus more to taste
- 3 cloves garlic, minced or grated
- ⅓ cup slivered almonds
- ½ cup coarse breadcrumbs
- 1 pound spaghetti
- ½ cup pasta water
- ¼ cup grated Parmesan cheese, plus more for serving
- 1 tablespoon lemon zest
- ¼ cup lemon juice
- handful chopped herbs (parsley, cilantro, or dill)

Add olive oil and 3 tablespoons butter to a large skillet over medium heat. When the butter has melted, add the leeks, cabbage, salt, and 1 teaspoon pepper. Reduce heat to medium-low and cook, covered, for 12 minutes without stirring. Uncover and stir, then add the garlic and cook 3 minutes more.

Meanwhile, toast the almonds in a dry cast iron skillet over medium-low heat for 4 minutes, until fragrant and just beginning to brown. Be careful not to burn. Set almonds aside in a small bowl and wipe out the skillet.

Add remaining 1 tablespoon butter and the breadcrumbs to the skillet and toast over medium heat until crispy and brown, being careful not to burn.

Cook spaghetti according to package instructions, then drain, reserving ½ cup pasta water.

Add pasta and pasta water to the cabbage along with the Parmesan cheese, lemon zest, lemon juice, and remaining 2 teaspoons pepper. Toss the pasta to coat and add the almonds, breadcrumbs, and a handful of fresh herbs. Finish with additional pepper to taste and serve with additional Parmesan cheese.

Banana Bread Cookies with Cream Cheese Frosting

Makes about 2 dozen cookies

These tasty nuggets are like banana bread but in the form of a cookie. The cream cheese frosting makes them a little delicate to store, but they do freeze beautifully. Of course, that's if there are any left over!

Cookies

- 1 cup (2 sticks) unsalted butter, at room temperature
- ¾ cup granulated sugar
- ¼ cup packed brown sugar
- 1 teaspoon vanilla extract
- 1 large egg, at room temperature
- 1 cup mashed bananas
- 2 cups all-purpose flour
- 1 teaspoon baking soda
- ½ teaspoon cinnamon
- ½ teaspoon kosher salt

Frosting

- 8 ounces cream cheese, at room temperature
- 4 tablespoons unsalted butter, at room temperature
- ½ teaspoon vanilla extract
- 4 cups confectioners' sugar

Heat oven to 350 degrees. Line a baking sheet with parchment paper.

In a large bowl, beat 1 cup butter with granulated sugar and brown sugar until light and fluffy, about 3 minutes. Add 1 teaspoon vanilla, egg, and mashed bananas and mix for 2 minutes more. Add flour, baking soda, cinnamon, and salt and continue beating until a dough forms. Scoop tablespoon-size balls of dough and place on the prepared baking sheet, about 8 per sheet. Bake cookies for 10 minutes or until the edges start to appear golden brown.

Meanwhile, use a blender or a handheld mixer to combine frosting ingredients, mixing until smooth. Let cookies cool, then spread the frosting on top.

February

WINTER ON TRUE NORTH ISLAND

The cabin on True North Island was built for use during the summer months. The builder put the cabin up on thick piers with no skirting or floor insulation. The large windows that wrap around three sides are single paned, rattle in a stiff wind, and seep cold air. The open ceiling with exposed beams has a layer of shiplap paneling and asphalt shingles. The only source of heat is a wood-burning stove. None of that has stopped us from going there in the winter.

Winter on Burntside Lake is a special time. Few people are about, and it can be quiet, still, and beautiful. The snow piles up on the pine and balsam branches, tracks reveal rabbit hops, deer that eat the pine seedlings, and wolves that roam the lake at night — in search of both the rabbits and the deer. We put out birdseed for the chickadees and blue jays. We take long cross-country ski excursions to places almost impossible to reach during the summer. There seems to always be a bald eagle that has forgotten to move south and searches the forest for squirrels, rabbits, or the remains of deer kills. Winter in the north woods can be deadly for creatures large and small.

And cold. One February we decided to go up on a weekend with another couple. We had Ellie, who was ten years old at the time, and the other couple had two girls roughly around Ellie's age. We took two cars and left at three in the afternoon. By the time we rolled into Burntside Lodge, it was 7 p.m. and dark outside except for a bright full moon. When we left Minneapolis, the temperature was around zero. When we packed up our food and gear on pull-behind sleds and put on our cross-country skis, the temperature was twenty degrees below zero. No wind, but deathly cold.

To this day, I have no idea what we were thinking. I'm typically not the kind of person who takes those chances, and even if my husband Kurt is, I'm the one to say no. I guess we were just excited to get up north for a long three-day weekend with our friends. Regardless, it didn't hit me that we were stepping out into a dangerous situation until we'd left the lodge parking lot and skied out onto the lake. We had two miles to ski. It then occurred to me that if one of those small girls had a meltdown — cried, sat down, and refused to move — this excursion could turn dangerous in a hurry.

So, I sang. Whatever I could remember, I sang it, like "Row, Row, Row Your Boat," getting everyone to enter the song at a different time, then "The Happy Wanderer," then, to make the kids laugh, I did all the lyrics to "Rapper's Delight." These verses got us a half mile. Our friends added songs they knew, and we had one mile down.

Then Kurt made up a story that took us the last mile. The story he invented was about the origins of the name of a Burntside Lake island, Lost Girl. He said that years ago there was a Lakota Indian camp just off the lodge where a family lived. This was true: Indian Island is deserted now, but there are still remnants of the encampment — a fire pit, hand-hammered tools, broken bottles, and the footings of a cabin. In Kurt's story, one morning a young daughter, ten years old, took off by herself in a small birchbark canoe. The wind was from the south, and the girl followed the wind in that direction. By the afternoon she had not returned, and her parents worried. They took a second canoe and paddled out to find her. Eventually the small canoe was discovered abandoned, banging against the rocks off an unnamed island. They searched the island that afternoon and found nothing. They camped on the island and made a fire, hoping the girl would eventually see the flames and come to them. Nothing. The parents camped on that island for the next week, searching every square inch. Eventually they found a single shoe. Maybe a wolf attacked her — but none of the tribe had ever had trouble with wolves, and even after a deer kill there'd be remnants, like scraps of fur, blood, a bone. The parents continued to search but could not find any signs of wolves or a kill, or of the girl. During the next month, they searched the surrounding islands and the mainland. Still, there was no sign of their daughter. The search had been futile, and the parents stopped actively looking. From then on, the island was called Lost Girl Island.

Then Kurt told about how his family first bought a lot on Lost Girl and set up a camp for one season. Kurt was the lost Indian girl's age at the time, and he described how one night while lying inside his tent, he could hear the wind. It blew hard but in a way that seemed to rise and fall in pitch, like a church organ. Then he swore the wind made words, and what he heard over and over was, "help, help, help."

Kurt finished the story just as we skied up to True North Island. The three girls had moved in rapt attention and silence, but just as he said, "help," two of the girls screamed, took off their skies, and ran to the door of the cabin. We were safe.

Once inside, we lit the stove and piled in as much wood as it would hold. By the time we were relatively warm, at a balmy fifty degrees, I'd made a big pot of chili and a skillet of cornbread. We sat around the stove with bowls on our laps. The food was comforting, but the girls were unusually quiet. I thought they might still be scared from the ghost story. I whispered to Kurt, and he confessed that the story was all made up. It was Ellie who asked, thinking of the island with the spooky name, "But then who was the lost girl?"

125

February

Hot Pickle Dip

Serves 6 at a party or 1 in front of the TV

I am crazy about pickles. I love eating them, cooking with them, and using the brine to flavor a dish. As an enhancer in salad dressings, egg salads, tuna salads, or pasta salads, as a meat tenderizer for chicken or beef — oh, and have I mentioned it's great in cocktails? — pickle juice continually appears in my home cooking. This hot pickle dip is a riff on a cold version I made on *Taste Buds with Stephanie*. If you can find Old Dutch Spicy Pickle Potato Chips, use them as the crunchy topping; Old Dutch Jalapeño Kettle Chips are also a great choice.

- 4 ounces cream cheese, at room temperature
- 4 ounces plain goat cheese
- ½ cup sour cream
- ½ cup homemade or bottled ranch dressing
- ¾ cup chopped dill pickles
- ¼ cup chopped pepperoncini
- 1 clove garlic, minced or grated
- ½ teaspoon fresh dill (or 1 teaspoon dried), plus more for garnish
- 1 teaspoon kosher salt
- ½ cup shredded mozzarella cheese
- ½ cup shredded white cheddar cheese
- ½ cup crushed potato chips
- sliced green onions, green parts only, for garnish

Heat oven to 350 degrees.

In the bowl of a food processor, pulse cream cheese, goat cheese, sour cream, and ranch dressing until combined. Add dill pickles, pepperoncini, garlic, dill, salt, and cheeses, and pulse a few times more to blend, leaving some texture. Transfer mixture to an 8-inch square baking dish and bake for 25 minutes, until bubbly.

Garnish with crushed potato chips, green onions, and fresh dill.

Oven-Baked Chicken Wings

Serves 6

I went on a quest during the pandemic to make crispy chicken wings in the oven at home that would taste like those ordered in a restaurant. I was desperately missing a Buffalo-style wing dipped in homemade ranch sauce from my local restaurant, but it was the pandemic, and folks were only doing take-out wings, which were not as good. By the time we brought them home, the wings had steamed in the cardboard container and lost their crispiness. After much trial and error, I've developed the perfect oven-baked wing. I tested baking soda, cornstarch, and flour and settled on a flour–spice shake to dry out the wings. Just like at a restaurant, the skin is crispy and crackling and the meat is well done but still moist. I have adapted these wings for an air fryer recipe (available at stephaniesdish.com), but I still rely on the trusty oven-baked version. You can mix up your sauces and dry-rubbed spice blends, but whatever you do, take the refrigeration step: that's what dries out the skin, making for the perfect crispy wing.

Chicken Wings
1 cup all-purpose flour

2 teaspoons kosher salt

1 teaspoon chili powder

½ teaspoon garlic powder

½ teaspoon onion powder

½ teaspoon cayenne pepper

2 pounds chicken wings

½ cup (1 stick) unsalted butter

½ cup hot pepper sauce

Dipping Sauce
1 clove garlic, minced or grated

½ cup buttermilk

3 tablespoons plain Greek yogurt

2 tablespoons mayonnaise

1 teaspoon dried dill

1 teaspoon Dijon mustard

6 dashes hot sauce (Tabasco)

pinch kosher salt

2–3 tablespoons chopped herbs (parsley, cilantro, dill, or basil), optional

For the Chicken Wings
Line a sheet pan with aluminum foil and spray with cooking spray, or line a pan with a silicone baking mat.

Place the flour, salt, and spices into a plastic zip-top bag and shake to mix. Add the chicken wings to the bag and toss until well coated. Place the wings on the prepared pan and refrigerate for at least 1 hour.

Heat oven to 400 degrees. Bake wings for 30 minutes.

Melt the butter in a small saucepan and whisk in hot sauce. Remove wings from oven, dip in the hot sauce, and return to the sheet pan. Cook for 15 minutes more, until brown and crispy.

For the Dipping Sauce
Combine sauce ingredients, mixing well. Adjust seasonings to your liking.

Oven-Baked Jalapeño Poppers

Serves 6

Another home cook's recipe quest (see page 127). But seriously, the pandemic was rough on those who love fried bar snacks! These jalapeño poppers stood in for my favorites from our local Mexican deli, run by the same family since 1970, El Burrito Mercado. Their poppers have a tempura-type breading, and because I could never replicate that treatment at home, I used bacon to give a crispy, crunchy bite. These are great with the homemade dipping sauce used with my Oven-Baked Chicken Wings (page 127).

- 4 ounces cream cheese, at room temperature
- 4 ounces goat cheese, at room temperature
- 1 teaspoon garlic powder
- ½ teaspoon onion powder
- ¼ teaspoon dried dill
- ¼ teaspoon dried chives
- ¼ teaspoon kosher salt
- pinch black pepper
- 6 jalapeños, sliced in half, stems intact, seeds removed
- ½ cup grated sharp cheddar cheese
- 12 slices bacon (not thick cut), cut in half

Heat oven to 400 degrees.

Mix the cream cheese, goat cheese, and seasonings in a small bowl. Fill the peppers with the cheese mixture. Avoid overfilling, or the cheese will ooze out while baking.

Place cheddar cheese in a flat bowl and press jalapeño peppers, filling side down, into cheese until about 1 teaspoon of cheese is stuck on the jalapeño. Wrap a piece of bacon around each jalapeño. Place the prepared jalapeños in a baking dish. Bake for 10–12 minutes or until bacon is browned and crispy. Serve warm or at room temperature.

Beer Cheese Wild Rice Soup

Serves 8

This soup is Minnesota in a bowl. In the North, we love cheese. We also love wild rice, which is hand-harvested by Native Americans throughout the region. This soup is a riff on the traditional wild rice soup, which is one of my most popular recipes on stephaniesdish.com.

- 1 cup uncooked wild rice
- 8 slices bacon
- 8 tablespoons unsalted butter, divided
- 1½ cups mushrooms, chopped into large chunks
- ½ cup chopped onion
- 1 cup all-purpose flour
- 6 cups chicken broth, divided
- ½ cup sour cream
- 3 tablespoons Worcestershire sauce
- 1 clove garlic, minced
- 1 teaspoon celery salt
- 1 teaspoon ground mustard
- 1 teaspoon black pepper
- 8 drops hot sauce (Tabasco)
- 4 cups freshly shredded extra-sharp cheddar cheese
- 1 (16-ounce) can dark beer (IPA, stout, or amber lager — or a nonalcoholic version)

In a large saucepan, combine wild rice with 4 cups water and bring to a boil. Reduce heat to low, cover, and simmer for 45 minutes, until soft. Drain excess liquid and set rice aside.

In a skillet over medium heat, cook bacon for about 10 minutes, until crisp. Drain bacon on a paper towel; when cool, break into half-inch pieces and set aside. Retain 1 tablespoon bacon fat in the pan, draining and discarding the rest. Melt 2 tablespoons butter in the pan and cook the mushrooms and onion until tender, about 8 minutes. Set aside.

Melt the remaining 6 tablespoons butter in a Dutch oven set over medium heat. Add the flour to the pot and cook, stirring, for 4 minutes, until a doughy paste forms. Add 1 cup chicken broth to the pan, bring to a low boil, and stir until the flour-butter mixture is dissolved. Add the remaining 5 cups chicken broth; reduce the heat to simmer and cook for 20 minutes. Stir in sour cream, Worcestershire sauce, garlic, celery salt, ground mustard, pepper, and hot sauce, followed by cooked wild rice, bacon, and mushrooms–onion mixture. Slowly add the cheese, ⅓ cup at a time, stirring until melted. Once all the cheese is incorporated, stir in the beer and cook for 15–30 minutes on low, stirring frequently and being careful not to boil. Taste and adjust seasonings before serving.

February

Spicy Chicken Sausage and Sweet Potato Soup

Serves 4

My friend Stephanie Meyer made a version of this soup for our first season of *Taste Buds with Stephanie*. I love how the recipe uses salsa verde as the main acid in the soup. I typically make twelve to twenty-four pints of green salsa each summer with the green tomatoes in my Ely Hilltop Garden, and I am always looking for new, creative ways to use it. This recipe is super delicious.

- 1 tablespoon extra-virgin olive oil
- 1 medium yellow onion, finely diced
- ½ pound bulk hot Italian or chorizo sausage
- 2 cloves garlic, minced or grated
- 1 teaspoon chili powder (or chipotle chili powder for more heat)
- 1 teaspoon dried oregano
- ½ teaspoon cumin
- 2 cups thinly sliced lacinato kale (center rib removed before slicing)
- 5 cups chicken broth
- 2 cups diced sweet potato cut into half-inch cubes
- ½ cup salsa verde
- 2 cups cooked chicken pulled into bite-size pieces
- juice of 1 lime
- ½ cup heavy cream, optional
- 2 teaspoons kosher salt

Add oil to a Dutch oven or large saucepan set over medium heat. When oil is hot, add onion and cook, stirring occasionally, until translucent and softened, about 5 minutes. Add sausage and cook, breaking it up with the side of a spoon, until sausage is cooked through, about 10 minutes. Add garlic, chili powder, oregano, cumin, and kale, and cook, stirring, for another 5 minutes. Stir in the chicken broth, sweet potato, and salsa and bring to a boil. Turn heat to low and simmer soup, uncovered, until sweet potato is tender, about 10 minutes. Stir in the chicken and lime juice and cream, if using, and bring back to a simmer. Remove from heat and season to taste with the kosher salt.

Broccoli Cheese Soup

Serves 4

I love broccoli cheese soup. A restaurant near my childhood home in Bloomington, Minnesota, served big sourdough bread bowls full of cheesy soup. When my daughter, Ellie, was little, we would take her to swimming lessons followed by Panera Bread for soup. Broccoli cheese was always our favorite.

½ cup (1 stick) unsalted butter

1 medium onion, diced

1 large carrot, peeled and diced

2 cloves garlic, minced or grated

⅓ cup all-purpose flour

1 teaspoon kosher salt, plus more to taste

1 teaspoon black pepper, plus more to taste

½ teaspoon ground mustard

¼ teaspoon nutmeg

3 large crowns broccoli, with stems, trimmed of any woody parts and cut into half-inch pieces

4 cups chicken broth

1 cup heavy cream

3 cups shredded cheddar cheese

Melt the butter in a large pot over medium heat, then add the onion and carrot. Cook for 3–4 minutes, then add the garlic, flour, salt, pepper, mustard, and nutmeg. Stir to combine and cook for a minute or so. Add the broccoli and chicken broth. Cover and reduce heat to low. Simmer until the broccoli is tender, 20–30 minutes. Using a potato masher or an immersion blender, mash up some of the broccoli into smaller bits. Stir in the cream, then stir in the cheese and allow it to melt. Season with salt and pepper to taste.

February

Buffalo Chicken Chili

Serves 6

This spicy, hearty chili is great for any game day and perfect for that day when the Minnesota Vikings once again play in a Super Bowl. The last time was in 1977. I was nine — too young to remember or care. I do recall when the Super Bowl was in Minneapolis. Our city population was decked out in matching winter coats as thousands of volunteers herded swarms of people like cats through the skyway system in subzero weather. The entire event was a blast for a week before the big game.

This chili is like Buffalo wings in a bowl. The fun part is personalizing the soup with various fixings like shredded cheese, sour cream, diced onions, pickled jalapeños, or a pile of tortilla chips. If the Vikings do ever play in another Super Bowl, I'll break out the blue cheese crumbles.

- 2 tablespoons extra-virgin olive oil
- 1 pound ground chicken
- 1 medium onion, chopped
- ½ cup chopped red bell pepper
- ½ cup chopped orange bell pepper
- ½ cup chopped celery
- 3 cloves garlic, minced or grated
- 2 tablespoons chili powder
- 2 teaspoons cumin
- 2 teaspoons kosher salt
- 1 teaspoon smoked paprika
- 1 teaspoon black pepper
- 2 (15.5-ounce) cans great northern beans, rinsed and drained
- 1 (14-ounce) can chopped tomatoes with chili seasoning (Ro-Tel)
- 1 (28-ounce) can crushed tomatoes
- 12 ounces beer (any variety — including nonalcoholic — is fine)
- ½ cup Buffalo sauce (Frank's RedHot)
- 1 tablespoon sugar
- **for serving:** blue cheese crumbles, sour cream, chopped green onions, chopped celery, tortilla chips

Heat olive oil in a large stockpot over medium-high heat. Brown the ground chicken, breaking up the meat until cooked through, about 5 minutes. Add onion, bell peppers, celery, garlic, chili powder, cumin, salt, paprika, and pepper, and cook, stirring, until the vegetables soften, about 5–6 minutes. Stir in beans, tomatoes, beer, hot sauce, and sugar, and bring to a boil. Reduce heat to medium-low and simmer, uncovered, for about 25–30 minutes, stirring occasionally. Top each bowl with garnishes as desired.

Easiest From-Scratch Focaccia

February

Serves 6

I could be a better bread baker. In truth, I struggle with technique. I even took a sourdough class, hopping on the craze like everyone else during the pandemic. All my sourdough loaves came out looking like flat flying saucers. I kept my starter alive in the refrigerator, feeding it week after week, but still the look of my loaves didn't improve. Eventually, I bagged the sourdough and settled on making focaccia instead.

Focaccia sandwiches, especially breakfast sandwiches, are fantastic. Cheers to my friends at Marty's Deli in Northeast Minneapolis, who have perfected the art of the focaccia sandwich. Here's how to make focaccia at home so you can construct your favorite breakfast sandwich.

4 cups all-purpose flour

2 teaspoons kosher salt

2 teaspoons quick-rise instant yeast

2 cups lukewarm water

1 tablespoon honey

4 tablespoons extra-virgin olive oil, divided, plus more for coating

2 teaspoons herbs and spices (red pepper flakes, thyme leaves, whole rosemary leaves, dill leaves)

kosher salt or sea salt flakes (Maldon)

In a large bowl, whisk together the flour, salt, and instant yeast. Use a spatula to mix in the water and honey until the liquid is absorbed and the ingredients form a sticky dough ball. Rub the surface of the dough ball generously with olive oil (make sure to get it really slick so it does not dry out during the initial rise). Cover the bowl with plastic wrap, place it in a warm spot, and let dough rise at least 2 hours or up to 4 hours.

Spray a 9×13-inch pan with nonstick cooking spray. Pour 2 tablespoons oil in the prepared pan. Place the dough in the pan and roll it in the oil to coat all over. Stretch the dough to fill the pan and let the dough rise, uncovered, for 30 minutes to 2 hours. The longer the rise, the airier the final bread product.

Heat oven to 425 degrees and place a rack in the middle of the oven.

Pour remaining 2 tablespoons oil over the dough. Rub your hands lightly in the oil to coat; then, using all of your fingers, press straight down to create deep dimples in the dough. If necessary, as you dimple gently stretch the dough to fill the pan. Sprinkle with herbs and kosher or flaky sea salt. Transfer the dough to the oven and bake for 25–30 minutes, until the underside is golden and crisp. Remove the pan from the oven and transfer the focaccia to a wire rack. Let cool for 10 minutes before cutting and serving.

Easy Shortcut Focaccia

Serves 6

"Thaw and go" makes this focaccia a helpful Hansen Hack. When poking your fingers into the dough, only go halfway, so the dough retains its shape and rise. The resulting dimpled pockets will hold the rich olive oil and fragrant herb toppings.

15 bake-and-serve frozen dinner rolls (Rhodes)

3 tablespoons extra-virgin olive oil

2 cloves garlic, minced or grated

2 teaspoons fresh thyme leaves

2 teaspoons chopped fresh rosemary leaves

1½ teaspoons kosher salt

Heat oven to 350 degrees. Spray a 9x13-inch pan with cooking spray. Place the frozen rolls in the prepared pan. Spray a sheet of plastic wrap with cooking spray and cover the baking dish. Let sit at room temperature overnight so the rolls will rise.

With your fingers, push the dough down gently, creating dimples. Coat the top of the dough with olive oil, top with the garlic, thyme, and rosemary leaves, and finish with the kosher salt. Bake for 25 minutes, until golden brown.

Roasted Brussels Sprouts Caesar Salad

Serves 4

What makes a Caesar salad? Is it the components or the dressing? Is it any dish that is finished with Caesar dressing? I have read all the rants. While the purists who insist on romaine and Parmesan cheese and croutons are probably not wrong, I do love my husband's Caesar dressing — so much so that I want to put it on everything: pasta salad, sandwiches, pizza, or chopped salads. I find a variety of lettuces are all greatly improved with a splash of this garlicky dressing.

This salad uses roasted and raw brussels sprouts, so you get those caramelized flavors as well as some crunch. Make sure you use the anchovies. All kidding aside — to answer the question, "What is a Caesar salad?": it must have anchovies or anchovy paste. Just don't tell your finicky friends!

Dressing
- 1 ounce oil-packed anchovy fillets, drained
- 2 cloves garlic, minced or grated
- 2 large egg yolks
- ¼ cup finely grated Parmesan cheese
- 2 tablespoons lemon juice
- 2 teaspoons mayonnaise
- 1 teaspoon Dijon mustard
- 1 teaspoon kosher salt
- freshly ground black pepper
- ½ cup extra-virgin olive oil

Salad
- 2 pounds brussels sprouts
- 2 tablespoons extra-virgin olive oil, divided
- salt and pepper
- 2 cups cubed stale bread
- ⅓ cup shredded Parmesan cheese

For the Dressing
To the bowl of a food processor, add the anchovies, garlic, egg yolks, ¼ cup Parmesan, lemon juice, mayonnaise, Dijon mustard, salt, and pepper. Blend to combine. Then, with the motor running, slowly drizzle in the olive oil until the dressing is emulsified and slightly thick.

For the Salad
Heat oven to 450 degrees.

Shred the brussels sprouts in a food processor fitted with a slicing blade. Transfer half to a serving bowl and set aside. (Alternatively, use pre-shredded brussels sprouts.)

Toss the other half of the shredded sprouts with 1 tablespoon olive oil and season with salt and pepper. Spread them out on half of a sheet pan.

Toss bread cubes in remaining 1 tablespoon olive oil and spread on the other half of the sheet pan. Roast the sprouts and the croutons in the oven for 15 minutes. Add the roasted sprouts and croutons to the serving bowl with the raw sprouts, toss with the dressing, and serve sprinkled with ⅓ cup Parmesan cheese.

Brussels Sprouts and Butternut Squash Salad with Tahini Vinaigrette

Serves 6

Fall and winter salads are my favorite. Years ago my friend Pam Powell, who owns Salad Girl salad dressings and published the cookbook *Salad Days*, taught me the elements of a good salad. Start with your base, which can be greens or grains, and then add a combination of something crispy, crunchy, salty, and sweet. With this technique in mind, you can make salads in a variety of ways with whatever ingredients you have on hand.

Salad
- 1 small butternut squash, peeled and cubed
- 2 tablespoons extra-virgin olive oil, divided
- kosher salt
- black pepper
- 12 brussels sprouts, rinsed and halved
- 2 shallots, thinly sliced
- 1 teaspoon fresh thyme leaves
- 4 cups baby spinach
- 1 cup cooked farro
- ½ cup dried cherries
- ⅓ cup pepitas (green pumpkin seeds), toasted
- 4 ounces crumbled goat cheese

Dressing
- ¼ cup tahini
- 3 tablespoons lemon juice
- 3 tablespoons extra-virgin olive oil
- 1 tablespoon maple syrup
- 1 clove garlic, minced or grated
- 2 teaspoons sea salt
- 1 teaspoon black pepper

Heat oven to 400 degrees and line 2 sheet pans with parchment paper or silicone mats.

On one tray, toss the butternut squash with 1 tablespoon olive oil, ½ teaspoon salt, and ¼ teaspoon pepper. On the second tray, combine the brussels sprouts, shallot, and thyme. Season with ½ teaspoon salt and ¼ teaspoon pepper, drizzle with remaining tablespoon oil, and toss well. Place both trays in the oven and roast for 30 minutes, rotating their position halfway through the baking time.

In a medium bowl, whisk together dressing ingredients. If the dressing seems too thick, add a tablespoon of water.

In a large bowl or on a large platter, combine the spinach and farro and top with the roasted brussels sprouts mixture, roasted butternut squash, cherries, and pepitas. Pour the dressing over the salad, tossing well to combine. Top with crumbled goat cheese.

Arugula and Wild Rice Salad with Pear Vinaigrette

137

February

Serves 6

When you build a salad with greens or grains and something crispy, crunchy, salty, and sweet (see page 50), you only need a delicious vinaigrette to tie it all together.

A basic ratio for dressings is the three-to-one, or three parts oil to one part vinegar. I then add an emulsifier, a sweetener, and a seasoning to most of my dressings. Using this basic formula, you can make many combinations, including for the salad below.

Salad

½ pound bacon, diced

5 ounces arugula

1 cup cooked wild rice

¾ cup finely grated Parmesan cheese

½ cup slivered almonds

2 just-ripe Bartlett pears, quartered and cut into slices; reserve ½ sliced pear for the dressing

Dressing

⅓ cup extra-virgin olive oil

3 tablespoons lemon juice

1 teaspoon honey

reserved sliced pear

kosher salt, to taste

black pepper, to taste

Cook bacon in a dry pot over medium-high heat until crispy, about 10–15 minutes. Remove with a slotted spoon and drain excess fat. Scrape bacon bits into the serving bowl for the salad.

For the dressing, in a blender combine olive oil, lemon juice, honey, reserved pear, salt, and pepper. Blend until smooth. (Alternatively, use an immersion blender.)

To the serving bowl add arugula, cooled bacon, cooked wild rice, Parmesan, almonds, and dressing, tossing to combine. Serve topped with pear slices and additional black pepper as desired.

Oil	Vinegar	Emulsifiers	Sweetener	Seasonings
olive	red wine	Dijon mustard	honey	herbs
walnut	white wine	egg yolk	maple syrup	salts
sesame	white vinegar	anchovy paste	honey	soy sauce
olive	balsamic	tomato paste	honey	soy sauce
sunflower	white vinegar	tahini	pomegranate molasses	orange zest
canola	citrus juice	yogurt	honey	shallots
olive	red wine	tahini	honey	capers
avocado	champagne	avocado	honey	shallots
sesame	lime juice	miso	honey	garlic
sesame	lime juice	nut butter	honey	garlic and red pepper flakes
olive	champagne	Dijon mustard	orange juice	curry powder
canola	lemon juice	mayonnaise	honey	tarragon
olive	lime juice	yogurt	orange juice	orange zest
almond	lemon juice	yogurt	pomegranate molasses	lemon zest
olive	lemon juice	blueberries	orange juice	basil
olive	lemon juice	humus	honey	lemon zest

Grandma's Scalloped Cabbage

Serves 6

My grandma Bea was most known for her hot beef sandwiches and cookies. My husband Kurt's grandma DeBower was also a noted cook, making fried chicken or plum dumplings with sauerkraut and pork ribs. However, Kurt's mom, Dolores, is, I think, the best. She can go into a kitchen that appears to have empty shelves and come away with a fully prepared meal. She has long repurposed vegetable scraps and bones into broth and always has a can of bacon grease handy to flavor any dish.

This humble cabbage recipe, a shoo-in for the local Lutheran church cookbook, is something all of our grandmas probably made. The recipe might vary by what type of breadcrumb or which type of cheese, but the general idea is the same. When I started growing cabbages in the Ely Hilltop Garden, this recipe was added to my repertoire as an accompaniment to roast chicken.

4 cups thinly sliced or shredded green cabbage

3 tablespoons extra-virgin olive oil

3 tablespoons all-purpose flour

1 teaspoon kosher salt

½ teaspoon black pepper

1 cup whole milk

3 dashes hot sauce (Tabasco)

1 cup shredded white cheddar cheese

¾ cup breadcrumbs

2 tablespoons unsalted butter, melted

½ teaspoon paprika

sliced chives or green onions, for garnish

Heat oven to 350 degrees. Place cabbage in a greased 2-quart baking dish.

Heat oil in a large saucepan over medium heat. Whisk in flour, salt, and pepper until smooth, then gradually whisk in the milk. Bring to a boil. Once boiling, add hot sauce and cook until thickened, 1–2 minutes, stirring constantly. Stir in cheese. Pour over cabbage.

In a small bowl, combine breadcrumbs and melted butter, then scatter mixture over the casserole. Sprinkle paprika over the top. Bake, uncovered, until bubbly, 20–30 minutes. Garnish with chives or green onions and serve immediately.

Miso Mashed Potatoes with Horseradish

Serves 4

I like serving these mashed potatoes with Gochujang Kimchi Meatloaf Muffins (page 143) or goulash (page 140). The horseradish gives them a spicy kick, but the miso adds a salty umami flavor that amplifies the traditional mash. I like a thicker, chunky mashed potato, but you can add additional buttermilk if you prefer a thinner, smoother dish.

3 pounds small Yukon gold potatoes, peeled and cut into 1-inch chunks

4 tablespoons unsalted butter

¼ cup half-and-half

3 tablespoons prepared horseradish

2 tablespoons buttermilk

2 tablespoons miso (Hikari Minute; or 1 tablespoon white miso paste diluted in ¼ cup water)

3 teaspoons kosher salt

black pepper, to taste

Add the potatoes to a large pot and cover with water by 2 inches. Bring to a boil, then reduce heat to medium and let cook for 20 minutes or until the potatoes are easily pierced with a knife. Drain the water and return the potatoes to the pot. Mash the potatoes with a potato masher. Add in the remaining ingredients and mix well. Taste and season with additional salt and pepper.

February

Hungarian Goulash with Horseradish

Serves 6

My husband, Kurt, loves goulash. When we were in Prague a few years back, he ate it almost every day, sometimes twice a day, and he was always amazed at the variations in this humble recipe. Goulash is a traditional soup or stew. The primary seasoning in goulash is paprika, and it usually includes potatoes served alongside as pancakes, dumplings, or mashed (see Miso Mashed Potatoes with Horseradish, page 139). Before heading out west in the camper van, Kurt will make a giant pot of goulash, freezing enough in mason jars to last him for four to six microwaved meals. What can I say? The man loves goulash.

2 tablespoons extra-virgin olive oil

1 clove garlic, peeled and lightly crushed

2½ pounds boneless beef chuck, cut into 1½-inch cubes

2 teaspoons kosher salt, plus more to taste

1 teaspoon black pepper, plus more to taste

1 cup diced onion

½ cup diced carrots

¼ cup diced celery

2 tablespoons sweet paprika

1 teaspoon caraway seeds, crushed with a rolling pin

1 (6-ounce) can tomato paste

2–3 cups chicken, beef, or vegetable broth

¼ cup white vinegar

1 tablespoon prepared horseradish

2 tablespoons chopped fresh dill, for garnish

Heat a large Dutch oven over medium-high heat for 3 minutes. Add the oil and the crushed garlic clove and cook, stirring constantly, for 1 minute. Remove and discard the garlic. Add the meat to the pan a few pieces at a time, browning well on all sides, about 10 minutes total. Season each batch with salt and pepper while browning. Remove meat from pan and set aside.

Add the onion, carrots, and celery to the pan and cook, stirring, until the onion is transparent, about 5 minutes. Add the paprika, caraway seeds, and tomato paste and stir, cooking the mixture for about 2 minutes, until the tomato paste starts to brown. Add 2 cups of broth and the vinegar, bring mixture to a boil, and cook for 1 minute, then return the meat to the pot. Reduce heat to low and cover. Cook, undisturbed, for 30 minutes.

Check the stew: If it looks dry, add 1 cup broth and continue cooking, covered, for 1 hour more. If you're pleased with the consistency, continue to cook, covered, over low heat until ready to serve. If it's too soupy, remove the cover, increase the heat to high, and boil off some liquid. Taste and add salt and pepper as desired. Stir in prepared horseradish. Garnish with fresh dill.

February

Ground Turkey Red Curry

Serves 4

One year when I was seven or eight, I left the house for school to catch the bus, and as I opened the front door I was confronted by a large white turkey tethered to the porch railing by a rope. It looked menacing, like a wild fluffy dog, and I shut the door immediately. I ran to get my dad, who followed me to the front door. The turkey was still there, but what I hadn't seen was the sign in the yard: "A Turkey for a Turkey!" It seems my dad's friends had a sense of humor. The turkey was gone by the time I got home from school, but to this day I believe our Thanksgiving turkey that year was the same poor bird.

Minnesota is one of the largest producers of turkeys. As proteins have gotten progressively more costly over the years, I've found myself substituting the less expensive ground turkey or ground chicken for ground pork or beef in many recipes. Feel free to vary the vegetables or even substitute the protein of your choice — it will still be delicious.

2 tablespoons coconut oil

1 medium red onion, cut into thin slices

1 pound ground turkey

2 cloves garlic, minced or grated

2-inch knob ginger, minced or grated

¼ cup red curry paste

1 (14-ounce) can unsweetened full-fat coconut milk

1 medium-large zucchini, diced into bite-size pieces

1 medium yellow squash, diced into bite-size pieces

4 cups baby spinach

2 teaspoons kosher salt

½ teaspoon black pepper

½ teaspoon red pepper flakes

¼ cup lime juice (from about 2 limes)

rice for serving

garnishes: finely chopped cilantro, finely chopped mint, sliced red chili peppers, lime wedges, peanuts

Melt the coconut oil in a Dutch oven or deep skillet over medium-high heat. Add the onion and cook, stirring, until it begins to soften, about 5 minutes. Add the turkey and cook, breaking up the meat, for about 4 minutes, until just about cooked through. Add the garlic and ginger and cook for about 1 minute more. Add the red curry paste and stir to combine. Add the coconut milk, zucchini, and squash and stir to combine. Reduce the heat to medium-low, cover the pan with a lid, and allow the vegetables to steam for about 3 minutes. Remove the lid, stir in the spinach, and cook, covered, for 2 minutes more. Turn off the heat and stir in the salt, pepper, red pepper flakes, and lime juice. Taste and adjust seasonings.

Serve with rice (about ½ cup per person) and garnish with cilantro, mint, red chilies, lime wedges, and peanuts, as desired.

Gochujang Kimchi Meatloaf Muffins

February

Serves 6

Kimchi is something I came to like later in life. Upon opening a jar of fermented kimchi, some people are put off by the smell. Over time, though, as the odor dissipates, you're left with a crunchy, spicy, ready-made vegetable mélange that not only tastes good but is good for you (gut, heart, immune system — you name it). Kimchi is right at home in this meatloaf muffin, and because this recipe uses pork in addition to beef, you get a bit of fat in each muffin cup that creates a brown and crispy skin on top.

Meatloaf Muffins

1 medium onion, grated on a box grater

1 small carrot, grated on a box grater

3 cloves garlic, minced or grated

½ cup kimchi chopped fine like slaw

1 tablespoon chopped cilantro

2 teaspoons minced or grated ginger

⅓ cup panko breadcrumbs

1 large egg, lightly beaten

1 tablespoon Worcestershire sauce

1 tablespoon soy sauce

1 tablespoon gochujang Korean chili paste

1 teaspoon kosher salt

½ teaspoon black pepper

1 pound ground pork

1 pound lean ground beef

chili sauce (Sriracha), for serving

Glaze

¼ cup apricot jam

¼ cup ketchup

2 tablespoons gochujang Korean chili paste

1 tablespoon soy sauce

1 tablespoon rice vinegar

1 tablespoon orange juice

Heat oven to 350 degrees. Coat cups of a 12-portion muffin pan with cooking oil spray.

In a large bowl, use a spoon to mix the onion, carrot, garlic, kimchi, cilantro, ginger, breadcrumbs, egg, Worcestershire, 1 tablespoon soy sauce, 1 tablespoon gochujang, salt, and pepper. Add the pork and beef and knead with your hands to incorporate all the ingredients. Using an ice cream or cookie scoop, fill each muffin cup with approximately ⅓ cup of the meat mixture, pressing down and smoothing the tops. Place the muffin tin on a sheet pan to catch drips and bake for 25 minutes.

In a small saucepan over medium heat, blend together glaze ingredients and cook for 2 minutes, until well combined; set aside.

Remove pan from the oven and spoon 1 tablespoon of glaze onto each meat muffin. Bake for an additional 5 minutes, until the internal temperature reads 165 degrees. Turn the oven to broil on high, move an oven rack 6 inches below the broiler, and broil muffins for 2 minutes, until the glaze is bubbly and starting to brown. Remove the meat muffins from the pan and arrange on a plate or platter with a swirl of chili sauce.

144

Juicy Lucy Cheeseburger Tater Tot Hot Dish

February

Serves 8

What two foods are iconic in Minnesota? I'd say a Juicy Lucy and hot dish. My first cookbook, *True North Cabin Cookbook*, did not include a burger or a hot dish, so I decided to kill two birds with one stone. Let's be honest: I'm no culinary genius; I'm more of a home cook and, at heart, an eater. I could have made my own cream sauce, ketchup, and fried potatoes, but in true Minnesota home-cook fashion I used canned soups, Heinz ketchup, and frozen tater tots. We're in the no-snob zone here!

- **1 tablespoon extra-virgin olive oil, plus more for baking**
- **2 pounds ground beef**
- **1 large onion, diced**
- **⅔ cup diced dill pickles**
- **3 cloves garlic, chopped**
- **2 teaspoons kosher salt**
- **1 teaspoon black pepper**
- **1 teaspoon smoked paprika**
- **¼ cup mustard (spicy brown or yellow)**
- **⅓ cup ketchup (Heinz)**
- **1 (10.5-ounce) can cheddar cheese soup**
- **1 (10.5-ounce) can cream of jalapeño condensed soup (or substitute cream of chicken soup)**
- **2 cups dill pickle chips**
- **2 cups shredded cheddar cheese**
- **2 pounds frozen tater tots**

Heat oven to 375 degrees.

Heat olive oil in a large skillet over medium heat. Brown the beef for 5 minutes; drain any excess fat. Add onions, pickles, and garlic to the ground beef and continue cooking until no pink remains and the onions are translucent. Add salt, pepper, smoked paprika, mustard, ketchup, and soups to the skillet, stirring to combine. Cover the bottom of a 9x13-inch pan with the beef mixture. Layer the pickle chips evenly across the beef. Top with the shredded cheese. Arrange the tater tots in a layer along the top of the casserole. Bake for 30 minutes, then remove from the oven. Brush or spray olive oil over the top of the tater tots to ensure crispness and bake 15 minutes more, until casserole is bubbly.

Creamy Lemon Pasta with Crispy Breadcrumbs

Serves 4

Early in my relationship with Kurt, we lived in a brick walk-up apartment in Loring Park, and he would make us creamy pasta for dinner. I have always loved the idea that with some butter, cream, and cheese, you could make a luxurious, comforting plate of noodles. These days, when Kurt and I go sailing we always have an emergency meal in case we get stuck in a remote anchorage or a storm takes us off our intended course. That emergency meal is a carton of heavy cream, a hunk of Parmesan cheese, and a box of noodles. The recipe is very simple, but there are so many variations: add garlic, peppers, shrimp, sausage, tomatoes, or chicken. This version includes lemon juice and a sprinkle of breadcrumbs for a crunchy, buttery topping.

Breadcrumbs

1 tablespoon unsalted butter

½ cup panko or finely ground fresh breadcrumbs

kosher salt

black pepper

1 tablespoon chopped parsley

Pasta

12 ounces spaghetti

zest and juice of 1 lemon

1 cup heavy cream

3 tablespoons unsalted butter

⅔ cup finely grated Parmesan cheese

1 tablespoon black pepper

kosher salt to taste

For the Breadcrumbs

Melt butter in a small skillet over medium-low heat. As soon as the butter is melted and frothy, stir in the breadcrumbs. Continue stirring until crumbs are evenly crisp and golden brown.

Stir in a pinch of salt, a pinch of pepper, and parsley. Set aside.

For the Pasta

Cook pasta in a large pot of boiling salted water, stirring occasionally, until al dente. Reserve ¼ cup pasta water and drain the remaining water. Set pasta aside.

To a Dutch oven over medium heat add lemon zest and cream and cook, whisking often, until the liquid is just beginning to simmer, about 2 minutes. Reduce heat to medium-low. Whisk in butter, 1 tablespoon at a time, until melted and the sauce is creamy and emulsified. Remove from heat.

Add reserved ¼ cup pasta water to the cream sauce and return to medium heat. Using tongs, transfer spaghetti to the pot. Cook, tossing often and adding Parmesan little by little, until the cheese is melted and the sauce is creamy. Stir in half the lemon juice; season with pepper and salt and remaining lemon juice if desired. Top with breadcrumbs and serve.

147

February

Marry Me One-Pot Shrimp

Serves 4

Marry Me Chicken was all the rage on the internet in 2016 when the website Delish first published the recipe. The idea is that the dish is so tasty, it might inspire someone to propose to the cook. As I brainstormed a recipe for *Taste Buds with Stephanie* to make for *The Bachelorette*'s Michelle Young, I came up with this riff. Her boyfriend (and my friend) Jack Leius prepared and served it to her at her parents' home — while we filmed, of course. Who knows: when they get married (they are engaged!), maybe they'll credit this recipe.

1 tablespoon extra-virgin olive oil

1 tablespoon unsalted butter

1 pound shrimp, peeled and deveined

kosher salt

black pepper

2 cloves garlic, minced or grated

1½ cups whole milk

1½ cups chicken broth

8 ounces fettuccine

4 cups baby spinach

1 (3-ounce) package sun-dried tomatoes, chopped

1 teaspoon Italian seasoning

¼ cup grated Parmesan cheese, plus more for garnish

zest and juice of ½ lemon

Heat oil and butter in a large pot over medium-high heat. Add shrimp, season with salt and pepper, and cook until pink and cooked through, about 5 minutes. Add garlic and cook for 1 minute, then remove shrimp from the pot and set aside.

Add the milk and chicken broth to the pot and bring to a boil; then add the pasta. Cook for about 8 minutes, until the pasta is toothy, stirring so it does not stick together. Add spinach, sun-dried tomatoes, Italian seasoning, Parmesan, 1 teaspoon kosher salt, and ½ teaspoon black pepper, and mix until the spinach is wilted and everything is well coated. Add the shrimp back in and stir in lemon zest and lemon juice until fully incorporated. Serve with extra Parmesan cheese if desired.

Orange Madeleines

February

Makes 16 cakes

Madeleines are one of the simplest baked goodies to make, but you do need a special pan, which is like a muffin tin but pressed into fluted seashell shapes. Husband Kurt bought me a madeleine pan for Christmas, and while I use it only a few times a year, I love the way these little cakes taste. Madeleines are butter cakes with a crispy edge, and they can take on lots of flavor, like the orange version here. The classic version is vanilla, but lemon or chocolate is yummy too. Dust madeleines with confectioners' sugar, leave them plain — or dip in melted chocolate for a fancy finish.

- ½ cup (1 stick) unsalted butter, melted, 1 tablespoon reserved
- ½ teaspoon vanilla extract
- 1 tablespoon honey
- 1 tablespoon orange liqueur (Cointreau)
- ¾ cup all-purpose flour
- 1 teaspoon baking powder
- ½ teaspoon kosher salt
- ⅓ cup granulated sugar
- zest of 1 medium orange
- 2 large eggs
- 1 tablespoon whole milk
- confectioners' sugar for dusting, optional

Heat oven to 375 degrees. Using a pastry brush, grease the cups of a madeleine pan with 1 tablespoon of the melted butter.

Add the vanilla, honey, and orange liqueur to the remaining melted butter, stirring to mix.

In a medium bowl, sift the flour and the baking powder, then stir in the salt.

In the bowl of a stand mixer, combine the sugar and orange zest. Start the mixer on low, then add the eggs, milk, and butter mixture and mix for 2 minutes. Add the dry ingredients and mix until just combined. Use a 1½–tablespoon cookie scoop to portion the batter into the prepared pan. Bake for 9 minutes, until edges begin to brown. Lift the cakes from the cups and dust with confectioners' sugar, if using, or enjoy plain. These are best warm on the day you make them.

Gluten-Free Bourbon Brownies

Serves 12

These brownies are a big hit on my website, stephaniesdish.com, and they're the perfect dessert to make for everyone to enjoy when you have a gluten-free guest. The bourbon gives them a great depth of flavor and adds to their grown-up profile.

10 tablespoons unsalted butter, plus more for the pan

¼ cup bourbon

¼ cup unsweetened cocoa powder

2 cups semisweet chocolate chips, divided

4 large eggs

½ cup confectioners' sugar

Heat oven to 325 degrees. Grease an 8-inch square baking pan, then line with parchment paper and grease the parchment.

Heat the butter and bourbon in a large saucepan over medium heat, stirring occasionally, until the butter melts. Stir in the cocoa powder until smooth. Remove from heat and immediately add 1½ cups chocolate chips. Stir until smooth. Let cool slightly.

Add the eggs, 1 at a time, beating well after each addition. Stir in the confectioners' sugar until well combined. Transfer to the prepared pan and spread in an even layer. Sprinkle the remaining ½ cup chocolate chips on top. Bake until the top is glossy and a toothpick inserted 1 inch from the edge comes out clean, about 20 minutes. Cool completely in the pan on a wire rack. Lift out of the pan using the parchment paper. Cut into 12 bars.

151

February

March

BREAST VACATION EVER

Are you the type of person who looks back and only sees all the bad stuff? Or do you cherish the good? The good is what I try to think about when reflecting upon my battle with breast cancer.

I found the lump in my breast when I was in Duluth for the weekend, attending one of Ellie's downhill ski races at Spirit Mountain. It's like my parents remembering where they were when President Kennedy was shot, or people of my generation remembering where we were when the World Trade Center fell. Every detail is etched in my memory. Our hotel room overlooked the ship channel and the iconic Aerial Lift Bridge and had a pullout couch for Ellie, a gas fireplace, and a whirlpool tub. I was in the tub when I felt the lump. I touched my right breast and there it was, the size of a lima bean. I had my husband, Kurt, feel it. Knowing my family's history of breast cancer, all he said was, "You'd better get that checked."

Some of you have experienced this: a biopsy that showed cancer in the lump, followed by a PET (aka positron emission tomography) scan indicating involvement of my lymphatic system. Stage 3 cancer. Radiation and chemotherapy were necessary, but then came the hardest decision: a lumpectomy, mastectomy, or double mastectomy — the worst array of "choices."

My mother had only recently died of breast cancer and was given a similar choice. Maybe out of vanity, or maybe because she didn't want the very invasive surgery, she chose the lumpectomy. The recurrence was two years later, and by that time her cancer was stage 4 and had spread to her lungs. No doubt I had some undiscovered genetic marker lying in wait all those years that, at the age of forty-two, decided to make its presence known. I can be a vain person, and I loved my breasts, but I really did not want to die, and I thought maybe if I took the hard left-hand turn and got the double mastectomy, I might have better odds than my mother did of beating the cancer and living.

The surgery was scheduled for the next month. Kurt, the man of very few words, said, "Let's get out of here." We both sail and had done bareboat charter trips in the Caribbean and Lake Superior. We rented a forty-foot catamaran out of St. Martin and were on our way for seven days ahead of the surgery — the "Breast Vacation Ever."

For that week, it was just Kurt, Ellie, and me. We rounded the island of St. Martin and anchored at a place called Orient Bay Beach. We took the dinghy ashore. There, half the

154

beach is nude with the other side optional. I went topless for the first time ever, determined to show off my breasts while I still had them. For lunch we ate sushi at a beach bar and drank beer, then piña coladas (virgin coladas for Ellie). The next day we sailed east to St. Barts and anchored off a remote and protected beach where we knew there'd be privacy and great snorkeling. Kurt made jambalaya with andouille sausage, chunks of halibut, and shrimp.

The day after that, we anchored outside the marina at Gustavia at a place called Shell Beach. We explored the small town in the afternoon after having lunch at Le Select, a small burger stand that allegedly was Jimmy Buffett's inspiration for "Cheeseburger in Paradise." I walked into a small jewelry store run by a woman and her mother who design and string Tahitian pearl necklaces. I bought a leather strand necklace with just one large pearl the color of heat-tempered steel.

The next day we sailed on to Sint Maarten, a town that shares its island with St. Martin — one Dutch, the other French — and anchored off Philipsburg. That night we had dinner at a favorite restaurant, L'Escargot, run by an older French couple who on Thursdays put on a sort of vaudeville burlesque show (the couple did impersonations of Kenny Rogers and Dolly Parton, singing with their French accents). We ate escargot, of course, along with a homemade baguette; I ordered duck à l'orange. We stayed late and watched the show. On our final night, we anchored off Grand Case and ate at one of the street food stands that made barbecued chicken, pork ribs, or goat served with rice, beans, and pigeon peas. Ellie, always an adventurous eater, ordered a side of mac and cheese with her barbecued goat.

A week after arriving back in Minneapolis, I was in the hospital. My new necklace rested just above the breasts soon to be removed and replaced with implants. Something about that pearl gave me strength. It reminded me of the Breast Vacation Ever, the good times we had.

We've gone back to St. Martin and St. Barts twice, and each time I've gone to the same shop with the woman and her mother and added a pearl to the strand. It's been over thirteen years since the double mastectomy, and no recurrence. I still wear the pearls every day in the summer, a short strand with the three pearls from St. Martin and a long strand with ten more added just last year. Each pearl represents another year alive. I alternate them with a gold necklace that was my mom's that has a charm with her initials, a gold Roman numeral ten for the years I have been a survivor, and a charm I bought myself called the Tree of Life that signifies my ongoing survivorship. If you see me wearing these necklaces — my good luck charms, my talismans — you'll know what they mean to me. I touch them to remind myself to be the kind of person who looks back and cherishes all the good that has come from my breast cancer diagnosis and who looks forward to all the good things yet to come. Facing a life-and-death situation, you get absolute clarity on what's really important in life. I am reminded of that fact daily when I look in the mirror and see my necklaces.

Boozy Shamrock Shakes

Serves 2

I love a boozy shake ever since my father gave me a taste of his grasshopper back at Simpson's Supper Club in Waupaca, Wisconsin. That was fifty years ago! This version is formulated especially for St. Patrick's Day. Garnish with a green foil–wrapped Andes Mint — just like you might find on a silver tray weighing down your supper club check.

3 cups vanilla bean ice cream

1 cup whole milk

⅓ cup crème de menthe

4 drops green food coloring

whipped cream and chocolate mints (Andes), for garnish

Combine the ice cream, milk, crème de menthe, and food coloring in the base of a blender. Blend until thick and creamy, about 30 seconds. Pour the mixture into 2 tall glasses and top with whipped cream and an Andes mint.

Tuna Pâté

Serves 6

This recipe is perfect as a last-minute appetizer. I always have a can of tuna in my pantry, and while this combination doesn't sound like a showstopper, it's surprisingly delicious and always at home on a cheese or charcuterie board. I like to present the pâté in a glass ramekin or slathered on a toasted baguette with capers, fresh dill, and crispy flakes of Maldon sea salt.

1 (5-ounce) can tuna packed in water, drained

2 scallions, roughly chopped

¼ cup whole milk Greek yogurt

1 tablespoon mayonnaise

zest and 1 tablespoon juice from ½ lemon

½ tablespoon very finely chopped fresh dill, plus a few sprigs for garnish

1 teaspoon sea salt (Maldon)

a few grinds freshly cracked black pepper

caper berries, for garnish

toasted baguette slices for serving

In a mini food processor, blend tuna and scallions until mixed and chopped but with some texture remaining. Transfer to a bowl. Add yogurt, mayonnaise, lemon zest, lemon juice, dill, salt, and pepper and mix well. Top with fresh dill sprigs and caper berries and serve alongside toasted baguette slices.

March

Thai Winter Squash Soup

Serves 6

During the winter when I am eating lots of potato, noodle, and beef dishes, I find that I crave Southeast Asian flavors like ginger, turmeric, lemongrass, and all the fresh herbs I can get my hands on. I make this soup to chase away the winter blues and liven up my palate.

- 1 tablespoon extra-virgin olive oil
- 1 pound ground pork
- 1 large red onion, chopped
- 3 tablespoons minced or grated ginger
- 2 cloves garlic, minced or grated
- 1 jalapeño or Thai red chili, sliced (optional: remove seeds to reduce heat)
- 2 tablespoons chopped lemongrass (or substitute lemongrass paste; see tip page 115)
- 1 tablespoon Thai red curry paste
- 2 teaspoons cumin
- 2 large zucchini, cut into half-moons
- 6 cups vegetable broth
- ¼ cup honey
- juice of 2 limes
- 2 teaspoons kosher salt
- 1 teaspoon black pepper
- 2 tablespoons chopped cilantro leaves

In a large pot over medium heat, heat the oil and cook the pork, stirring to break apart, for 4 minutes, until almost cooked through; drain the grease. Add the onion and ginger to the pot and continue to cook over medium heat, stirring occasionally, until onions are softened. Add garlic, jalapeño, lemongrass, curry paste, and cumin and cook for 2 minutes, until fragrant. Add zucchini and broth and simmer for 15 minutes, until squash is soft. Stir in honey, lime juice, salt, and pepper. Top with chopped cilantro.

Coconut Curry Soup with Salmon

Serves 4

This is a stew or a soup (depending on your point of view), but either way it's delicious when served with a scoop of rice and garnished with green onions, chilis, basil, and peanuts. Don't forget the extra squeeze of lime!

- 1 (1-pound) skinless salmon fillet, cut into 1-inch pieces
- ½ teaspoon kosher salt
- ½ teaspoon black pepper
- ¼ cup avocado oil
- 1 medium onion, finely chopped
- 4 green onions, thinly sliced (reserve dark green parts for garnish)
- 4 lemongrass stalks, outer layers removed, finely chopped (or substitute ¼ cup lemongrass paste; see tip page 115)
- 3 cloves garlic, minced or grated
- half-inch knob ginger, minced or grated
- 8 ounces mushrooms, sliced into 1-inch pieces
- 2 (13.5-ounce) cans unsweetened full-fat coconut milk
- 3 tablespoons Thai red curry paste
- 1 tablespoon fish sauce
- 1 tablespoon honey
- 1 bunch lacinato kale, chopped into 1-inch pieces
- zest and juice of 2 limes
- ¼ cup shredded basil (reserve some for garnish)

For Serving
- 2 cups cooked jasmine rice
- 1 lime, cut into wedges
- 1 Thai red chili, sliced
- ⅓ cup crushed peanuts
- reserved green onions
- reserved basil

Pat the salmon dry with a paper towel and sprinkle with salt and pepper.

Heat avocado oil in a large Dutch oven or soup pot over medium heat. Cook the chopped onions, white parts of green onion, lemongrass, garlic, and ginger for 8 minutes, stirring occasionally. Add mushrooms and allow to brown for about 5 minutes before adding the coconut milk, curry paste, fish sauce, and honey; stir to combine. Stir in kale and salmon, and simmer for 5 minutes. Remove soup from heat and stir in lime zest, lime juice, and basil.

Divide soup among four bowls. Add ½ cup rice to each bowl. Garnish with squeezed lime wedges, Thai chilis, crushed peanuts, and reserved green onions and basil.

Fish Chowder with Bacon

Serves 6

I love a good fish chowder. One of my favorite versions is in Las Vegas at the oyster bar inside the Palace Station Hotel. The bar seats twenty, and there are eight kettles to make soups, fish stews, or what they call pan roasts, which have a creamy tomato base.

This fish chowder uses flaky cod, the spice of Old Bay, and the enhancement of bacon. Of course you can use clams or shrimp, halibut or scallops. You can't go wrong.

4 slices bacon

2 tablespoons unsalted butter

1 cup diced onion

1 cup diced celery

2 tablespoons minced or grated garlic

¼ cup all-purpose flour

3 cups clam juice

1 pound Yukon gold potatoes, cut into half-inch pieces

1 tablespoon finely chopped fresh thyme

2 tablespoons seafood seasoning (Old Bay)

1 bay leaf

2 cups heavy cream

1 tablespoon hot sauce

1 tablespoon Worcestershire sauce

1 teaspoon kosher salt

1 teaspoon black pepper

1¼–1½ pounds cod, cut into 1-inch chunks

juice of ½ lemon

chopped parsley, for garnish

Cook the bacon in a large Dutch oven until crispy. Transfer bacon to a paper towel–lined plate, leaving 1–2 tablespoons of bacon fat in the pot. Add the butter to the pot and heat over medium. Add the onions, celery, and garlic and cook, covered, for 5–7 minutes, until softened. Add the flour, and cook, stirring constantly, for about 2 minutes. Stir in the clam juice, scraping any browned bits off the bottom of the pan. Add potatoes, thyme, seafood seasoning, and bay leaf. Bring the mixture to a boil and reduce the heat to medium-low. Simmer for 15 minutes. Add the cream, hot sauce, Worcestershire sauce, salt, and pepper. Return soup to a simmer and add the cod. Simmer for about 7 minutes, until the cod is cooked through. Crumble the bacon and stir in with the lemon juice. Garnish with chopped parsley.

Dill Pickle and Ham Soup

Serves 6

I know it seems weird to put pickles in soup. It seemed weird to me too, but then I was surprised by how delicious it is. I typically make pickle soup in the spring with the leftovers from the Easter ham. The pickle juice gives it a sweet and sour vibe that really plays well with the lushness of the sour cream. Serve with Irish Soda Bread (page 162) for a hearty lunch or mid-day cabin meal.

1 tablespoon extra-virgin olive oil
4 tablespoons unsalted butter
1 medium onion, chopped
2 medium carrots, grated on a box grater
1 cup shredded cabbage
1 cup finely chopped dill pickles
4 cloves garlic, minced or grated
2 cups cubed ham
6 cups chicken broth
⅓ cup pickle juice
4 large red potatoes, cut into half-inch cubes
¼ cup chopped fresh dill, plus more for garnish
1½ teaspoons seafood seasoning (Old Bay)
1 cup sour cream
1 teaspoon kosher salt
1 teaspoon black pepper

Add olive oil and butter to a Dutch oven or large pot over medium heat. When the butter has melted, add the onion, carrots, and cabbage and cook until the cabbage is wilted and starting to take on some color, about 5 minutes. Add chopped pickles, garlic, and ham and stir for 1 minute, until the garlic is fragrant. Stir in the broth and pickle juice. Add the potatoes and bring to a boil. Cook for 12–15 minutes, until the potato is cooked through, then reduce heat to simmer. Stir in the dill, seafood seasoning, sour cream, salt, and pepper. Heat through and serve with fresh chopped dill on top.

Irish Soda Bread

Serves 4–6

Even if you're challenged by bread baking like me, you can make soda bread. The round loaf comes out crusty on the outside and moist on the inside. This easy recipe is perfect alongside any of the soups in this book. If there's any left over, it makes great toast, slathered with grainy mustard and served with corned beef hash.

3¼ cups all-purpose flour (see tip)

¼ cup granulated sugar

1 tablespoon baking powder

2 teaspoons baking soda

1 teaspoon sea salt

4 tablespoons unsalted butter

2 cups buttermilk

Heat oven to 375 degrees. Grease a deep 8-inch baking pan or cast iron pot.

In a large bowl, whisk together flour, sugar, baking powder, baking soda, and salt. Add the butter to the bowl and cut it into the dry ingredients with a fork or pastry cutter (aim for pea-size chunks, like for pie dough). Add buttermilk and mix with a spatula until the dough comes together.

Turn out the dough on a floured surface and briefly knead to ensure the ingredients are combined. It will be a sticky dough. Round the ball into a plump loaf about 5 inches wide, dust with flour, and place in the prepared pan. Use an X-ACTO knife, razor blade, or sharp knife to make an X shape in the top, cutting at least ½ inch deep. Bake for 30 minutes, until golden brown on top and a toothpick or skewer inserted in the middle comes out clean. Cool completely on a wire rack before cutting into the loaf.

TIP: You can use half all-purpose flour and half whole wheat flour if you wish: the loaf will be very dense but tasty.

Twice-Baked Potato Casserole

Serves 6

This recipe is much easier to cook for a potluck or large gathering than traditional twice-baked potatoes, where you bake the potatoes, hollow the skins, and refill them to bake a second time. Though I do love the crispy potato skin boats of a twice-baked potato, this casserole is a time-saver, great for large groups, and creamy-delicious.

I typically use an 8-inch square pan or a round soufflé dish, but you can easily double this recipe for a deep 9x13–inch pan.

- 2½ pounds Yukon gold potatoes, peeled and cut into 1½-inch cubes
- kosher salt
- 4 tablespoons unsalted butter
- ½ teaspoon black pepper
- ⅓ cup whole milk
- ½ cup sour cream
- 1⅓ cups shredded sharp cheddar cheese, divided
- ⅓ cup grated Gruyère cheese
- ¼ cup finely grated Parmesan cheese
- 4 thick bacon strips, chopped and cooked until crisp

Heat oven to 350 degrees. Grease a 2-quart baking dish.

Place the potatoes in a large pot, cover with water, and add 1 tablespoon salt. Bring to boiling over high heat and cook until the potatoes are tender and can be easily smashed with a fork, about 25 minutes.

Drain the potatoes in a colander and return to the pot. Add butter, 1 teaspoon salt, and pepper, and mash until chunky. Add milk and sour cream and mash until smooth. Stir in 1 cup cheddar cheese and the Gruyère cheese.

Scoop potato mixture into prepared baking dish; sprinkle with remaining ⅓ cup cheddar and Parmesan cheese, and top with the bacon. Bake, uncovered, until the filling is heated through and the cheese is melted, 35–40 minutes. Let rest 10 minutes before serving.

Dill Pickle Pot Roast

Serves 6

I learned how to make this pot roast by accident. My first years of pickling at the Ely Hilltop Garden were met with limited success. The canned pickles tasted good, but they were lacking that crisp bite. I was on a quest for ways to use my soggy failures. In addition to the creative Tuna Pâté (page 157) and Dill Pickle and Ham Soup (page 161), I saw a recipe that used pickles to brine and tenderize the cut of meat. I wondered if this technique would work, and if you could make a gravy of sorts. The answer is yes!

This melt-in-your-mouth pot roast is delicious piled on a giant mound of mashed potatoes. You can also make this in the slow cooker, but leave the top off for the last hour or so to evaporate some of the liquid.

2 tablespoons canola oil

3 pounds beef chuck roast

1 large yellow onion, diced

1 cup finely chopped dill pickles

¼ cup finely chopped pepperoncini

⅓ cup beef broth

1 tablespoon black pepper

2 teaspoons kosher salt

1 cup sour cream

1 tablespoon chopped fresh dill

1 tablespoon chopped parsley

Heat oven to 350 degrees.

Heat oil over high heat in a large Dutch oven or oven-safe pot with a lid. Brown the roast in the oil, about 4 minutes per side, until a brown crust forms. Add the onions, pickles, pepperoncini, beef broth, pepper, and salt to the pot, stirring to combine. Cover and bake for 2½ hours.

Stir in the sour cream and cook uncovered for another 30 minutes to brown the roast and thicken the gravy.

Remove the roast from the pot and slice against the grain to achieve the most tender texture. Place slices on a serving platter. Add the chopped herbs to the sauce and taste and adjust seasonings before topping the slices with the gravy.

Oven-Baked Corned Beef Brisket

Serves 8

If you wait until after St. Patrick's Day, the unsold corned beef goes on clearance. It's the perfect time of year to stock the freezer. For this recipe, discard the seasoning packet that usually comes with the brisket in favor of my customized blend, and cook the brisket low and slow in the oven. The brisket comes out fork-tender. Serve sliced with a spicy grainy mustard or pulled for sandwiches. It's an inexpensive crowd-pleaser!

1 tablespoon kosher salt

1 tablespoon coarse black pepper

2 teaspoons smoked paprika

1½ teaspoons onion powder

1½ teaspoons garlic powder

½ teaspoon ground coriander

1 (4- to 5-pound) flat-cut corned beef brisket

1 tablespoon extra-virgin olive oil

3 tablespoons barbecue sauce

Heat oven to 275 degrees.

In a small bowl, combine salt, pepper, paprika, onion powder, garlic powder, and coriander.

Rub brisket with olive oil, then massage the seasoning mix into the meat. Place brisket on a rack set in a roasting pan. Cover the pan tightly with aluminum foil. Roast for 4 hours. Remove from oven and glaze with barbecue sauce. Return to oven, uncovered, and cook 1 additional hour, until tender. Slice against the grain and serve.

Chicken and Biscuits

Serves 4–6

I first had chicken and biscuits at my friend Renee's cabin after a day of snowmobiling. Her mom, Connie, would dollop mounds of Bisquick batter on top of chicken stew, and they'd puff up like doughy clouds. I remember eating these delicious biscuits out of steaming bowls while waiting for our hats and gloves to dry on the radiator so we could go back out for another snowmobile ride. Over the years, I've learned to replicate Connie's puffy biscuits but without the Bisquick. I usually use leftover pulled chicken or grocery-store rotisserie chicken. Something about repurposing leftovers for a great meal is mighty satisfying.

Stew

- **3 carrots, peeled and cut into quarter-inch rounds**
- **2 cups peeled sweet potato or butternut squash cut into half-inch cubes**
- **1 large onion, chopped into half-inch cubes**
- **2 tablespoons extra-virgin olive oil**
- **2 tablespoons unsalted butter**
- **3 tablespoons all-purpose flour**
- **1 tablespoon concentrated chicken soup base (Better than Bouillon) or 1 bouillon cube**
- **3 cups chicken broth, warmed**
- **3 cups shredded chicken, pulled off the bone or from poached chicken breasts**
- **1 tablespoon chopped fresh rosemary**
- **1 tablespoon fresh thyme leaves**
- **kosher salt and black pepper, to taste**

Biscuit Dough

- **2 cups all-purpose flour**
- **2 teaspoons baking powder**
- **1 teaspoon granulated sugar**
- **1 teaspoon kosher salt**
- **½ teaspoon baking soda**
- **½ cup (1 stick) unsalted butter, melted and cooled**
- **1 cup buttermilk, chilled**

For the Stew

Heat oven to 400 degrees. Toss the vegetables with the olive oil on a sheet pan and roast for 25 minutes.

Melt the butter in a Dutch oven over medium heat, then whisk in the flour, 1 tablespoon at a time, cooking until a doughy paste forms. Add soup base or bouillon and then chicken broth, ½ cup at a time, and whisk, forming a gravy. After about 10 minutes, when the gravy coats the back of a spoon, add vegetables, chicken, rosemary, and thyme leaves.

Increase oven temperature to 450 degrees. Continue to cook the filling on low for 15 minutes. If it gets too thick, add more broth. Season with salt and pepper to taste.

For the Biscuits

Mix the flour, baking powder, sugar, salt, and baking soda in a bowl. In a separate bowl, combine the butter and buttermilk. Add the wet ingredients to the dry ingredients and mix until a shaggy dough forms. Using a ¼-cup scoop, drop portions of biscuit dough all over the top of the filling. Bake for about 25 minutes or until the tops of the biscuits are golden brown.

March

Grilled Jerk Chicken with Coconut Rice and Mango Salsa

Serves 4

This recipe always reminds my daughter, Ellie, of the few holidays we spent in the Caribbean. Ellie was five when she first went. Husband Kurt had started the process of becoming a certified sailing captain, and we'd rented a boat with the instructor. I guess you could call him an Old Salt. Originally from New York City, Captain Steve had been in the British Virgin Islands for many years, and the deep lines through his tanned face and missing incisor showed it. He cautioned that we should never drink more than one beer per hour while sailing. Then his instructions and tests came late at night while Ellie was asleep and the rum was flowing. We dropped Captain Steve back at the marina and spent Christmas Eve safely moored in Virgin Gorda Sound, where we watched the festive lit boat parade and sang Christmas songs. The next day, we had presents for Ellie that I'd lugged all the way from Minnesota. For Christmas dinner, instead of our traditional prime rib, I made a version of this jerk chicken dish for the first time.

Chicken

- 2 pounds boneless, skinless chicken thighs
- 2 tablespoons extra-virgin olive oil
- 1 tablespoon brown sugar
- 2 teaspoons kosher salt
- 1 teaspoon paprika
- 1 teaspoon minced or grated garlic
- 1 teaspoon onion powder
- ½ teaspoon cinnamon
- ½ teaspoon dried thyme
- ½ teaspoon allspice
- ½ teaspoon cayenne pepper
- pinch ground cloves
- zest and juice of 1 lime

Coconut Rice

- 1 (14.5-ounce) can unsweetened full-fat coconut milk
- 1 cup chicken broth
- 1 tablespoon honey
- 2 teaspoons kosher salt
- 1½ cups jasmine rice
- 1 tablespoon lime juice, plus lime wedges for serving

Mango Salsa

- 2 medium ripe mangos, peeled and diced (see tip)
- ¼ cup diced red onion
- ¼ cup finely chopped cilantro, plus more for garnish
- zest and juice of 1 lime
- 1 small jalapeño, finely chopped
- 1 avocado, cubed (or substitute a tomato)
- ½ teaspoon kosher salt

For the Chicken
Place the chicken in a plastic zip-top bag along with the oil, sugar, spices, lime zest, and lime juice. Shake to coat the chicken, and let sit to marinate for a minimum of 30 minutes or up to 12 hours.

Heat the grill to medium-high. Place the chicken thighs on the grill and cook until the internal temperature is 165.

For the Coconut Rice (see note)
In a medium pot set over high heat, stir together the coconut milk, broth, honey, and salt and bring to a boil. Add the rice; reduce heat to low, cover, and simmer for 16–18 minutes, until tender. While the rice is cooking, stir every 3–4 minutes to ensure the coconut milk doesn't burn on the bottom of the pan. When the rice is done, fluff with a fork, toss with lime juice, and set aside.

For the Mango Salsa
In a medium bowl, mix together the mango, onion, cilantro, lime zest, lime juice, jalapeño, avocado, and salt. Chill until ready to use.

Serve the chicken on top of the rice; garnish with the salsa or serve alongside, with additional cilantro and lime wedges.

NOTE: You can make rice in an Instant Pot. Add ingredients to the pot and stir. Cook on Manual for 10 minutes, or use the Rice feature. Manual release the steam when done, fluff with a fork, and serve.

TIP: If you've never cut a mango before, it's helpful to watch a YouTube video for how to do it.

Cajun Shrimp Pasta

Serves 4

My husband Kurt's creamy pasta alfredo in my first cookbook has been a go-to recipe for years, great paired with a nice grilled ribeye or roast chicken. This Cajun version cooks the shrimp right in the skillet so it's a one-pot meal, perfect for a quick weeknight dinner.

1 pound spaghetti

2 tablespoons extra-virgin olive oil, divided

1 pound raw shrimp, peeled and deveined

3 teaspoons Cajun seasoning, divided

1 shallot, minced

1 red bell pepper, cut into strips

1 (14.5-ounce) can fire-roasted diced tomatoes

¾ cup heavy cream

1 teaspoon kosher salt

½ teaspoon black pepper

1 tablespoon chopped parsley, for garnish

lemon wedges, for garnish

Cook the pasta according to package instructions, then drain, reserving about ⅓ cup of pasta water. Set aside.

Add 1 tablespoon olive oil to a large skillet over medium-high heat. When oil is hot, add the shrimp. Sprinkle with 2 teaspoons Cajun seasoning and cook briefly, stirring, until just cooked through, about 2–3 minutes. Remove to a plate and keep warm.

Add the remaining 1 tablespoon olive oil to the pan along with the shallot and red pepper. Cook, stirring, until soft, about 7 minutes, then reduce heat to medium and add the diced tomatoes and cream. Stir in the remaining 1 teaspoon Cajun seasoning. When the cream starts to bubble, reduce heat to low. Let sauce simmer for a couple of minutes to thicken, then add pasta and shrimp, stirring to coat. Add some pasta water to thin the sauce if needed. Season with salt and pepper, to taste. Garnish with parsley and lemon wedges.

Linguine and Clam Sauce

Serves 2

This is a simple pantry dish to have on hand because it takes mainly dry goods — an onion, a lemon, pasta, canned clams. It can be made with your favorite dried spices and hot red pepper flakes, but I find a fresh lemon offers the right amount of acid to balance the salty clam juice.

8 ounces linguine

1 tablespoon unsalted butter

2 tablespoons extra-virgin olive oil

1 small onion, diced

1 clove garlic, minced or grated

½ teaspoon crushed red pepper flakes

1 tablespoon lemon zest

3 tablespoons lemon juice

1 teaspoon kosher salt

½ teaspoon dried or fresh rosemary

½ teaspoon dried oregano

½ teaspoon fresh thyme leaves

2 (6.5-ounce) cans minced clams

garnishes: parsley, ½ cup Parmesan cheese, black pepper, lemon wedges

Cook pasta according to package instructions until al dente, then drain, reserving ⅓ cup of pasta water.

While the pasta is cooking, add butter and olive oil to a large skillet over medium-high heat. When butter has melted, add the onion and cook, stirring, for 3 minutes. Add garlic and red pepper flakes and cook, stirring, for 2 minutes more. Add lemon zest, lemon juice, salt, rosemary, oregano, thyme, and clams with juice. Bring to a simmer and cook for 5 minutes. Add pasta to the skillet and toss, coating the pasta with the clam sauce and adding some of the reserved pasta water if the mixture seems dry. Top with parsley, Parmesan cheese, and fresh cracked black pepper. Serve with lemon wedges.

One-Pot Turkey Meatballs with Lemon Orzo

Serves 4

There's something about one-pot meals that is so satisfying. One dish to cook in and one dish to clean. Everyone can help themselves from the communal pot and settle in with a glass of wine and some crusty bread. In this recipe, the meatballs are browned in the skillet before the orzo and braising liquid are added; the simmering broth finishes cooking everything at the same time. Change up this cooking strategy for other weeknight one-pot meatball meals like:

Italian: veal meatballs; add tomatoes and oregano.

Asian: pork meatballs; use lemongrass, ginger, and a bit of fish sauce instead of the lemon juice; swap pho broth for the chicken broth.

Mediterranean: chicken meatballs; add thyme, rosemary, and prunes, raisins, or green olives.

There are tons of creative options once you pick your protein.

- 1 medium onion, three-quarters of it chopped, one-quarter finely chopped
- 2 cloves garlic, minced or grated
- ¼ cup panko breadcrumbs
- ¼ cup grated Parmesan cheese
- 1 heaping tablespoon ricotta
- 1 tablespoon chopped parsley
- 1 tablespoon chopped fresh oregano (or substitute 2 teaspoons dried)
- 2 teaspoons kosher salt, divided
- 1 pound ground turkey
- 3 tablespoons extra-virgin olive oil
- 1½ cups dried orzo
- zest of 1 lemon (reserve some for garnish)
- ¼ cup lemon juice
- 2½ cups chicken broth
- 4 cups baby spinach
- ⅓ cup heavy cream
- garnishes: oregano, parsley, lemon zest

In a large bowl, mix finely chopped onion, garlic, panko, Parmesan, ricotta, parsley, oregano, 1 teaspoon salt, and ground turkey. Use a tablespoon or cookie scoop to form into 1½– to 2-inch meatballs.

Heat the oil in a Dutch oven over high heat and brown the meatballs on all sides, about 5–10 minutes, rotating them occasionally with tongs to ensure even browning. Add the remaining chopped onions and cook for 3 minutes, continually scraping the browned bits off the bottom of the pan. Stir the orzo, lemon zest, lemon juice, and chicken broth into the meatball and onion mixture. Reduce heat to simmer; add spinach on top and cook, covered, for 6 minutes. Uncover the pot and stir in heavy cream and remaining 1 teaspoon salt. Cook, covered, for 6 minutes more, until the orzo is cooked through. Garnish with chopped oregano, parsley, and lemon zest.

Skillet Baked Ziti with Meatballs

Serves 6

I've cooked this meal in Ely for dinner parties with Burntside Lake friends: it's always a huge hit. In my giant cast iron skillet, the meatballs are nestled into the ziti with hunks of fresh mozzarella cheese and tomato sauce. Serve with your favorite red table wine, a simple salad, and a crusty loaf of bread. It makes a delicious and hearty shoulder season meal, perfect for when chilly weather is lingering.

- 1 pound ground beef
- ½ pound ground pork
- ⅓ cup panko breadcrumbs
- 2 large egg yolks
- 3 cloves garlic, minced or grated, divided
- 2 teaspoons dried oregano, divided
- 1 teaspoon kosher salt
- ½ teaspoon black pepper
- 1 tablespoon extra-virgin olive oil
- ½ cup diced onion
- 1 (28-ounce) can crushed tomatoes
- 1 pound ziti
- 3 tablespoons chopped parsley leaves
- 2 tablespoons chopped fresh basil
- 1 (8-ounce) ball mozzarella cheese, torn into pieces

Heat oven to 375 degrees. Spray a 12- to 14-inch cast iron pan with cooking spray.

In a large bowl, combine beef, pork, panko, egg yolks, half the garlic, 1 teaspoon oregano, salt, and pepper. Stir until well combined, then roll into 1-inch meatballs, forming about 24 meatballs.

Heat olive oil in a Dutch oven over medium-high heat. When the oil is hot, add the meatballs in batches and brown for about 10 minutes, rotating them occasionally with tongs to ensure even browning. Set meatballs aside. Drain excess oil from the skillet, leaving about 1 tablespoon behind. Add onion and cook for 5 minutes, until translucent. Add remaining garlic and cook for 1 minute, stirring constantly, until fragrant. Add the tomatoes and remaining 1 teaspoon oregano and simmer until thickened, about 10 minutes.

Cook pasta according to package instructions for al dente; drain well and set aside.

Add the meatballs to the prepared pan and pour in the sauce. Bring to a boil, then reduce heat and simmer until flavors have blended, about 5 minutes. Remove from heat. Stir in the pasta, parsley, and basil. Tuck torn mozzarella pieces into the skillet among the pasta and meatballs. Bake until bubbly, about 25–30 minutes. Let stand 10 minutes before serving.

Cowboy Bread

Serves 12

I vividly remember the lunchroom at Normandale Hills Elementary in Bloomington, Minnesota. I recall my teacher, Mrs. Berg, reading the daily lunch menu. My top five favorites were pizza burgers, cheese pizza, pork with mashed potatoes and gravy, tacos, and spaghetti. The spaghetti was always served with a cowboy bread dessert nestled in its square on our mint green plastic tray. Years later, someone published a few of the Bloomington school lunch recipes, and this is my adapted version of the cowboy bread I still love today.

- ⅔ cup unsalted butter, at room temperature
- 2½ cups all-purpose flour
- 2 cups packed brown sugar
- ½ teaspoon kosher salt
- 2 teaspoons baking powder
- ½ teaspoon baking soda
- ½ teaspoon nutmeg
- 1½ teaspoons cinnamon, divided
- 1 cup buttermilk
- 2 large eggs

Heat oven to 375 degrees and spray a 9x13–inch baking pan with cooking spray.

In a large bowl, combine butter, flour, brown sugar, and salt until crumbly. Reserve ½ cup of the crumble to sprinkle on top. Add baking powder, baking soda, nutmeg, and ½ teaspoon cinnamon to the mixture and mix well. Add buttermilk and eggs and stir to combine.

Pour the batter into the prepared pan. Evenly distribute the reserved crumble on top and sprinkle with remaining 1 teaspoon cinnamon. Bake for 25–30 minutes, until top is golden brown and crackly. Serve warm or at room temperature.

Blueberry-Lemon Bread

Makes 1 large loaf, 3 mini loaves, or 1 dozen muffins

With this versatile recipe you can make muffins, a large loaf in a 5x9-inch pan, or mini loaves. Swirling the blueberry compote or rough jam throughout the batter yields a beautiful streaky pattern of color. I like to wrap those cute mini loaves in waxed paper, tie them up with colorful string or ribbon, and give them as gifts.

Blueberry Compote
- 1 pint blueberries
- ¼ cup granulated sugar
- 1 tablespoon lemon juice

Bread
- 1 cup sugar
- zest of 1 lemon
- 1½ cups all-purpose flour
- 1 teaspoon baking powder
- ½ teaspoon kosher salt
- ½ cup full-fat plain unsweetened yogurt
- ¼ cup whole milk
- ½ cup (1 stick) unsalted butter, melted and cooled
- 2 large eggs, lightly beaten
- 2 tablespoons lemon juice
- ½ teaspoon vanilla extract

For the Blueberry Compote
In a small saucepan over medium heat, mix the blueberries, sugar, and 1 tablespoon lemon juice and cook until the berries soften, burst, and release their juices, about 10 minutes. Set aside.

For the Bread
Heat oven to 350 degrees and grease a 5x9-inch loaf pan, mini loaf pans, or muffin tins.

In a large bowl, combine the sugar and lemon zest, stirring until the sugar starts to turn a bit yellow and is fragrant. Stir in the flour, baking powder, and salt.

In a medium bowl, whisk together the yogurt, milk, cooled melted butter, eggs, 2 tablespoons lemon juice, and vanilla extract. Add the wet ingredients to the dry ingredients and stir until just combined.

Add half the batter to prepared pans or baking tin. With a spoon, dollop the compote onto the batter, then cover with remaining batter, encasing the compote in the center. Use a knife, trussing needle, or chopstick to swirl the mixture until ribbons of fruit are incorporated throughout. Bake until a toothpick inserted into the center comes out clean, about 1 hour and 10 minutes for a traditional loaf pan, 40 minutes for mini loaf pans, or 20 minutes for muffins.

Remove bread from the oven and allow to cool on a wire rack for 20–30 minutes. Run a knife along the edges of the pan to loosen, then turn upside down and remove bread from the pan.

Salted Peanut Butter Rice Crispy Treats

Makes 12 bars

Growing up we would make Rice Krispies bars as an after-school snack (who didn't?). I wish I had known then about this sweetened condensed milk trick. It gives the bars a creamy texture and keeps them soft and ooey-gooey for days afterward. The traditional bars become dried out and hard (if they last that long). As a chocolate option, try substituting Nutella for the peanut butter—it's decadent and delicious with a pinch of flaky sea salt. This recipe was a huge hit when I made it on *The Jason Show*.

3 tablespoons unsalted butter

1 (14-ounce) can sweetened condensed milk

¼ cup peanut butter

1 (10-ounce) bag mini marshmallows

6 cups crispy rice cereal

1 teaspoon flaky sea salt (Maldon)

2 tablespoons crushed peanuts

Spray an 8-inch square baking dish with nonstick cooking spray.

Melt butter in a large pot over medium heat. Add sweetened condensed milk and peanut butter, stirring to combine. Bring the mixture to a simmer, stirring constantly. Add marshmallows and stir until melted. Remove from heat and add the rice cereal. Use a clean rubber spatula to stir until everything is well coated. Transfer the mixture to the prepared baking dish and press into an even layer. Combine the sea salt with the peanuts and sprinkle over the bars while still warm. Cool to room temperature before cutting and serving.

March

April

EASTER

April

For years, Kurt, Ellie, and I traveled southwest to Schuyler, Nebraska, for Easter. My mother-in-law, Dolores, had built a small Craftsman-style home in the farming town after she'd retired from the Houston Grand Opera. We'd always take the long way that ran along the Minnesota River, then down through the small Minnesota towns of St. James, Windom, and Worthington and into Iowa. We'd pass the largest ice cream plant in the world in Le Mars — Blue Bunny — then through Sioux City into Nebraska. Sometimes there'd still be a coating of snow on the ground, but often the tractors were out in the fields planting seed. Then we'd hit Schuyler with, at the time, the largest meatpacking plant in North America. Dolores lived a few blocks from this monstrosity. (During my pregnancy, the smell made me plug-my-nose nauseous.)

When Ellie was small, we decorated Easter Bunny cookies, frosted hot cross buns, and dyed and hid Easter eggs. After that, I would set Dolores's dining table with heirloom silverware, her best china, and crystal stemware on a linen tablecloth. She usually had some jelly beans or malted milk chocolate eggs in a little dish at each place setting. The traditional meal was mashed potatoes, roasted asparagus, and roasted leg of lamb with gravy and no mint jelly (thank goodness!).

Guests would sometimes join us in the early afternoon. This dining table would be filled with a few men scattered among some very strong women, not unlike Dolores herself. She'd grown up on a farm just outside Schuyler, where her mother was the town nurse and her father the sheriff. She went to a one-room schoolhouse that held all the children in the first eight grades, then moved to an aunt's house in town for high school. She left the small town to attend St. Olaf in Northfield, Minnesota, where she met her husband, Richard. She didn't finish college until twenty years later, and then received her master's degree in women's studies. She found a secretarial position at a nonprofit organization in St. Paul called the Schubert Club, which put on small classical music performances. She moved up from there to run the Saint Paul Chamber Orchestra, followed by the Houston Symphony. Then Richard died, but not before squandering all their savings on toys like boats, cars, and airplanes. Still, Dolores had management skills that would do her well in life. She was a strong woman who got started in her professional career in her early forties and worked well into her eighties. She settled back in Houston to avoid feeling like a "third wheel" if she hung around the Twin Cities after Richard's death. She became the managing director of the Houston

Grand Opera. Upon retirement, she was able to build her dream home and live comfortably for the rest of her years.

Also at the table was her mother, Edna, who'd grown up on a large farm in those days before electricity, cars, computers, and iPhones. Edna was the only one of three daughters to survive an influenza epidemic. Edna married Ernest, who became the sheriff, only to lose his job at the outset of World War II because of his German heritage. He joined the navy, and while he was stationed in San Diego Edna raised their two girls and at the same time trained to become a nurse. Ernest would die twenty years later, but by then Edna was the head nurse at the local hospital. They'd always kept their checking accounts separate, a practice almost unheard of in that day and age. Edna made her own money, enough to get her through when the farm struggled. She was a strong woman too.

Am I a strong woman? You bet! I come from a strong woman. My mom divorced when I was a teenager and, like many women who had been homemakers, entered the workforce to help support us. I watched as she searched for a job during a time of double-digit unemployment. Finally, she found a position at Dayton's department store, working forty hours a week at the Estée Lauder counter, where she sold makeup kits and perfumes and gave mini makeovers and tutorials. She really enjoyed that job, but it was challenging to be on her feet for eight hours a day. As a result of this trajectory, I inherited money issues. My mother instilled in me the belief that I should have my own income and rely only on myself for financial stability. Like Dolores and Edna, I maintain my own checking and savings accounts, have my own credit cards, and have always worked hard, sometimes excessively; much of my self-worth is predicated on my achievements in the workplace. As for my daughter, Ellie, my lesson for her has always been to be self-sufficient and not rely on the largesse of others. She's on her way.

So, back to Easter. Leg of lamb, mashed potatoes, green beans, creamed pearl onions, and hot cross buns. Of course the cross on the buns is a Christian symbol, but originally the buns were to celebrate the goddess Easter and the cross represented the four phases of the moon. Easter is also a celebration of renewal and fertility. I like to think of those past Easter suppers as a celebration of the strong women in my life who renewed and reinvented themselves. Dolores, Edna, Kathy, Cubbie, Stephanie, and so many of my extended lady friend groups, and my own mother, Anne. Throughout my life the women around me have been my compass.

181

April

Mason Jar Basil Lemonade

Serves 4

Lemonade is certainly the drink that makes me, and most others, think of summer. The problem is that in Minnesota, "Sometimes it snows in April," to quote our own music idol, Prince. Yes, in April we can get snow, but we can also get a reprieve, a false hint of summer — which is precisely why this basil lemonade recipe appears here. Making this lemonade is an ode to the warm season to come. If we just hang on, before too long every day will be a lemonade day!

1 lemon, rinsed and cut into chunks
¼ cup fresh basil
3 tablespoons granulated sugar
1½ cups water
1½ cups ice

Place the lemon pieces, basil, and sugar in a quart-size (32-ounce) mason jar. Seal and shake the jar for 30 seconds. Open the jar and muddle the ingredients to break down the mixture further. Add ice and water, seal and shake for 30 seconds more, and enjoy.

Optional:
Add 1½ ounces vodka, gin, or tequila for a cocktail.

Top with 2 ounces sparkling water for a mocktail.

Cheddar and Chive Shortbreads

Serves 12

I first made these shortbreads for a dinner party and called them crackers, but really they are more like savory cookies. Crumbly, buttery, and a bit salty, these delicious biscuits are great to serve with cocktails, olives, and a charcuterie board to get the evening started. I roll these and store the dough in waxed or parchment paper so I can slice and bake them fresh as the guests arrive.

- **5 ounces creamy cheese (Boursin), at room temperature**
- **¼ cup grated Parmesan cheese**
- **¼ cup shredded sharp white cheddar cheese**
- **4 tablespoons unsalted butter, at room temperature**
- **1 teaspoon kosher salt**
- **½ teaspoon black pepper**
- **1 large egg**
- **2 tablespoons chopped chives**
- **½ cup all-purpose flour**
- **½ cup white whole wheat flour**

In the bowl of a stand mixer fitted with the paddle attachment, combine creamy cheese, Parmesan, cheddar, butter, salt, and pepper and beat until just combined. Add egg and chives, then beat to combine. Add flours and mix on low speed until dough forms, about 4 minutes.

Divide the dough in half and shape each piece into a 6-inch log, 1½ inches in diameter. Wrap the logs tightly in plastic wrap and freeze until firm, about 1 hour.

Heat oven to 400 degrees and line 2 baking sheets with parchment paper.

Use a sharp knife to cut logs into quarter-inch-thick slices. Arrange about 1 inch apart on prepared baking sheets and bake for 15 minutes, until golden. Enjoy immediately or freeze for later.

April

Orzo Vegetable Bean Soup

Serves 8

This soup is full of spring vegetables and finished with heaping cups of orzo, cannellini beans, and chickpeas to make it extra hearty. Lemon gives it an added fresh kick.

1 tablespoon extra-virgin olive oil

1 medium onion, diced

1 medium carrot, peeled and diced

2 ribs celery, diced

3 cloves garlic, finely chopped

1 medium zucchini, diced

1 yellow squash, diced

1 teaspoon crushed red pepper flakes

1 teaspoon fresh thyme leaves

1 teaspoon dried oregano

8 cups vegetable or chicken broth

1 (14-ounce) can chickpeas, rinsed and drained

1 (14-ounce) can cannellini beans, rinsed and drained

1 cup dried orzo

juice of 1 lemon

2 cups roughly chopped kale

2 cups roughly chopped baby spinach

3 teaspoons kosher salt

2 teaspoons black pepper

¼ cup basil leaves, stems removed, stacked, rolled, and cut into thin strips

Heat the olive oil in a Dutch oven over medium heat and cook the onion, carrot, and celery for 5 minutes, until vegetables are softened and onion is translucent. Add the garlic, zucchini, and squash and cook for 2 minutes more. Stir in the red pepper flakes, thyme, and oregano and continue to cook for another minute. Add the broth, chickpeas, beans, and orzo. Stir to combine, bring to a boil, then lower the heat and simmer for 10 minutes, until the orzo is cooked. Stir in the lemon juice, kale, and spinach, and simmer for 1–2 minutes, until the kale wilts. Finish with salt and pepper and fresh basil.

Clam Chowder

Serves 6

When I was growing up, my family would go to the Red Lobster behind Southtown Mall in Bloomington for fancy lunches. I always ordered the clam chowder and dunked in their signature cheddar bay biscuits to get every creamy drop of soup. I love making this recipe in the middle of winter or early spring when I'm craving seafood. The sensory memory of those past lunches always puts a smile on my face.

- **4 slices bacon, chopped into half-inch pieces**
- **1 large onion, diced**
- **3 ribs celery, diced**
- **3 (6.5-ounce) cans minced clams**
- **1 (8-ounce) bottle clam juice**
- **5 cups diced potatoes (about 8 yellow potatoes)**
- **2 cups chicken broth**
- **2 cups heavy cream**
- **2 teaspoons kosher salt**
- **1 teaspoon black pepper**

In a large Dutch oven over medium heat, brown the bacon. Add onions and celery and cook until onions are translucent, about 5 minutes. Add clams and their juice, clam juice, potatoes, and broth and simmer until potatoes are soft, about 10–15 minutes. Stir in heavy cream, salt, and pepper.

Creamy Chicken Broccoli Soup

Serves 6

Sometimes my favorite soups are made even more delicious thanks to the garnish. That's the case with this creamy chicken and broccoli soup. The garnish not only elevates its visual appeal but also enhances the flavor.

Here are some garnish ideas that will complement any soup:

Croutons — for a crunchy contrast.

Fresh herbs — try chopped parsley, chives, or dill for a vibrant flavor.

Grated cheese — a sprinkle of sharp cheddar or Gruyère adds richness to the Parmesan called for here.

Dairy — a dollop of sour cream or Greek yogurt swirled into the soup can add tanginess and extra creaminess.

Lemon — a bit of freshly grated lemon zest or a squeeze of juice can brighten any soup.

1 tablespoon extra-virgin olive oil

1 medium onion, chopped

1 cup chopped carrots

1 cup chopped celery

3 cloves garlic, minced or grated

2 teaspoons kosher salt

1½ teaspoons ground thyme

1 teaspoon ground sage

1 teaspoon black pepper

4 cups broccoli florets and stems cut into half-inch pieces

2 cups shredded or cubed cooked chicken

6 cups chicken broth

1⅔ cups whole milk, divided

3 tablespoons all-purpose flour

3 tablespoons lemon juice

finely chopped parsley, for garnish

Parmesan cheese, for garnish

Heat the olive oil in a Dutch oven over medium heat. Add onions, carrots, celery, garlic, salt, thyme, sage, and pepper. Cook, stirring, until the vegetables soften and the onions are translucent, about 5 minutes. Stir in the broccoli and cook for another 5 minutes. Add chicken and chicken broth. Bring the mixture to a boil, then reduce to a simmer.

Whisk ¼ cup of milk and the flour in a small bowl until the flour is fully incorporated. Slowly add the rest of the milk to the slurry, stirring to combine, then stir the milk mixture into the soup until combined. Let the soup simmer, uncovered, for 10–15 minutes; it will thicken and reduce slightly. Stir in the lemon juice; taste and adjust seasonings. Serve each bowl with a sprinkle of fresh parsley and a tablespoon of grated Parmesan cheese.

April

Roasted Asparagus Quinoa Salad

Serves 8

We planted our first asparagus patch at the Ely Hilltop Garden about five years ago. It started with scraggly looking roots that, once they became established, are somehow the first thing in the garden to poke their way through the soil. Year after year, they return as the harbingers of spring. As the season progresses the asparagus plants produce tall, fernlike foliage and red berries. Asparagus is a perennial that can remain productive for twenty years or more. This herby, lemony quinoa salad is a perfect way to use those fresh new stalks. Pair with salmon fillets or roasted lamb chops for the first taste of spring.

1 pound asparagus, ends snapped off

3 tablespoons plus 1 teaspoon extra-virgin olive oil

salt

black pepper

1 cup uncooked quinoa

zest of 1 lemon

¼ cup lemon juice

2 cloves garlic, minced or grated

1 (14.5-ounce) can chickpeas, drained

⅔ cup crumbled feta cheese

2 tablespoons chopped fresh dill

2 tablespoons chopped parsley

1 tablespoon chopped mint

Heat oven to 425 degrees. Place the asparagus on a sheet pan. Toss with 1 teaspoon of the olive oil, season with salt and pepper, and roast for 12–14 minutes or until tender. Let cool for a few minutes, then cut asparagus into 1-inch pieces.

Meanwhile, in a small saucepan, combine quinoa with 2 cups water. Bring mixture to a boil over medium-high heat, then reduce heat to maintain a gentle simmer. Cook, uncovered, until the quinoa has absorbed all of the water, about 15 minutes. Cover and set aside until the quinoa has cooled to room temperature.

Combine the remaining 3 tablespoons olive oil, lemon zest, lemon juice, and garlic in a large bowl. Season with salt and pepper and whisk to combine. Add in chickpeas, feta, asparagus, and quinoa, tossing to combine. Finish by tossing in the fresh herbs and seasoning with more salt and pepper to taste.

Arugula, Parmesan, and Pine Nut Salad

Serves 4

We start eating this delicious salad as soon as the fresh arugula, the first lettuce at the Ely Hilltop Garden, appears. I love serving slices of medium-rare grilled ribeye beef over this salad. The natural peppery pop of the arugula and the tartness of the lemon enhance the meat's charcoal-grilled flavor.

1 tablespoon pine nuts

4 ounces arugula

2 tablespoons shaved Parmesan cheese

1 tablespoon extra-virgin olive oil

juice of 1 lemon

1 teaspoon kosher salt

½ teaspoon black pepper

In a small skillet over medium heat, gently toast the pine nuts, shaking the pan occasionally to prevent burn spots. It takes about 3 minutes, but watch carefully as they burn easily. Set aside.

Add arugula and Parmesan to a large salad bowl. Drizzle with olive oil and lemon juice, sprinkle with salt and pepper, and toss to combine. Add the pine nuts and toss again. Serve immediately.

April

Kathy's Cheesy Potatoes

Serves 8

We won the stepparent lottery when my dad married Kathy. We didn't know it then because we were ungrateful teenagers with attitudes, but Kathy has stood the test of time and all the challenges of three sassy lassies and has been a wonderful addition to our family. Kathy is a great grandma to our kids too. She never missed birthdays or special occasions and would drive eight hours to spend summer weekends with us in Ely, Minnesota. Ellie requests her delicious cheesy potatoes for holidays, and in recent years Kathy has brought extras just for Ellie, frozen in aluminum pans with preparation instructions written on the Press'n Seal. Our holidays wouldn't be complete without Kathy and her cheesy potatoes.

2 pounds frozen diced hash brown potatoes, thawed

1 (10.5-ounce) can condensed cream of chicken soup

1 cup (2 sticks) butter, melted, divided

2 cups shredded cheddar cheese

2 cups sour cream

½ cup chopped onion

1 teaspoon kosher salt

½ teaspoon black pepper

3 cups crushed crackers (Ritz)

Heat oven to 350 degrees. Grease a 9x13–inch pan.

In a large bowl, combine hash browns, soup, ½ cup melted butter, cheddar cheese, sour cream, onion, salt, and pepper, mixing well. Transfer the mixture to the prepared pan and press firmly with a spatula.

In a saucepan over medium heat, cook and stir the crushed crackers in the remaining ½ cup melted butter for 5 minutes. Sprinkle crumbs over the top of the casserole. Bake for 1½ hours. Let rest 5 minutes before serving.

Gluten-Free Ham and Cheese Egg Bake

April

Serves 8

Every home cook needs a scrumptious egg bake recipe in their arsenal of standby dishes: easy to make, perfect for feeding a crowd, and great for using up the dribs and drabs in your refrigerator. It's like a blank canvas; you can mix in anything you love — cheese, veggies, meats, herbs — and it all comes together in a fluffy, savory dish that's like an omelet, casserole, and quiche all rolled into one. I make this scrumptious egg bake with ham left over from our Easter dinner.

2 tablespoons unsalted butter, plus more for the baking dish

3 leeks (white parts only), diced

1 medium onion, diced

1 cup finely chopped cooked ham

12 large eggs

1 teaspoon kosher salt

1 teaspoon black pepper

1 teaspoon dry mustard

2 cups whole milk

1 cup half-and-half

2 cups shredded Swiss cheese, divided

¼ cup chopped chives

Heat oven to 350 degrees and grease a 9×13–inch baking dish.

Melt butter in a large skillet over medium heat. Add leeks and onions and cook, stirring, until tender, about 10 minutes. Add ham and cook 5 minutes more.

In a large bowl, beat eggs with salt, pepper, and dry mustard. Whisk in milk and half-and-half.

Transfer leeks and ham mixture to prepared baking dish. Top with 1 cup of the cheese. Pour egg mixture over the cheese, then sprinkle the remaining 1 cup cheese on top. Bake until gently set in the center, 50–55 minutes. If the top gets too brown, cover with foil.

Allow to rest on a wire rack for 5–10 minutes before serving or risk a room full of burned tongues. (It packs serious heat!) Top with chives and serve in squares or spoonfuls.

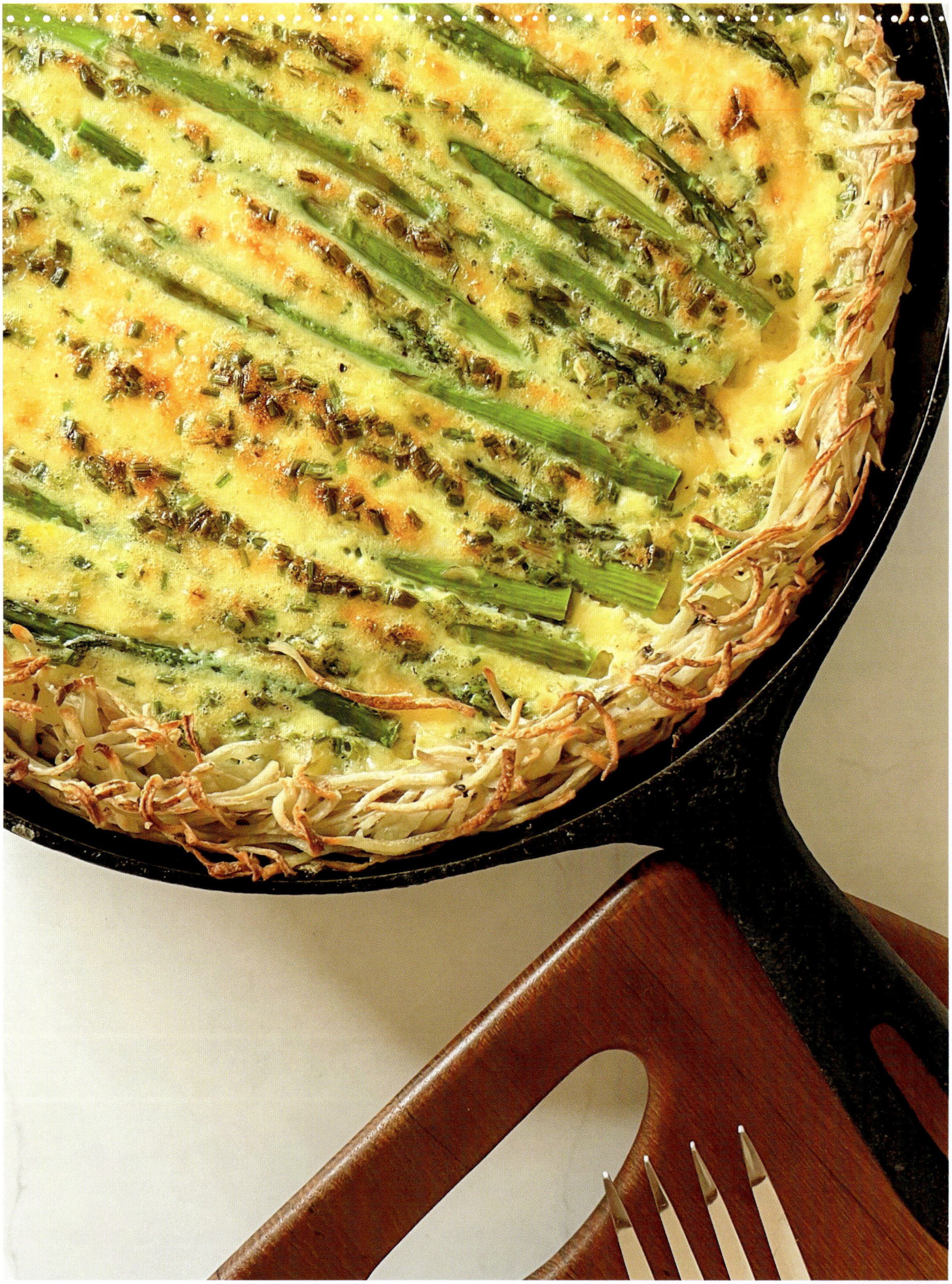

Asparagus Quiche with Hash Brown Crust

April

Serves 10-12

I first saw a hash brown crust on a quiche at a coffee shop in Minneapolis, and I recall thinking, *Brilliant: a gluten-free alternative to a traditional quiche crust*. I promptly tried it for our Easter brunch, and it tasted great and was a showstopper on the table. The key to getting the hash browns crispy is to press the potato strands firmly against the sides of the skillet so they can fry along all the edges.

4 medium russet potatoes (about 2 pounds), peeled

kosher salt

black pepper

2 tablespoons extra-virgin olive oil

4 tablespoons unsalted butter, divided

1 medium onion, diced

7 large eggs

1 cup heavy cream

½ cup whole milk

1 tablespoon finely chopped chives

1 teaspoon dry mustard

½ teaspoon garlic powder

1½ cups shredded Gruyère cheese

4 ounces goat cheese, crumbled

½ bunch asparagus (about 14 spears), ends trimmed to be about 2 inches shorter than the diameter of the pan

Heat oven to 400 degrees.

Shred potatoes using the grater disk on a food processor or the largest holes on a box grater. In a large bowl, toss the potatoes with 1 teaspoon salt and ½ teaspoon pepper. Transfer the potato shreds into a clean dish towel and wring out the excess liquid over the sink. Place potatoes in a bowl and set aside.

Heat oil and 2 tablespoons butter in a 10-inch cast iron skillet until the butter melts. Add potatoes and, using a ½ cup measure or juice glass with a flat bottom, immediately start forming a crust by pushing potatoes flat against the bottom and sides of the pan. Continue cooking, pressing potatoes up the sides of the pan until they are bound together and the bottom of the crust is beginning to brown, about 12 minutes. Remove pan from stovetop and place in the oven for 15 minutes to further crisp the crust. Set crust aside. Reduce oven temperature to 375 degrees.

Meanwhile, melt the remaining 2 tablespoons butter in another small skillet over medium heat. Add the onions and cook, stirring, until translucent, 5–6 minutes. Set aside.

In another large bowl, whisk eggs, cream, milk, chives, mustard, garlic powder, 1 teaspoon salt, and ½ teaspoon pepper until well combined.

Spread onions over the bottom of the crust, top with cheeses, and pour in the egg mixture. Arrange asparagus decoratively on top. Bake until the quiche is set and the crust is well browned, 35–40 minutes. Let cool to room temperature before cutting into wedges and serving from the pan. Alternatively, run a knife along the edges of the pan, invert the quiche onto a baking sheet, and flip it back over to serve on a pie plate or serving platter so all can admire the handiwork of your crust.

Crispy Skillet Hash Brown Cake with Kale Pesto

Serves 8

I love hash browns fried in an iron skillet, and kale pesto is the perfect sauce to adorn these delicious, crispy potatoes. This pesto recipe was another improvisation for kale when I had to find creative uses for my abundant Hilltop crop or winter CSA share. Of course, this combination topped with fried eggs would be ideal for breakfast or brunch, but it's also great served next to a ribeye cooked medium-rare.

Kale Pesto

- **2 cups packed kale leaves**
- **3 cloves garlic**
- **½ cup walnuts**
- **¼ cup extra-virgin olive oil**
- **1 tablespoon lemon juice**
- **2 teaspoons kosher salt**
- **1 teaspoon black pepper**

Hash Brown Cake

- **1 pound russet potatoes (about 4 medium potatoes), scrubbed**
- **1 large onion**
- **2 large eggs, lightly beaten**
- **⅓ cup panko breadcrumbs**
- **2 teaspoons kosher salt, plus more for sprinkling**
- **1 teaspoon black pepper**
- **1 teaspoon lemon zest**
- **¼ cup plus 2 tablespoons extra-virgin olive oil, divided**
- **sour cream for serving**

For the Kale Pesto

Combine kale, garlic, walnuts, ¼ cup olive oil, lemon juice, 2 teaspoons salt, and 1 teaspoon pepper in the bowl of a food processor and pulse, scraping down the sides. The pesto will not be completely smooth.

For the Hash Brown Cake

Heat oven to 475 degrees.

Grate unpeeled potatoes and onion on the large holes of a box grater. Place vegetable mixture on a clean towel and squeeze firmly over the sink to remove as much liquid as you can. Transfer the mixture to a large bowl. Add eggs, panko, 2 teaspoons salt, 1 teaspoon pepper, and lemon zest, stirring to combine.

Add ¼ cup olive oil to a 10-inch cast iron skillet and swirl to coat. Heat over medium-high until shimmering. Spoon potato mixture into the skillet. Using a metal spatula, press the mixture to cover the bottom of the skillet in an even layer. Lower the heat to medium and cook until the edges begin to brown, about 15 minutes.

Brush the top of the cake with the remaining 2 tablespoons oil. Transfer the pan to the oven and bake for 15 minutes, until the bottom is browned and the edges are crisp.

Switch the oven to broil on high, and broil until the top is golden brown in spots, 4–5 minutes. Remove from the oven and allow to cool for 5 minutes.

Run a knife along the edge of the pan to loosen the cake, then place a large plate on top of the skillet and invert to remove the cake. Sprinkle lightly with kosher salt. Top each piece of sliced cake with a dollop of kale pesto and sour cream.

195

April

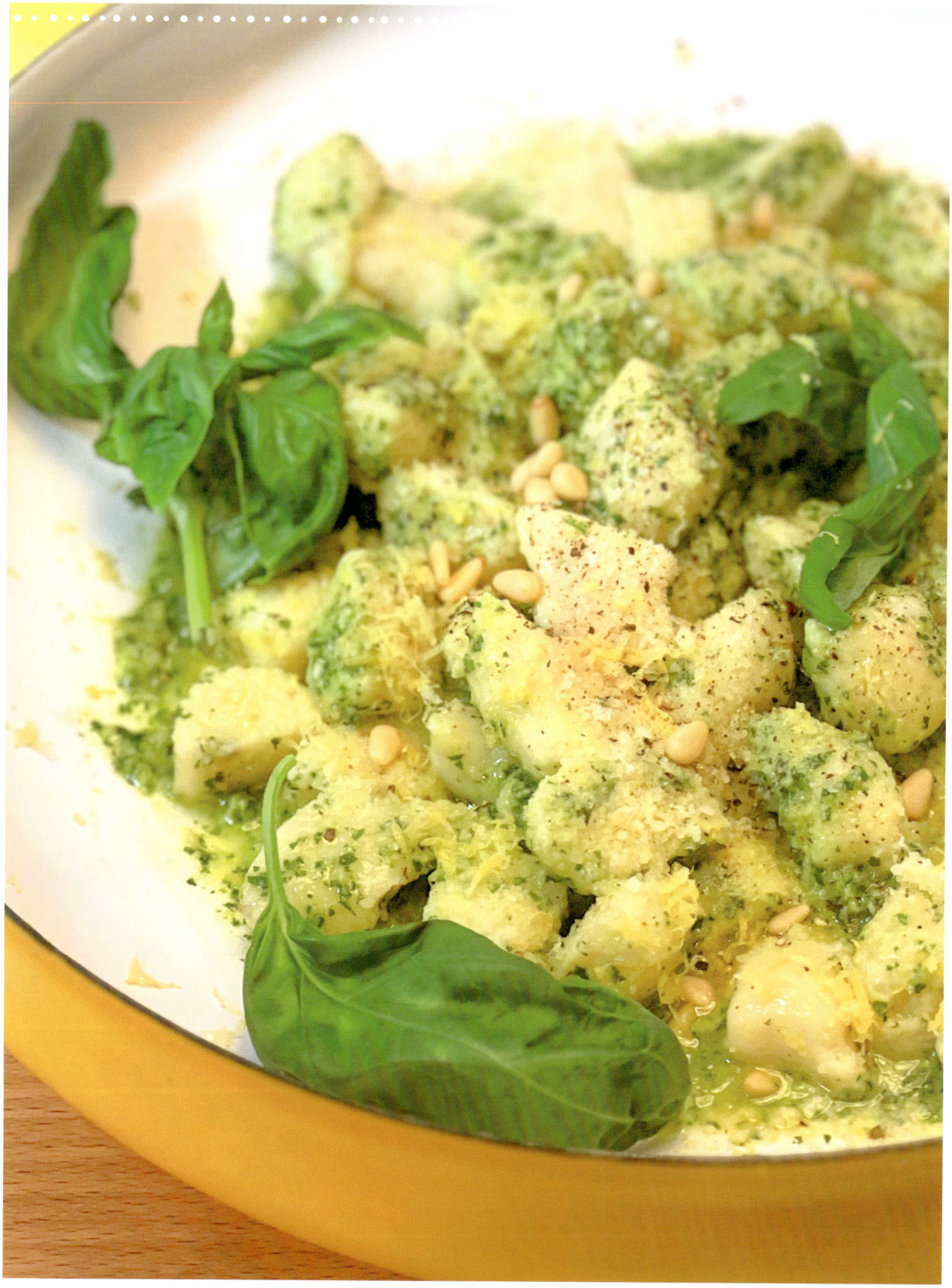

Gnocchi with Spring Pesto

Serves 4

I love making gnocchi in the spring, and it's not hard, I promise! It requires some practice to get the right texture, but the ingredients and process are simple. See tips below.

Pesto
- 1 cup tightly packed arugula
- 1 cup tightly packed herb leaves (a combination of parsley, basil, and about 6–8 mint leaves)
- 2 cloves garlic, minced or grated
- ⅓ cup grated Parmesan cheese
- ¼ cup walnuts, pine nuts, pecans, or almonds, lightly toasted
- 1 teaspoon kosher salt
- ½ cup extra-virgin olive oil

Gnocchi
- 2 pounds russet potatoes, scrubbed
- about 1 cup all-purpose flour
- 1 large egg, beaten
- 1½ tablespoons kosher salt
- Parmesan cheese, for garnish
- basil, for garnish

For the Pesto
Place arugula, herbs, garlic, Parmesan cheese, nuts, and salt in the bowl of a food processor. Pulse 5–7 times to combine. With the machine running, slowly add olive oil and process until the mixture is smooth. Set aside.

For the Gnocchi
Boil the potatoes, skin on, until tender, about 25 minutes. Drain and dry thoroughly.

When the potatoes are cool enough to handle but still warm, use a paring knife to peel. Grate the potatoes on a box grater. Set aside and let potatoes cool completely. You should have about 2½ cups of potato.

Mound the potatoes on a clean work surface and sprinkle with ¾ cup of the flour. Make a well in the center of the mound. Add egg and salt. Using a fork, incorporate the egg and salt into the potato–flour mixture until a shaggy dough forms. Sprinkle 2 tablespoons flour onto the dough and knead until smooth, about 2 minutes, pressing any loose flour into the dough. Roll the dough into a rope. If it falls apart, add a tablespoon more flour and try again.

Bring a large pot of salted water to a boil.

Divide the dough into 4 pieces, roll into ropes, and cut crosswise into 1-inch pieces. Working in batches, place gnocchi pieces in boiling water and cook until they puff up and float to the surface. Use a slotted spoon to remove the gnocchi from the water and set aside in a large bowl. Reserve ⅓ cup pasta water.

Add pesto to the gnocchi and toss gently. Add a bit of pasta water if needed to yield desired consistency. Taste and season with salt, pepper, Parmesan, and fresh torn basil.

TIPS: Choose starchy potatoes, like russets, and boil them whole with the skin on until tender. Keeping the skin on prevents the potatoes from absorbing too much water.

Once cooked, peel the potatoes and mash them while still warm. It's best to use a potato ricer or a fork to get a smooth texture without overworking the potatoes, which can make for gluey gnocchi.

Avoid overworking the dough, as it can become tough.

April

Roast Rack of Lamb

Serves 4

We usually have lamb for Easter, and then again for Memorial Day when we open the cabin and celebrate spring and the first signs of summer. People eat lamb at Easter because of its strong religious symbolism in both Christianity and Judaism, representing sacrifice, redemption, and renewal. I just think it tastes good accompanied by my Green Sauce (page 199). Serve the lamb atop a pile of grains or arugula dressed with lemon juice.

- **¼ cup extra-virgin olive oil**
- **4 cloves garlic**
- **1 cup lightly packed fresh herbs (parsley, thyme, rosemary, oregano, or basil)**
- **2 teaspoons lemon zest**
- **1 rack lamb**
- **2 teaspoons kosher salt**
- **1 teaspoon black pepper**

To the bowl of a small food processor, add the olive oil, garlic, herbs, and lemon zest and combine until everything is finely chopped. Season the lamb all over with salt and pepper. Rub lamb rack thoroughly with the marinade. Let the lamb marinate for up to 1 hour at room temperature.

Heat oven to 450 degrees. Arrange the lamb rack fat side up on a sheet pan. Place the sheet pan in the top third of the oven for 15 minutes. Flip the rack of lamb; return to the oven and cook for 5 more minutes for medium-rare.

Remove from the oven and let rest for 10 minutes. Cut the lamb chops in between the bones and arrange on a platter for serving.

Green Sauce

Makes about 1 cup

Everyone needs a good dipping sauce in their life. My green sauce finds its way into many dishes and onto many tables. Once you master this sauce, you will use it all the time.

Here are some suggestions:

- As a dip for veggies or pita bread
- Thinned out as a salad dressing
- Added to plain Greek yogurt as a base for chicken salad
- Dolloped onto a baked sweet potato
- As a base for potato salad, egg salad, or tuna salad
- Drizzled over roasted vegetables
- As a sauce for roasted salmon
- With fried fish instead of tartar sauce

2 jalapeños, stems and seeds removed, plus 1 jalapeño, stem removed but seeds intact, all three roughly chopped

3 cloves garlic, minced or grated

1 cup cilantro leaves

⅓ cup mayonnaise

¼ cup sour cream

¼ cup plain unsweetened Greek yogurt

juice of 1 lime

1 teaspoon white vinegar

1 teaspoon lemon juice

1 teaspoon kosher salt

pinch red pepper flakes

2 tablespoons extra-virgin olive oil

Add all ingredients except the olive oil to bowl of a food processor or blender and pulse to combine. Stop and scrape down the sides of the bowl, then continue processing until smooth. With the machine running, drizzle in the olive oil. Use the sauce right away or refrigerate. The chilled sauce will thicken; to thin, add buttermilk, lemon juice, or water and mix well.

April

Old Bay Crab Cakes with Mustard Sauce

Serves 4

I first had crab cakes and Old Bay Seasoning when I lived in Fell's Point in Baltimore. Old Bay is a popular and versatile spice blend that originated in the Chesapeake Bay area and is particularly known for its use in seafood dishes. Old Bay will always remind me of the spectacular crab cakes at Chart House in the Baltimore Inner Harbor where I worked. I also loved the peel-and-eat shrimp served at our neighborhood dive bar, John Steven Ltd. They'd dump a dozen large steamed shrimp drenched in Old Bay on a paper plate, with a side of cocktail sauce and a jumbo bottle of Tabasco alongside. I haven't been back to Baltimore in some time. Both restaurants are now closed, but my flavor memories live on.

Mustard Sauce

½ cup mayonnaise

3 tablespoons Dijon mustard

1 teaspoon lemon zest

1 tablespoon lemon juice

½ teaspoon kosher salt

pinch black pepper

pinch smoked paprika

Crab Cakes

¼ cup finely chopped onion

1 tablespoon finely chopped celery

1 tablespoon finely chopped green onion

1 cup mayonnaise

2 teaspoons seafood seasoning (Old Bay)

1 teaspoon chopped fresh tarragon

1 teaspoon Dijon mustard

1 large egg

2 cups crustless cubed white bread

1 pound jumbo lump crabmeat, drained of any liquid

For the Mustard Sauce

In a small bowl, combine mayonnaise, mustard, lemon zest, lemon juice, salt, pepper, and paprika until well mixed. Taste and adjust seasonings if needed.

For the Crab Cakes

Heat oven to 400 degrees. Prepare a sheet pan with cooking oil.

Whisk together the onion, celery, green onion, mayonnaise, seafood seasoning, tarragon, Dijon mustard, and egg to make a dressing.

In a large bowl, toss the bread with the dressing, mixing until the bread absorbs the dressing. Gently mix in the crab, being careful not to break up the larger pieces. The mixture should hold its shape when formed into a ball by hand. Divide the mixture into 8 crab cakes. Place the cakes on the prepared sheet pan. Bake until golden brown, about 10–12 minutes. Serve warm or at room temperature accompanied by the mustard sauce.

201

April

Baked Haddock with Buttered Breadcrumbs

Serves 6

Ina Garten, the Barefoot Contessa, loves to cook with haddock. It's a firm, mild, and flaky fish that soaks up the flavor of any accompanying sauce. Haddock also reminds me of my grandmother. For years, I spent weeks in the summer at her house in Waupaca, Wisconsin. A special treat was dinner at Simpson's Supper Club, where I'd always order the broiled haddock served with butter and slices of lemon. This treatment adds cracker crumbs, which soak up all that butter and give the dish a crispy, luscious bite.

- 2 tablespoons extra-virgin olive oil
- 6 (6- to 8-ounce) haddock fillets, skinned
- 2 teaspoons kosher salt
- 1 teaspoon black pepper
- ¾ cup (1½ sticks) unsalted butter
- 1½ cups cracker crumbs (saltines, Ritz, or Club)
- 1 teaspoon paprika
- zest of 1 lemon
- juice of 2 lemons
- ⅓ cup dry white wine
- 1 teaspoon hot sauce
- lemon wedges for serving

Heat oven to 400 degrees. Add the oil to a 9x13-inch baking dish and spread to cover the bottom of the pan. Place the fish fillets in the pan and sprinkle with salt and pepper. Bake for 10 minutes.

Meanwhile, melt the butter in a skillet.

In a small bowl, combine the cracker crumbs, paprika, and lemon zest. Moisten them with 3 tablespoons of the melted butter.

Remove the fish from the oven. Stir lemon juice, wine, and hot sauce into the remaining melted butter and then pour over the fillets. Pat the crumb mixture evenly onto the fillets, pressing gently to adhere. Return the pan to the oven for 10 minutes, until the fillets are just cooked through in the center. Sprinkle with salt and serve with the pan juices and lemon wedges.

Roasted Salmon with Lemon

Serves 4-6

A whole side of salmon can be simple and delicious to serve for dinner parties of four to eight people. This preparation looks lovely presented on a large platter garnished with citrus slices and fresh herbs. I like to serve it over a pile of perfectly cooked grains like millet, farro, rice, or herbed couscous.

1 clove garlic, minced or grated

3 tablespoons extra-virgin olive oil

1 tablespoon Dijon mustard

zest and juice of 1 lemon, plus 1 lemon, thinly sliced

1 teaspoon black pepper

1 teaspoon kosher salt

1 (3- to 5-pound) salmon fillet

fresh herbs, for garnish

lemon wedges, for garnish

Heat oven to 500 degrees. Line a sheet pan with foil or parchment paper.

Whisk together the garlic, olive oil, mustard, lemon zest, lemon juice, salt, and pepper. Place the salmon in the prepared pan and drizzle on the marinade; let sit for 15 minutes. Top with the lemon slices. Place the salmon in the oven and cook for 12 minutes or until the temperature on an instant-read thermometer reaches 125–135 degrees, depending on preferred level of doneness. Let rest for 15 minutes before serving. Garnish with herbs and lemon wedges.

April

Roasted Salmon Caesar

Serves 2

My husband Kurt's Caesar salad dressing (see page 135) is the best, and one batch makes enough for a large salad with plenty left over. The idea for this roasted salmon was inspired by the extra lemony, tangy Caesar dressing — an excellent topping for fish.

1 (6- to 8-ounce) salmon fillet
1 teaspoon kosher salt
1 teaspoon black pepper
¼ cup Caesar dressing (page 135)
1 tablespoon grated Parmesan cheese

Heat oven to 400 degrees. Line a large sheet pan with parchment paper, place the salmon on the pan, and sprinkle with salt and pepper. Spread Caesar dressing on the salmon fillet. Top with Parmesan cheese. Roast in the oven for 18–20 minutes, until the flesh becomes opaque and flakes easily with a fork.

Pan-Roasted Chicken Thighs with Roasted Grapes

Serves 4

Grapes in Minnesota are polarizing. We had to suffer through a disgrace when some national media outlet dubbed our most recognized state food as grape salad. Allow me to declare here and now: NO! Grape salad is NOT a beloved dish in Minnesota. We don't love it during the holidays, and we don't love it during potlucks. In fact, grape salad didn't originate in Minnesota, so who decided we needed to be the state that was saddled with this unpopular side dish?

But I digress. If you are going to use grapes in cooking, try a savory treatment like grapes pressed into focaccia, roasted alongside pork, or in this tasty chicken skillet dish. It's excellent with mashed potatoes.

1 tablespoon Dijon mustard

3 teaspoons kosher salt

2 teaspoons dried sage

1 teaspoon smoked paprika

1 teaspoon black pepper

6 boneless skin-on chicken thighs

1 tablespoon extra-virgin olive oil

4 small (or 2 large) shallots, sliced into rings

1 cup chicken broth

4 small clusters red grapes still attached to the stem, about ½ cup each

4 sprigs thyme

Heat oven to 425 degrees. In a medium bowl, stir together the mustard, salt, sage, paprika, and pepper. Toss the chicken thighs in the mixture, massaging to coat.

Heat a heavy-bottomed or cast iron pan on the stovetop over medium heat for 3 minutes. Add olive oil and heat until shimmering. Add the chicken thighs, skin side down, and cook, undisturbed, until golden brown and crispy, about 10 minutes. Flip each chicken thigh to be skin side up. Nestle the sliced shallots between the chicken pieces. Pour in the chicken broth and use a wooden spoon to scrape up any browned bits. Top with the grape clusters and thyme sprigs.

Transfer the pan to the oven and cook until the thickest part of each chicken thigh registers 185 degrees, about 15–20 minutes. Turn the broiler to high and broil for 2 minutes to get the grapes all nice and roasty. Remove the chicken from the oven and let rest for 5 minutes before serving.

Rhubarb Almond Bread

Serves 12

I love rhubarb, and while it doesn't usually show up in my garden until at least May, I couldn't resist putting this delicious bread in the book. In peak rhubarb season, I harvest from the two large rhubarb patches at my house and cabin. I also receive countless other rhubarb stalks from friends, family, and even TV show viewers who bring them to live events. I use this glorious bounty to make rhubarb shrubs, syrups, cookies, tarts, pies, and bars.

This simple quick bread is a great spring treat.

- 1½ cups all-purpose flour
- 2 teaspoons baking powder
- 1 teaspoon kosher salt
- 1 cup granulated sugar
- 1 tablespoon lemon zest
- ¾ cup full-fat Greek yogurt
- ½ cup vegetable oil
- 2 large eggs
- 1 teaspoon almond extract
- 1½ cups rhubarb chopped into quarter-inch pieces
- ¼ cup sliced almonds
- confectioners' sugar, optional

Heat oven to 350 degrees. Spray a 5x9-inch loaf pan with cooking spray.

In a medium bowl, whisk together flour, baking powder, and salt.

In a large bowl, mix sugar and lemon zest using your fingers, rubbing in the zest until well distributed. Then add the yogurt, oil, eggs, and almond extract, stirring to combine. Add the dry ingredients to the wet ingredients, mixing until just combined; fold in the rhubarb. Pour the batter into the prepared pan. Sprinkle the top with the sliced almonds. Bake for 55–60 minutes, until the top of the cake is golden brown and a toothpick inserted into the center comes out clean. Allow the bread to cool completely, then dust with confectioners' sugar if desired.

Gooey Butter Bars

Serves 12

This recipe came to me from a coworker at one of my first jobs, the *Twin Cities Reader*, where I wrote personal ads — the precursor to dating apps. My coworker made these ooey-gooey treats for one of our company potlucks. She claimed they originated in St. Louis, where her grandmother lived. I cannot confirm the origin, but if you're looking for love, maybe sweeten the deal with these Gooey Butter Bars.

- 2½ cups all-purpose flour
- 1½ cups granulated sugar
- 1 tablespoon baking powder
- ½ teaspoon kosher salt
- 5 large eggs
- ¾ cup (1½ sticks) butter, melted
- 8 ounces cream cheese, at room temperature
- 1 teaspoon vanilla extract
- 4 cups confectioners' sugar, plus more for serving

Heat oven to 350 degrees. Line a 9x13–inch pan with parchment paper and spray with nonstick cooking spray.

In the bowl of a stand mixer fitted with the paddle attachment, combine flour, sugar, baking powder, and salt. Add 2 eggs and melted butter; mix until well combined and crumbly. Transfer mixture to the prepared pan and press evenly to cover the bottom. Set aside. Wipe out the bowl for the next step.

Mix the cream cheese until smooth. Add 3 remaining eggs, 1 at a time, and mix until well blended. Stir in the vanilla. Gradually add the confectioners' sugar, mixing until well combined and smooth. Pour over the crust. Bake for 50 minutes or until golden brown.

Lift the cake out of the pan and cut into 12 generous bars. Sprinkle with sifted confectioners' sugar if desired.

April

Lemon Bars

Serves 12

My mother-in-law, Dolores, loves lemon bars. I make them for her in the spring when it feels like we're desperately craving light after the dark winter months. With their bright yellow color, lemon bars always feel cheerful. For added decoration, zest a lemon over the top or add dried or fresh edible flowers (pansies work well).

Crust
- 1 cup (2 sticks) unsalted butter, melted
- 2¼ cups all-purpose flour
- ½ cup granulated sugar
- 1 teaspoon kosher salt
- 2 teaspoons vanilla extract

Filling
- 2 cups granulated sugar
- ¼ cup plus 2 tablespoons all-purpose flour
- 6 large eggs
- zest of 2 lemons
- juice of 4 lemons
- ¼ cup confectioners' sugar for serving

For the Crust
Heat oven to 325 degrees. Line a 9x13–inch glass baking dish with parchment paper, leaving about an inch of overhang on all sides.

In a large bowl, mix the melted butter, flour, sugar, salt, and vanilla with a wooden spoon. Transfer the dough to the prepared pan and press firmly and evenly to create the crust. Bake for 25 minutes, until the edges are just starting to brown. Remove from the oven, and while the crust is still warm, use a fork to pierce it all over.

For the Filling
In a large bowl, mix the sugar and flour and whisk in the eggs, lemon zest, and lemon juice until completely combined. Pour the filling over the crust and bake for 25 minutes. Let cool in the pan for 2 hours, then use the parchment paper to carefully lift out the bars. Sprinkle with confectioners' sugar and cut into squares. Refrigerate or freeze bars if not serving right away.

April

Acknowledgments

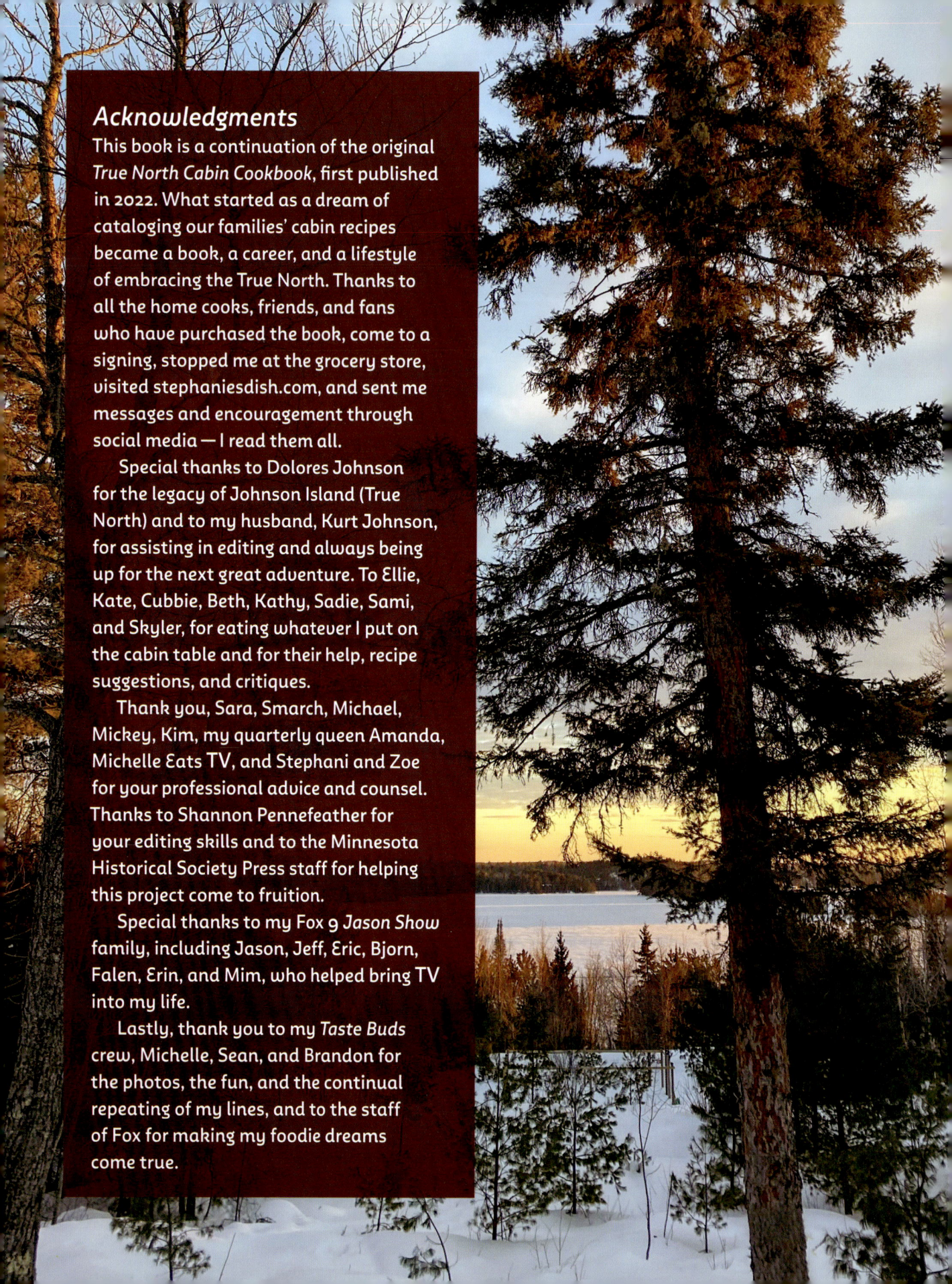

This book is a continuation of the original *True North Cabin Cookbook*, first published in 2022. What started as a dream of cataloging our families' cabin recipes became a book, a career, and a lifestyle of embracing the True North. Thanks to all the home cooks, friends, and fans who have purchased the book, come to a signing, stopped me at the grocery store, visited stephaniesdish.com, and sent me messages and encouragement through social media — I read them all.

Special thanks to Dolores Johnson for the legacy of Johnson Island (True North) and to my husband, Kurt Johnson, for assisting in editing and always being up for the next great adventure. To Ellie, Kate, Cubbie, Beth, Kathy, Sadie, Sami, and Skyler, for eating whatever I put on the cabin table and for their help, recipe suggestions, and critiques.

Thank you, Sara, Smarch, Michael, Mickey, Kim, my quarterly queen Amanda, Michelle Eats TV, and Stephani and Zoe for your professional advice and counsel. Thanks to Shannon Pennefeather for your editing skills and to the Minnesota Historical Society Press staff for helping this project come to fruition.

Special thanks to my Fox 9 *Jason Show* family, including Jason, Jeff, Eric, Bjorn, Falen, Erin, and Mim, who helped bring TV into my life.

Lastly, thank you to my *Taste Buds* crew, Michelle, Sean, and Brandon for the photos, the fun, and the continual repeating of my lines, and to the staff of Fox for making my foodie dreams come true.

INDEX

A

Aebleskivers, 84
apples: Apple Cider–Braised Lamb Shanks with Parmesan Risotto, 110–11; Apple Donut Cake, 36; Braised Red Cabbage with Apples, 17; Butternut Squash Soup with Crispy Prosciutto Croutons, 46; Double Potato Gratin with Apples and Onions, 19; Kale, Pomegranate, and Apple Salad with Roasted Pumpkin Seeds, 50; Salted Caramel Apple Bars, 34–35; Tarte Tatin, 37; Wild Rice Stuffing, 56
artichokes: Artichoke Dip, 99; Christmas Eve Cheesy Artichokes, 77
arugula: Arugula, Parmesan, and Pine Nut Salad, 189; Arugula and Wild Rice Salad with Pear Vinaigrette, 137; Arugula Clementine Salad with Dried Cherries, 102; Gnocchi with Spring Pesto, 197
Asian Pear Spinach Salad with Maple Pecans and Ginger Vinaigrette, 49
asparagus: Asparagus Quiche with Hash Brown Crust, 193; Roasted Asparagus Quinoa Salad, 188
Autumn Harvest Sheet Pan Roasted Veggies, 14
avocados: Arugula Clementine Salad with Dried Cherries, 102; Grilled Jerk Chicken with Coconut Rice and Mango Salsa, 168–69

B

bacon: Arugula and Wild Rice Salad with Pear Vinaigrette, 137; Bacon Vinaigrette, 103; Beer Cheese Wild Rice Soup, 129; Clam Chowder, 185; Fish Chowder with Bacon, 160; Oven-Baked Jalapeño Poppers, 128; Spinach Salad with Instant Pot Jammy Eggs and Bacon Vinaigrette, 103; Swedish Meatloaf with Brown Gravy, 118–19; Twice-Baked Potato Casserole, 163
Baked Brussels Sprouts with Lemon and Goat Cheese, 15
Baked Haddock with Buttered Breadcrumbs, 202
Baked Party Brie, 72
Banana Bread Cookies with Cream Cheese Frosting, 121
beans: Big Beefy Chili, 13; Buffalo Chicken Chili, 132; Mom's Chili Mac, 48; Orzo Vegetable Bean Soup, 184; Weeknight Enchilada Soup, 12
beef: Beef Barley Soup, 76; Big Beefy Chili, 13; Dill Pickle Pot Roast, 164; Gochujang Kimchi Meatloaf Muffins, 143; Hungarian Goulash with Horseradish, 140; Juicy Lucy Cheeseburger Tater Tot Hot Dish, 145; Lila's Swedish Meatballs with Gravy, 80; Mom's Chili Mac, 48; Mom's Meatloaf, 27; Old-School Beef Stroganoff, 114; Oven-Baked Corned Beef Brisket, 165; Pan-Seared Ribeye Steaks with Shallot Cream Sauce, 57; Reverse-Seared Prime Rib with Horseradish Cream, 82; Short Rib Bolognese, 26; Skillet Baked Ziti with Meatballs, 174; Swedish Meatloaf with Brown Gravy, 118–19
beer: Beer Cheese Wild Rice Soup, 129; Big Beefy Chili, 13; Buffalo Chicken Chili, 132; Short Rib Bolognese, 26
Beth's Chex Party Mix, 74
Beth's Spinach Dip, 98
beverages: Boozy Shamrock Shakes, 156; Cranberry French 75, 42–43; Cranberry Old-Fashioned, 69; Eggnog, 70; Homemade Irish Cream, 68; Mason Jar Basil Lemonade, 182; Pomegranate Old-Fashioned, 43; Pumpkin Spice Cream, 8; Pumpkin Spice Espresso Martini, 9; Thanksgiving Punch, 44
Big Beefy Chili, 13
biscuits: Chicken and Biscuits, 166; Herb Drop Biscuits, 11
Blueberry-Lemon Bread, 176
Boozy Shamrock Shakes, 156
bourbon: Eggnog, 70; Gluten-Free Bourbon Brownies, 150
Braised Red Cabbage with Apples, 17
breads: Biscuits, 166; Blueberry-Lemon Bread, 176; Cowboy Bread, 175; Easiest From-Scratch Focaccia, 133; Easy Shortcut Focaccia, 134; Irish Soda Bread, 162; Popovers with Honey Butter, 83; Rhubarb Almond Bread, 206
breakfasts: Aebleskivers, 84; Eggnog Croissant Christmas Casserole, 85; Savory Sausage Breakfast Bread Pudding, 86
Brie, Baked Party, 72
broccoli: Broccoli Cheese Soup, 131; Creamy Chicken Broccoli Soup, 186
Broiled Scallops à la Simpson's with Oven-Baked Lemon Risotto, 104–5
brussels sprouts: Autumn Harvest Sheet Pan Roasted Veggies, 14; Baked Brussels Sprouts with Lemon and Goat Cheese, 15; Brussels Sprouts and Butternut Squash Salad with Tahini Vinaigrette, 136; Roasted Brussels Sprouts Caesar Salad, 135; Roasted Brussels Sprouts with Pomegranate Seeds, 55
Buffalo Chicken Chili, 132
Butternut Squash Soup with Crispy Prosciutto Croutons, 46

C

cabbage: Braised Red Cabbage with Apples, 17; Cabbage Almond Pasta with Toasted Breadcrumbs, 120; Dill Pickle and Ham Soup, 161; Grandma's Scalloped Cabbage, 138; Sesame Almond Chicken Salad, 51
Caesar Dressing, 135
Cajun Shrimp Pasta, 170
Caramels, Cookie Exchange Salted, 92
carrots: Autumn Harvest Sheet Pan Roasted Veggies, 14; Beef Barley Soup, 76; Broccoli Cheese Soup, 131; Butternut Squash Soup with Crispy Prosciutto Croutons, 46; Chicken and Biscuits, 166; Creamy Chicken Broccoli Soup, 186; Dill Pickle and Ham Soup, 161; Gochujang Kimchi Meatloaf Muffins, 143; Ham Hock and Split Pea Soup, 75; Hungarian Goulash with Horseradish, 140; Lentil and Sausage Stew with Spinach and Lemon, 112; Orzo Vegetable Bean Soup, 184; Roast Chicken with Autumn Vegetables, 24–25;

Roasted Carrot Hummus, 45; Short Rib Bolognese, 26; Thai Pork Noodle Goulash, 115; Thanksgiving Leftovers Turkey Wild Rice Soup, 47

Cheddar and Chive Shortbreads, 183

cheese, cheddar: Beer Cheese Wild Rice Soup, 129; Broccoli Cheese Soup, 131; Cheddar and Chive Shortbreads, 183; Grandma's Scalloped Cabbage, 138; Hot Pickle Dip, 126; Juicy Lucy Cheeseburger Tater Tot Hot Dish, 145; Kathy's Cheesy Potatoes, 190; Mom's Chili Mac, 48; Oven-Baked Jalapeño Poppers, 128; Pork Shoulder Ragu with Cheesy Polenta, 117; Twice-Baked Potato Casserole, 163

cheese, feta: Kale, Pomegranate, and Apple Salad with Roasted Pumpkin Seeds, 50; Roasted Asparagus Quinoa Salad, 188

cheese, goat: Artichoke Dip, 99; Asparagus Quiche with Hash Brown Crust, 193; Baked Brussels Sprouts with Lemon and Goat Cheese, 15; Brussels Sprouts and Butternut Squash Salad with Tahini Vinaigrette, 136; Cheesy Sausage Lasagna, 106; Eggnog Croissant Christmas Casserole, 85; Herb Drop Biscuits, 11; Hot Pickle Dip, 126; Oven-Baked Jalapeño Poppers, 128

cheese, Gruyère: Asparagus Quiche with Hash Brown Crust, 193; Gruyère Puff Pastry with Sun-Dried Tomatoes, 73; Scalloped Potatoes with Gruyère Cheese, 78; Stuffed Chicken Breasts, 108–9; Twice-Baked Potato Casserole, 163

cheese, mozzarella: Cheesy Sausage Lasagna, 106; Hot Pickle Dip, 126; Skillet Baked Ziti with Meatballs, 174

cheese, ricotta: Cheesy Sausage Lasagna, 106; Lila's Swedish Meatballs with Gravy, 80; One-Pot Turkey Meatballs with Lemon Orzo, 172–73; Swedish Meatloaf with Brown Gravy, 118–19

Cheesy Sausage Lasagna, 106

cherries, dried: Arugula Clementine Salad with Dried Cherries, 102; Brussels Sprouts and Butternut Squash Salad with Tahini Vinaigrette, 136

Cherries in the Snow, 90

Chex Party Mix, Beth's, 74

chicken: Buffalo Chicken Chili, 132; Chicken and Biscuits, 166; Creamy Chicken Broccoli Soup, 186; Grilled Jerk Chicken with Coconut Rice and Mango Salsa, 168–69; Heavenly Chicken and Rice, 107; Oven-Baked Chicken Wings, 127; Pan-Roasted Chicken Thighs with Roasted Grapes, 205; Roast Chicken with Autumn Vegetables, 24–25; Sesame Almond Chicken Salad, 51; Sheet Pan Shawarma Two Ways, 22–23; Spicy Chicken Sausage and Sweet Potato Soup, 130; Stuffed Chicken Breasts, 108–9; Thai Chicken Rice Soup, 100

chickpeas: Orzo Vegetable Bean Soup, 184; Roasted Asparagus Quinoa Salad, 188; Roasted Carrot Hummus, 45; Sheet Pan Shawarma Two Ways, 22–23

Chili, Big Beefy, 13

chocolate: Gluten-Free Bourbon Brownies, 150; Mom's Toffee Bars, 88; Pumpkin Dark Chocolate Snack Cake, 29

Christmas Eve Cheesy Artichokes, 77

clams: Clam Chowder, 185; Linguine and Clam Sauce, 171

Clementine Salad with Dried Cherries, Arugula, 102

Coconut Curry Soup with Salmon, 159

Cookie Exchange Salted Caramels, 92

cookies: Banana Bread Cookies with Cream Cheese Frosting, 121; Easiest Roll-Out Sugar Cookies, 89; Ginger Molasses Cookies, 91

corn: Creamed Corn, 79; Weeknight Enchilada Soup, 12

Corned Beef Brisket, Oven-Baked, 165

Cowboy Bread, 175

Crab Cakes with Mustard Sauce, Old Bay, 200

cranberries: Cranberry French 75, 42–43; Cranberry Old-Fashioned, 69; Cranberry Orange Bread, 87; Cranberry Orange Sauce, 58; cranberry simple syrup, 43; Cranberry Wild Rice Salad with Candied Pecans and Bitter Greens, 52–53; Thanksgiving Punch, 44; Wild Rice Stuffing, 56

cream cheese: Artichoke Dip, 99; Banana Bread Cookies with Cream Cheese Frosting, 121; Cherries in the Snow, 90; Christmas Eve Cheesy Artichokes, 77; Cream Cheese Frosting, 121; Gooey Butter Bars, 207; Hot Pickle Dip, 126; Oven-Baked Jalapeño Poppers, 128; Pumpkin Bars with Cream Cheese Frosting, 61; Pumpkin Cheesecake, 62–63

Creamed Corn, 79

Creamy Chicken Broccoli Soup, 186

Creamy Lemon Pasta with Crispy Breadcrumbs, 146

Crispy Skillet Hash Brown Cake with Kale Pesto, 194

Curried Pumpkin Soup, 10

D desserts: Apple Donut Cake, 36; Banana Bread Cookies with Cream Cheese Frosting, 121; Cherries in the Snow, 90; Cowboy Bread, 175; Easiest Roll-Out Sugar Cookies, 89; Ginger Molasses Cookies, 91; Gluten-Free Bourbon Brownies, 150; Gooey Butter Bars, 207; Lemon Bars, 208; Mom's Toffee Bars, 88; Orange Madeleines, 149; Pecan Bars, 59; Pumpkin Bars with Cream Cheese Frosting, 61; Pumpkin Cheesecake, 62–63; Pumpkin Dark Chocolate Snack Cake, 29; Pumpkin Pudding, aka Crustless Pumpkin Pie, 60; Pumpkin Snickerdoodle Cookies, 33; Salted Caramel Apple Bars, 34–35; Salted Peanut Butter Rice Crispy Treats, 177; Tarte Tatin, 37

Dill Pickle and Ham Soup, 161

Dill Pickle Pot Roast, 164

dips: Artichoke Dip, 99; Beth's Spinach Dip, 98; Hot Pickle Dip, 126; Roasted Carrot Hummus, 45

Double Potato Gratin with Apples and Onions, 19

dressings/vinaigrettes: Bacon Vinaigrette, 103; Caesar Dressing, 135; Ginger Vinaigrette, 49; Pear Vinaigrette, 137; Tahini Vinaigrette, 136

E Easiest From-Scratch Focaccia, 133

Easiest Roll-Out Sugar Cookies, 89

Easy Shortcut Focaccia, 134

Eggnog, 70

Eggnog Croissant Christmas Casserole, 85

F Fish Chowder with Bacon, 160

Focaccia, Easiest From-Scratch, 133

Focaccia, Easy Shortcut, 134

G
Ginger Molasses Cookies, 91
Ginger Vinaigrette, 49
Gluten-Free Bourbon Brownies, 150
Gluten-Free Ham and Cheese Egg Bake, 191
Gnocchi with Spring Pesto, 197
Gochujang Kimchi Meatloaf Muffins, 143
Gooey Butter Bars, 207
Grandma's Scalloped Cabbage, 138
Gravy, Brown, 118–19
Green Sauce, 199
Grilled Jerk Chicken with Coconut Rice and Mango Salsa, 168–69
Ground Turkey Red Curry, 142
Gruyère Puff Pastry with Sun-Dried Tomatoes, 73

H
Haddock with Buttered Breadcrumbs, Baked, 202
ham: Dill Pickle and Ham Soup, 161; Gluten-Free Ham and Cheese Egg Bake, 191; Ham Hock and Split Pea Soup, 75
Heavenly Chicken and Rice, 107
Herb Drop Biscuits, 11
Homemade Irish Cream, 68
Horseradish Cream, 82
Hot Pickle Dip, 126
Hummus, Roasted Carrot, 45
Hungarian Goulash with Horseradish, 140

I
Irish Soda Bread, 162
Italian Sausage Soup, 101

J
Juicy Lucy Cheeseburger Tater Tot Hot Dish, 145

K
kale: Cheesy Sausage Lasagna, 106; Coconut Curry Soup with Salmon, 159; Cranberry Wild Rice Salad with Candied Pecans and Bitter Greens, 52–53; Crispy Skillet Hash Brown Cake with Kale Pesto, 194; Kale, Pomegranate, and Apple Salad with Roasted Pumpkin Seeds, 50; Kale Pesto, 194; Orzo Vegetable Bean Soup, 184; Skillet Shells with Sausage, Ricotta, and Greens, 20; Spicy Chicken Sausage and Sweet Potato Soup, 130
Kathy's Cheesy Potatoes, 190
Kimchi Meatloaf Muffins, Gochujang, 143

L
lamb: Apple Cider–Braised Lamb Shanks with Parmesan Risotto, 110–11; Roast Rack of Lamb, 198
Lasagna, Cheesy Sausage, 106
leeks: Cabbage Almond Pasta with Toasted Breadcrumbs, 120; Gluten-Free Ham and Cheese Egg Bake, 191
Lemon Bars, 208
lemongrass: Coconut Curry Soup with Salmon, 159; Thai Chicken Rice Soup, 100; Thai Pork Noodle Goulash, 115; Thai Winter Squash Soup, 158
Lentil and Sausage Stew with Spinach and Lemon, 112
Lila's Swedish Meatballs with Gravy, 80
Linguine and Clam Sauce, 171

M
Mac, Mom's Chili, 48
Mango Salsa, Grilled Jerk Chicken with Coconut Rice and, 168–69
Maple Pecans, 49
Maple Roasted Butternut Squash with Sage Browned Butter, 16
Marry Me One-Pot Shrimp, 148
marshmallows: Cherries in the Snow, 90; Salted Peanut Butter Rice Crispy Treats, 177
Mason Jar Basil Lemonade, 182
Miso Mashed Potatoes with Horseradish, 139
Mom's Chili Mac, 48
Mom's Meatloaf, 27
Mom's Oven Barbecue Spare Ribs, 113
Mom's Toffee Bars, 88
mushrooms: Beer Cheese Wild Rice Soup, 129; Coconut Curry Soup with Salmon, 159; Heavenly Chicken and Rice, 107; Old-School Beef Stroganoff, 114
Mustard Sauce, 200

N
nuts: Beth's Chex Party Mix, 74; Gnocchi with Spring Pesto, 197; Spiced Nuts, 71

O
Old Bay Crab Cakes with Mustard Sauce, 200
Old-School Beef Stroganoff, 114
One-Pot Turkey Meatballs with Lemon Orzo, 172–73
Orange Madeleines, 149
orzo: One-Pot Turkey Meatballs with Lemon Orzo, 172–73; Orzo Vegetable Bean Soup, 184
Oven-Baked Chicken Wings, 127
Oven-Baked Corned Beef Brisket, 165
Oven-Baked Jalapeño Poppers, 128

P
Pan-Roasted Chicken Thighs with Roasted Grapes, 205
Pan-Seared Ribeye Steaks with Shallot Cream Sauce, 57
parsnips: Autumn Harvest Sheet Pan Roasted Veggies, 14; Roast Chicken with Autumn Vegetables, 24–25
pasta dishes: Cabbage Almond Pasta with Toasted Breadcrumbs, 120; Cajun Shrimp Pasta, 170; Cheesy Sausage Lasagna, 106; Creamy Lemon Pasta with Crispy Breadcrumbs, 146; Italian Sausage Soup, 101; Linguine and Clam Sauce, 171; Marry Me One-Pot Shrimp, 148; Mom's Chili Mac, 48; Old-School Beef Stroganoff, 114; Short Rib Bolognese, 26; Skillet Baked Ziti with Meatballs, 174; Skillet Shells with Sausage, Ricotta, and Greens, 20; Thai Pork Noodle Goulash, 115
pears: Arugula and Wild Rice Salad with Pear Vinaigrette, 137; Asian Pear Spinach Salad with Maple Pecans and Ginger Vinaigrette, 49
pecans: Asian Pear Spinach Salad with Maple Pecans and Ginger Vinaigrette, 49; Cranberry Wild Rice Salad with Candied Pecans and Bitter Greens, 52–53; Pecan Bars, 59
pepperoncini: Dill Pickle Pot Roast, 164; Hot Pickle Dip, 126
peppers, bell: Big Beefy Chili, 13; Buffalo Chicken Chili, 132; Cajun Shrimp Pasta, 170; Italian Sausage Soup, 101; Lentil and Sausage Stew with Spinach and Lemon, 112; Mom's Chili Mac, 48; Sheet Pan Shawarma Two Ways, 22–23; Thai Chicken Rice Soup, 100
peppers, jalapeño: Big Beefy Chili, 13; Green Sauce, 199; Grilled Jerk Chicken with Coconut Rice and Mango Salsa, 168–69; Oven-Baked Jalapeño Poppers, 128; Thai

213

Index

Chicken Rice Soup, 100; Thai Winter Squash Soup, 158
peppers, poblano, Weeknight Enchilada Soup, 12
Pesto, Kale, 194
Pesto, Spring, 197
pickles, dill: Dill Pickle and Ham Soup, 161; Dill Pickle Pot Roast, 164; Hot Pickle Dip, 126; Juicy Lucy Cheeseburger Tater Tot Hot Dish, 145
Polenta, Pork Shoulder Ragu with Cheesy, 117
pomegranate seeds: Kale, Pomegranate, and Apple Salad with Roasted Pumpkin Seeds, 50; Pomegranate Old-Fashioned, 43; Roasted Brussels Sprouts with Pomegranate Seeds, 55; Thanksgiving Punch, 44
Popovers with Honey Butter, 83
pork: Gochujang Kimchi Meatloaf Muffins, 143; Lentil and Sausage Stew with Spinach and Lemon, 112; Lila's Swedish Meatballs with Gravy, 80; Mom's Meatloaf, 27; Mom's Oven Barbecue Spare Ribs, 113; Pork Chop and Scalloped Potato Casserole, 28; Pork Shoulder Ragu with Cheesy Polenta, 117; Savory Sausage Breakfast Bread Pudding, 86; Skillet Baked Ziti with Meatballs, 174; Thai Pork Noodle Goulash, 115; Thai Winter Squash Soup, 158
potatoes: Asparagus Quiche with Hash Brown Crust, 193; Autumn Harvest Sheet Pan Roasted Veggies, 14; Clam Chowder, 185; Crispy Skillet Hash Brown Cake with Kale Pesto, 194; Dill Pickle and Ham Soup, 161; Double Potato Gratin with Apples and Onions, 19; Fish Chowder with Bacon, 160; Gnocchi with Spring Pesto, 197; Kathy's Cheesy Potatoes, 190; Miso Mashed Potatoes with Horseradish, 139; Pork Chop and Scalloped Potato Casserole, 28; Roast Chicken with Autumn Vegetables, 24–25; Scalloped Potatoes with Gruyère Cheese, 78; Twice-Baked Potato Casserole, 163
prosciutto: Butternut Squash Soup with Crispy Prosciutto Croutons, 46; Maple Roasted Butternut Squash with Sage Browned Butter, 16
puff pastry: Gruyère Puff Pastry with Sun-Dried Tomatoes, 73; Tarte Tatin, 37

pumpkin puree: Big Beefy Chili, 13; Curried Pumpkin Soup, 10; Pumpkin Bars with Cream Cheese Frosting, 61; Pumpkin Cheesecake, 62–63; Pumpkin Dark Chocolate Snack Cake, 29; Pumpkin Muffins, 31; Pumpkin Pudding, aka Crustless Pumpkin Pie, 60; Pumpkin Snickerdoodle Cookies, 33; Pumpkin Spice Cream, 8; Pumpkin Spice Espresso Martini, 9

Q

Quinoa Salad, Roasted Asparagus, 188

R

Reverse-Seared Prime Rib with Horseradish Cream, 82
Rhubarb Almond Bread, 206
ribs: Mom's Oven Barbecue Spare Ribs, 113; Reverse-Seared Prime Rib with Horseradish Cream, 82; Ribeye Steaks with Shallot Cream Sauce, Pan-Seared, 57; Short Rib Bolognese, 26
rice: Apple Cider–Braised Lamb Shanks with Parmesan Risotto, 110–11; Broiled Scallops à la Simpson's with Oven-Baked Lemon Risotto, 104–5; Grilled Jerk Chicken with Coconut Rice and Mango Salsa, 168–69; Heavenly Chicken and Rice, 107; Stuffed Chicken Breasts, 108–9; Thai Chicken Rice Soup, 100
Rice Crispy Treats, Salted Peanut Butter, 177
ricotta cheese: Cheesy Sausage Lasagna, 106; Lila's Swedish Meatballs with Gravy, 80; One-Pot Turkey Meatballs with Lemon Orzo, 172–73; Swedish Meatloaf with Brown Gravy, 118–19
Roast Chicken with Autumn Vegetables, 24–25
Roasted Asparagus Quinoa Salad, 188
Roasted Brussels Sprouts Caesar Salad, 135
Roasted Brussels Sprouts with Pomegranate Seeds, 55
Roasted Carrot Hummus, 45
Roasted Parmesan Delicata Squash, 54
Roasted Salmon Caesar, 204
Roasted Salmon with Lemon, 203
Roast Rack of Lamb, 198

S

salads: Arugula and Wild Rice Salad with Pear Vinaigrette, 137; Arugula Clementine Salad with Dried Cherries, 102; Asian Pear Spinach Salad with Maple Pecans and Ginger Vinaigrette, 49; Brussels Sprouts and Butternut Squash Salad with Tahini Vinaigrette, 136; Cranberry Wild Rice Salad with Candied Pecans and Bitter Greens, 52–53; Kale, Pomegranate, and Apple Salad with Roasted Pumpkin Seeds, 50; Roasted Asparagus Quinoa Salad, 188; Roasted Brussels Sprouts Caesar Salad, 135; Roasted Salmon Caesar, 204; Sesame Almond Chicken Salad, 51; Spinach Salad with Instant Pot Jammy Eggs and Bacon Vinaigrette, 103
salmon: Coconut Curry Soup with Salmon, 159; Roasted Salmon Caesar, 204; Roasted Salmon with Lemon, 203
Salted Caramel Apple Bars, 34–35
Salted Peanut Butter Rice Crispy Treats, 177
sauces: Cranberry Orange Sauce, 58; Gravy, 80; Green Sauce, 199; Mustard Sauce, 200; Shallot Cream Sauce, 57; Tahini Sauce, 22–23
sausage: Cheesy Sausage Lasagna, 106; Italian Sausage Soup, 101; Skillet Shells with Sausage, Ricotta, and Greens, 20; Spicy Chicken Sausage and Sweet Potato Soup, 130
Savory Sausage Breakfast Bread Pudding, 86
Scalloped Potatoes with Gruyère Cheese, 78
Scallops à la Simpson's with Oven-Baked Lemon Risotto, Broiled, 104–5
seafood: Baked Haddock with Buttered Breadcrumbs, 202; Broiled Scallops à la Simpson's with Oven-Baked Lemon Risotto, 104–5; Cajun Shrimp Pasta, 170; Clam Chowder, 185; Coconut Curry Soup with Salmon, 159; Fish Chowder with Bacon, 160; Marry Me One-Pot Shrimp, 148; Old Bay Crab Cakes with Mustard Sauce, 200; Tuna Pâté, 157
Sesame Almond Chicken Salad, 51
Shallot Cream Sauce, 57

Sheet Pan Roasted Veggies, Autumn Harvest, 14
Sheet Pan Shawarma Two Ways, 22–23
Short Rib Bolognese, 26
shrimp: Cajun Shrimp Pasta, 170; Marry Me One-Pot Shrimp, 148
Skillet Baked Ziti with Meatballs, 174
Skillet Shells with Sausage, Ricotta, and Greens, 20
snacks: Aebleskivers, 84; Blueberry-Lemon Bread, 176; Cheddar and Chive Shortbreads, 183; Cowboy Bread, 175; Oven-Baked Jalapeño Poppers, 128; Rhubarb Almond Bread, 206; Spiced Nuts, 71
soups/stews: Beer Cheese Wild Rice Soup, 129; Big Beefy Chili, 13; Broccoli Cheese Soup, 131; Buffalo Chicken Chili, 132; Butternut Squash Soup with Crispy Prosciutto Croutons, 46; Clam Chowder, 185; Coconut Curry Soup with Salmon, 159; Creamy Chicken Broccoli Soup, 186; Curried Pumpkin Soup, 10; Dill Pickle and Ham Soup, 161; Fish Chowder with Bacon, 160; Ham Hock and Split Pea Soup, 75; Hungarian Goulash with Horseradish, 140; Italian Sausage Soup, 101; Lentil and Sausage Stew with Spinach and Lemon, 112; Mom's Chili Mac, 48; Orzo Vegetable Bean Soup, 184; Spicy Chicken Sausage and Sweet Potato Soup, 130; Thai Chicken Rice Soup, 100; Thai Winter Squash Soup, 158; Weeknight Enchilada Soup, 12
spaghetti: Cabbage Almond Pasta with Toasted Breadcrumbs, 120; Cajun Shrimp Pasta, 170; Creamy Lemon Pasta with Crispy Breadcrumbs, 146
Spiced Nuts, 71
Spicy Chicken Sausage and Sweet Potato Soup, 130
spinach: Asian Pear Spinach Salad with Maple Pecans and Ginger Vinaigrette, 49; Beth's Spinach Dip, 98; Brussels Sprouts and Butternut Squash Salad with Tahini Vinaigrette, 136; Ground Turkey Red Curry, 142; Italian Sausage Soup, 101; Lentil and Sausage Stew with Spinach and Lemon, 112; Marry Me One-Pot Shrimp, 148; One-Pot Turkey Meatballs with Lemon Orzo, 172–73; Orzo Vegetable Bean Soup, 184; Skillet Shells with Sausage, Ricotta, and Greens, 20; Spinach Salad with Instant Pot Jammy Eggs and Bacon Vinaigrette, 103
Split Pea Soup, Ham Hock and, 75
Spring Pesto, 197
squash: Autumn Harvest Sheet Pan Roasted Veggies, 14; Brussels Sprouts and Butternut Squash Salad with Tahini Vinaigrette, 136; Butternut Squash Soup with Crispy Prosciutto Croutons, 46; Ground Turkey Red Curry, 142; Maple Roasted Butternut Squash with Sage Browned Butter, 16; Orzo Vegetable Bean Soup, 184; Roasted Parmesan Delicata Squash, 54
Steaks with Shallot Cream Sauce, Pan-Seared Ribeye, 57
Stuffed Chicken Breasts, 108–9
sun-dried tomatoes: Baked Party Brie, 72; Gruyère Puff Pastry with Sun-Dried Tomatoes, 73; Marry Me One-Pot Shrimp, 148
Swedish Meatloaf with Brown Gravy, 118–19
sweet potatoes: Chicken and Biscuits, 166; Double Potato Gratin with Apples and Onions, 19; Spicy Chicken Sausage and Sweet Potato Soup, 130
syrup, maple: Curried Pumpkin Soup, 10; Double Potato Gratin with Apples and Onions, 19; Maple Roasted Butternut Squash with Sage Browned Butter, 16

T

tahini: Brussels Sprouts and Butternut Squash Salad with Tahini Vinaigrette, 136; Roasted Carrot Hummus, 45; Tahini Sauce, 22–23
Tarte Tatin, 37
Tater Tot Hot Dish, Juicy Lucy Cheeseburger, 145
Thai Chicken Rice Soup, 100
Thai Pork Noodle Goulash, 115
Thai Winter Squash Soup, 158
Thanksgiving Leftovers Turkey Wild Rice Soup, 47
Thanksgiving Punch, 44
Toffee Bars, Mom's, 88
Tuna Pâté, 157
turkey: Ground Turkey Red Curry, 142; One-Pot Turkey Meatballs with Lemon Orzo, 172–73; Thanksgiving Leftovers Turkey Wild Rice Soup, 47

Twice-Baked Potato Casserole, 163

V

veal, ground: Lila's Swedish Meatballs with Gravy, 80; Swedish Meatloaf with Brown Gravy, 118–19
Vegetables, Roast Chicken with Autumn, 24–25
Veggies, Autumn Harvest Sheet Pan Roasted, 14
vinaigrettes/dressings: Bacon Vinaigrette, 103; Caesar Dressing, 135; Ginger Vinaigrette, 49; Pear Vinaigrette, 137; Tahini Vinaigrette, 136

W

walnuts: Crispy Skillet Hash Brown Cake with Kale Pesto, 194; Maple Roasted Butternut Squash with Sage Browned Butter, 16
Weeknight Enchilada Soup, 12
whiskey: Cranberry Old-Fashioned, 69; Homemade Irish Cream, 68
wild rice: Arugula and Wild Rice Salad with Pear Vinaigrette, 137; Beer Cheese Wild Rice Soup, 129; Cranberry Wild Rice Salad with Candied Pecans and Bitter Greens, 52–53; Thanksgiving Leftovers Turkey Wild Rice Soup, 47; Wild Rice Stuffing, 56

Y

yogurt: Baked Brussels Sprouts with Lemon and Goat Cheese, 15; Blueberry-Lemon Bread, 176; Cranberry Orange Bread, 87; Green Sauce, 199; Rhubarb Almond Bread, 206; Sheet Pan Shawarma Two Ways, 22–23; Tuna Pâté, 157

Z

Ziti with Meatballs, Skillet Baked, 174
zucchini: Ground Turkey Red Curry, 142; Italian Sausage Soup, 101; Orzo Vegetable Bean Soup, 184; Swedish Meatloaf with Brown Gravy, 118–19; Thai Pork Noodle Goulash, 115; Thai Winter Squash Soup, 158

ABOUT THE AUTHOR

Stephanie Hansen is the author of *True North Cabin Cookbook*, the Regional Emmy Award–winning host of *Taste Buds with Stephanie*, and the brand amplifier and social commentator behind the *Weekly Dish* radio show, stephaniesdish.com, and *Dishing with Stephanie's Dish* podcast.